2,00

HIDING BEHIND A FACE

GW00598184

Stephen O'Byrnes

HIDING BEHIND A FACE

Fine Gael under FitzGerald

Gill and Macmillan

Published in Ireland by
Gill and Macmillan Ltd
Goldenbridge
Dublin 8
with associated companies in
Auckland, Dallas, Delhi, Hong Kong,
Johannesburg, Lagos, London, Manzini,
Melbourne, Nairobi, New York, Singapore,
Tokyo, Washington
© Stephen O'Byrnes 1986
5 4 3 2 1
0 7171 1448 1
Print origination in Ireland by Galaxy Reproductions Ltd
Printed in Great Britain by
Richard Clay (The Chaucer Press) Ltd, Bungay, Suffolk.
All rights reserved. No part of this publication may be
copied, reproduced or transmitted in any form or by any
means, without permission of the publishers.

FOR
NORAH AND MY
PARENTS

Contents

Acknowledgments

Politicians are always busy. And when they are in government they really have no time at all to spare. The research for this book was completed in the second half of 1985 and because of this time constraint therefore, I would like to express my appreciation to so many people in the Fine Gael party — Ministers, backbenchers, senators, retired and former deputies, party officials and other party activists and strategists (those much maligned 'Handlers') — who managed to make time available to discuss the fortunes of Fine Gael, and their own involvement, over the past decade in particular. Their story is the nucleus of this book.

But there were many others also deserving of appreciation. My thanks to Jim Maguire, *Irish Independent* librarian, for his constant help with cuttings, photographs and photocopying facilities. The counter staff of the National Library were ever helpful. Ms Eileen Pearson, general manager of *Magill*, kindly made various back issues of the magazine available. Ted McEnery of the Dáil Public Office tracked down any Dáil debates I required. My former colleague on the *Irish Independent*, Bruce Arnold, was extremely helpful with suggestions on content and priorities. A special word of appreciation to Ms Mary Downes of the Fine Gael press office for making the file of the party newspaper, *National Democrat*, available; it was an invaluable source on the party's restructuring since 1977. My editor at Gill and Macmillan, Fergal Tobin, guided my endeavours from conception to finished book form, and was ever courteous and patient. And speaking of patience, since this work was completed while maintaining the 'day job' at the *Irish Independent*, a special thank-you for my wife Norah, and my children, Ruth and Emily.

Stephen O'Byrnes
Dublin, 1986

'He is what he is. He does not hide behind a face.
I'm a Garret supporter. It is a very personal thing.'
Bono, lead singer with U2,
on Garret FitzGerald, 19 November 1982.

1

Cosgrave Blows Out!

The National Coalition government were in a dilemma. They were impossibly divided on whether to call a quick election or wait until the autumn. It was May 1977, and the fourteen ministers had divided evenly on the crucial tactical issue. Should they go in the summer, or wait until the autumn? That was the question. Seven said June; seven said October. It was all down to the Taoiseach's casting vote.

Liam Cosgrave had nothing to guide him except his own political judgment. Amazingly, he had not commissioned any opinion poll to help resolve the timing problem. Two of his ministers, Garret FitzGerald and Richie Ryan, had indicated their desire for an opinion poll to be done, and Jack Jones of the Market Research Bureau of Ireland had actually prepared some sample papers earlier in the year. But the call never came — not from the government, not from the Fine Gael party.

But there was other opinion poll data available. Indeed on a two-monthly basis, since the start of 1976, polls by Irish Marketing Surveys showed Fianna Fáil with a rating that scarcely dipped below 50 per cent, enough to give them a clearcut election victory. That information had been published by both RTE and the national newspapers. But opinion polling was not yet the guiding light of political strategists that it was soon to become. Hardly anyone believed those opinion polls in early 1977. Fianna Fáil certainly did not; the political correspondents of the national media did not; Liam Cosgrave did not.

Cosgrave saw no point in the coalition hanging on until October. He was a conventional man and he accepted the conventional wisdom. The conventional wisdom — which

1

blithely ignored opinion polls — was that the coalition could not lose.

Certainly the government was unpopular in some respects. It was unlucky to take office just before the first oil crisis brought to an end the amazing post-War boom in the Western economies. And it had gradually come to show a dour, cantankerous demeanour to the public, typified by Paddy Donegan's 'thundering disgrace' attack on President Ó Dálaigh in October 1976. And there was Cosgrave's own recent nasty outburst, at the 1977 Fine Gael árd fheis, against some elements in the media, whom he called 'blow-ins'. He told them they could 'blow out, or blow up' as far as he cared. The consensus was that the attack was primarily aimed at the *Irish Independent*'s English-born parliamentary reporter, Bruce Arnold. In fact, subsequently Garret FitzGerald, Alexis FitzGerald, Eddie Collins and Tom Fitzpatrick were among the senior Fine Gael figures who apologised to Arnold over the blow-in speech.

There had also been other running problems for the government. Richie Ryan, as Minister for Finance, had antagonised powerful and influential groups — businessmen and farmers — and the ensuing controversy saw him dubbed 'Richie Ruin' and 'Red Richie' in the media. Conor Cruise O'Brien simply could not refrain from becoming embroiled in controversy on the national question, or the behaviour of the media, or whatever was exercising his mind.

But none of this seemed to really matter in the early summer of 1977. The budget had been popular, inflation was falling, and the economy was coming round. On top of all that, the coalition had a trump card: the Tullymander. The last of the great Irish constituency gerrymanders, lovingly fashioned by Jimmy Tully, Minister for Local Government, to ensure the re-election of the coalition. Most pundits reckoned it was worth at least half-a-dozen extra seats.

So Liam Cosgrave weighed all this in his mind, and decided. He plumped for June. He was in a confident mood when he announced the dissolution of the 20th Dáil on 25 May. It had sat for a record number of days and hours, and he highlighted the fact also that it had passed 157 bills. He saw no point in waiting. They were ready to face the electorate.

2

Ten days later, on Saturday 4 June, the coalition election committee met in Government Buildings. They were anxiously awaiting a very special caller, Jack Jones of MRBI, with the findings of an opinion poll they had commissioned immediately *after* they called the election. Jones arrived about 10 o'clock. There to hear his findings were Richie Ryan, Garret FitzGerald, Alexis FitzGerald, Michael O'Leary, Conor Cruise O'Brien, Jim Dooge and Brendan Halligan. What Jones had to say was going to shatter them.

His national opinion poll findings were: Fianna Fáil, 58 per cent; Fine Gael/Labour, 39 per cent. There were still twelve days to go to polling, but the government were facing annihilation. Jones went on to tell them that the issues were taxation, prices and unemployment, and he warned them that unless they came up with some dramatic initiatives, 'this election will result in a landslide for Fianna Fáil'.

They listened to him in stunned silence. 'All you could hear was cups rattling on saucers as we tried to take in this dreadful news', according to Michael O'Leary. Over eight years later his recall was vivid, since it was an occasion 'burned' in his memory. Halligan asked Jones to repeat it all again, while he prepared to take it down. His own coalition win over Fianna Fáil in the Dublin South-West by-election, exactly a year earlier, had been one of the factors that had fuelled so much electoral optimism in the government. The election committee decided they had no option but to 'bury' the findings. They would have had the most demoralising impact on their campaign if they were generally known. There was nothing for it but to resume the uneven electoral struggle.

To make matters worse for Fine Gael — the majority government party — their capacity to operate a significant campaign was severely limited. Preparations for the election had almost been non-existent. Cosgrave had asked Richie Ryan to be national director of elections, although the latter protested that he was so busy as Minister for Finance that he hardly knew what was going on in his own constituency!

The party had no press officer to oversee the vital business of relations with the media. Cosgrave rang up Moore McDowell, a young UCD economist, and asked him to do the job for the

3

campaign. McDowell's foremost political qualification was that he was a grandson of the 1916 Volunteers' leader, Eoin MacNeill. Liaising with the Leinster House press corps was a total novelty for him. But he answered the call and did the best he could.

Fine Gael's poky headquarters in Hume St was an organisational disaster area. The launch of the government election manifesto on 27 May was a shambles. All that was available for the media were hastily-stencilled copies of the document, stapled together. Ministers were still seeking changes in the text right up to the time of its press conference launch. Originally the coalition had planned no manifesto; they would simply run on their record in government. But the glittering package of goodies from Fianna Fáil, abolishing rates and car tax and providing £1,000 grants for house-buyers, demanded a more structured response. Hence the hastily assembled programme.

Economist Brendan Dowling, who had worked with Garret FitzGerald since 1975, took holidays during the campaign to try and counteract the Fianna Fáil giveaway manifesto. However, he usually found it impossible to contact the various Fine Gael ministers in order to agree statements that could be used to counter Fianna Fáil claims. One day, Dowling needed fifty copies of a document, but found that headquarters had no photo-copying machine! FitzGerald and Ryan were reluctant to use government machinery for party purposes. It was only when an official in Finance wised them up that if it was Fianna Fáil, not only machinery but staff would be so deployed that Dowling got the go-ahead to use the department's copying machine.

One of the central issues of the election campaign was the cost of Fianna Fáil's manifesto, and whether the country could borrow the necessary money. On Sunday 5 June, the *Sunday Independent*'s main front-page story claimed 'We Can Borrow. Fianna Fáil plan is on, say bankers.' The story, by Vincent Browne, quoted various bankers and an unnamed EEC official to this effect. FitzGerald and Ryan were appalled, and they disagreed. They decided to get together to compile a detailed response. But it was the bank holiday weekend, and the party headquarters had simply shut down. The upshot was the waste of much valuable time rounding up a secretary, following which the two ministers spent much of Sunday cobbling together a response.

Moreover, Cosgrave's desultory forays into the country during the campaign contrasted woefully with Jack Lynch's barnstorming tour.

It was all faithfully reflected in the media coverage. Outgoing Fine Gael deputies and other party candidates all over the country were being bombarded daily by Fianna Fáil's American-style razzmatazz campaign, with tour buses, party hats and T-shirts, and a catchy party song. By comparison, Fine Gael headquarters back-up was almost non-existent. They even rationed election posters! Half-way through the campaign, Cosgrave retired from the countrywide hustings, pleading a sore throat. Lynch's campaign blazed on, embracing old hurling rivals, hugging babies and being warmly greeted by nuns.

Nevertheless, the coalition did manage to claw back some of Fianna Fáil's massive 19 per cent poll lead. Jones' third and final eve-of-poll national survey for the government showed the opposition down to 51 per cent against the combined coalition parties' 44 per cent (29 per cent for Fine Gael, and 15 per cent for Labour).

The actual outcome in the election on 16 June was: Fianna Fáil, 50.6 per cent; Fine Gael 30.5 per cent; and Labour, 11.6 per cent. Fianna Fáil had broken all election records for the Republic of Ireland, and had won 84 seats.

––––––––––

The knives were being sharpened for Liam Cosgrave. It was Thursday, 23 June 1977, exactly a week since the general election. Fine Gael had been routed, winning just 43 seats. It was their worst performance in twenty years and an eleven-seat drop on their 1973 showing. The depleted parliamentary party were gathering in Leinster House for the post-mortem.

Quite a few TDs had made up their mind. Cosgrave must go! It wasn't merely that Fianna Fáil had trounced them; with their 84 seats, they all but doubled Fine Gael. The National Coalition government had run a lousy campaign. Already some of the unrest had broken in the media. Garret FitzGerald had said publicly that he believed the government should not have gone to the country until the autumn, and on RTE Radio's 'This Week' programme, on Sunday 19 June, he equivocated on the possibility of a change of party leadership. On the same programme, his cabinet colleague, Richie Ryan, had no such doubts. He assured the nation that Liam Cosgrave would be leader of Fine Gael for many more years to come.

FitzGerald, in fact, had already been party to a number of private meetings to analyse the election debacle, and to consider how Cosgrave could be deposed. These meetings were held in his own Rathmines home, and in the Ailesbury Road home of his namesake and friend, Senator Alexis FitzGerald. A number of personal supporters of FitzGerald's from his Dublin South-East constituency predominated. The mood of antagonism towards Cosgrave was heightened by his rash of judicial and other appointments in these, his dying days as Taoiseach.

Nobody really expected Cosgrave to remain on as leader until the next general election. But they all expected him to hang on for a year or so, and to attempt to tee up the succession to suit somebody more in his own mould, like Richie Ryan.

The caucus suggested that FitzGerald should propose a vote of no confidence in Cosgrave at the parliamentary party meeting. FitzGerald disagreed. It would be too divisive. Finally, it was agreed a few days before the 23 June meeting that Alexis FitzGerald would propose the leadership be debated when the party held its next meeting in October, after the summer recess. That would be the marker around which opposition could rally in the following few months.

They also decided to notify some other TDs in advance of the meeting, like Paddy Harte and Eddie Collins, who were quite close to Garret FitzGerald. They were anxious that the general election inquest should not be a dogfight, with a babel of charges and allegations. Cosgrave and his cabinet allies might seize upon such discord to push through a confidence vote, and it would then be more difficult to challenge him later.

6

Other deputies who had also decided in the week following the general election that Cosgrave must go were Jim White and Paddy Harte of Donegal; John Donnellan, Gerry L'Estrange, Kieran Crotty, Eddie Collins and Brendan Griffin. White, Donnellan, Griffin, Crotty and Collins had shared the same party room since 1973, and they had all made it back to the new Dáil.

None of them really owed anything to Cosgrave, and some of them made contact with FitzGerald to indicate that they would back him as an alternative leader. There was also a great deal of telephone calling done between Fine Gael TDs in the run-up to the 23 June meeting, and some of them feared Cosgrave might get to hear of the moves which were afoot. However, the party leader was too long in politics, and too experienced a fox-hunter with the South County Dublin Hunt, not to scent his pursuers.

In the days succeeding the election defeat, he weighed up the situation. Now fifty-seven, he had been in the Dáil since he was twenty-three, and had long ago decided to quit politics at sixty. Down the years, he had seen too many colleagues hang on beyond their time, and he was determined it would not happen to him. Clearly, he reckoned, Fianna Fáil would go a full term, and he was anxious that his successor would have plenty of time to prepare for the next election. He also knew he would face severe criticism for the election debacle. An intensely private man, Cosgrave made up his mind, without consulting anybody, that it was time for him to stand down. On the morning of 23 June, before leaving his house in Templeogue for Government Buildings, he simply told his wife, Vera, that he was quitting that day as Fine Gael leader. Nobody else knew.

The day before, the outgoing Cathaoirleach of the Seanad, Jim Dooge, had gone to see Cosgrave. He had been a close mentor of the party leader and was also friendly with FitzGerald. Dooge, a world renowned hydrologist, had been in the Seanad since 1961, and had now decided to stand down to concentrate on his academic career. In response, Cosgrave gave no inkling of his own intentions.

The official reason for the 23 June meeting was to consider party nominations for the upcoming Seanad elections. However, nobody among the bulk of the party's 43 deputies and 23 senators gathering in their third floor room in Leinster House doubted that the election defeat would be raised.

The meeting commenced and proceeded to consider Seanad nominations for over an hour. Cosgrave sat at the top table, flanked by most of his outgoing ministers. Richie Ryan was missing. He was representing the government at a meeting of the International Monetary Fund in Washington. When they had finished dealing with the Seanad, Cosgrave suddenly stood up and calmly declared that he had decided to stand down that day as party leader. Everyone in the room was stunned. Nobody, but nobody, expected him to go while he was still Taoiseach: he would not be handing over government to Jack Lynch until 5 July. Cosgrave cited his age, and the fact that he would be over sixty at the next election. Now was the time to hand over to a new man to build up the party for that time. He was not prepared to join with Fianna Fáil in a Dutch auction for the support of the people. He forecast that the opposition's promises to the electorate would be a disaster for the country.

There was a finality and a certainty about him. Nobody, not even his close allies in cabinet, like Mark Clinton or Paddy Donegan, had the slightest inkling that he would resign at that time.

Donegan was quickly on his feet. He protested at the decision, and called for a unanimous vote of confidence in Cosgrave. This was put to the meeting, but nearly a dozen hands stayed down, including that of FitzGerald. His was most noticeable because as one of the outgoing government ministers, he was sitting at the top table.

But even a unanimous vote would not have changed Cosgrave's mind. A number of deputies then spoke to express their regret at his decision. When FitzGerald spoke, he recalled that relations between himself and the party leader had sometimes been strained, but that since they served in government together there had been no difficulties.

Cosgrave, in reply, thanked his colleagues, adverted to FitzGerald's remarks, and concurred with his sentiments. But he did not single out his Foreign Minister, or any other member of the party, as his preferred choice of successor. He did, however, accede to a call from some deputies, including Paddy Harte, to defer his decision to resign for a week so that they could have time to consider a successor. The parliamentary party agreed to reassemble on Friday, 1 July, to elect a new leader.

The timing of Cosgrave's departure certainly heaped the odds in favour of FitzGerald succeeding him. It caught Ryan unawares, helplessly sidelined on the other side of the Atlantic. A staunch supporter of Cosgrave, and preferred by the party leader over FitzGerald for the key finance portfolio in 1973, Ryan had every reason to be annoyed over Cosgrave's precipitate move.

Ryan was immediately seen by the media and some elements of the party as a contender. Indeed, every senior politician in Fine Gael, and notably its outgoing ministers, had to decide if they would seek the glittering prize. Speculation focused on Mark Clinton, Tom Fitzpatrick, Peter Barry and FitzGerald, as well as Ryan. Outgoing Attorney-General, John Kelly, indicated his willingness if his colleagues wanted him, while also stating that he would not canvass.

Soon, Clinton and Fitzpatrick dropped out. Clinton had been an extremely popular and hardworking Minister for Agriculture, and he had been very upset by what he perceived as the unfairness of the electorate to the Cosgrave government. The farmers, for whom he had personally worked so hard, had also turned against Fine Gael because of the government's decision to extend income tax to them. But, most importantly, Clinton was then sixty-two and was convinced that the job needed a younger man. Fitzpatrick was a popular figure in the party, and chairman of the national executive, but age was also against him. He was then in his sixtieth year.

Peter Barry was the outgoing Minister for Education, but most of his four and a half years in the Cosgrave government had been marked by an unspectacular ministerial posting at Transport and Power. He was a popular deputy, however, and was the party's principal standard-bearer in Cork. He would also be a focus of support for many non-Dublin deputies, more attracted to traditional Fine Gael values and attitudes.

9

The heavyweights in the contest, however, in terms of popular awareness of them, were undoubtedly Ryan and FitzGerald. But whereas the general public's estimation of FitzGerald was benign, Ryan's public profile was not. This was the consequence of being a tough and brave Minister for Finance in hard times. Very abrasive in debate, he suffered the additional handicap of having been national director of elections in the recent nightmare.

By comparison, FitzGerald had scarcely a blemish. Already rated the second most popular politician, next only to Jack Lynch in the opinion polls, he had carved out a substantial reputation for himself at Foreign Affairs since 1973. Never one to shy away from the political limelight, and for years eager to make it to the top, he was instantly installed as favourite to succeed.

After the 23 June meeting, FitzGerald was due to fly to Paris for the OECD meeting, and his wife Joan was waiting outside Leinster House for him. He did not go to Paris, but began informal discussions with likely supporters. Indeed one other candidate would state later that FitzGerald had begun canvassing before the meeting even broke up.

An *Irish Times* editorial the next day summed up the public perception of FitzGerald:

> In popularity with the public, in successful tenure of office, in possession (unlike so many others in the party) of a coherent philosophy, and in that invaluable physical attribute, the capacity for sustained hard work — in all these ways, Dr FitzGerald is ahead of any other rival.

The same paper, with commendable prescience, had three weeks earlier polled the public on who would most likely succeed Cosgrave. It was during the election campaign. If the next government was a coalition, and Cosgrave were to stand down as leader, who should lead it? The poll's response indicated 49 per cent support for FitzGerald; 12 per cent for the Labour leader, Brendan Corish; 5 per cent each for Clinton and Ryan, and 3 per cent for Paddy Cooney.

Cosgrave was aware that the timing of his departure virtually assured the succession for FitzGerald. But still he did not try to arrange his own departure either to stymie FitzGerald, or to give any of the other aspirants a better chance. Cosgrave would have had plenty of reasons for making it more difficult for FitzGerald. The differences between the two men went back a long way.

FitzGerald was first elected to the Oireachtas as a senator in 1965, the same year that Cosgrave became party leader. Initially, they got on well, despite their very different outlooks. Cosgrave, dour and conservative, and FitzGerald, effervescent and liberal-to-radical. Maybe they got on too well initially; John Healy, of the *Irish Times*, began to dub the Fine Gael leader 'FitzCosgrave', because of the alleged influence being wielded by the new economist senator. But gradually, as the right-wing former Minister for Finance, Gerry Sweetman, came to be the prime influence on Cosgrave, the relationship between him and FitzGerald waned.

Relations perceptibly cooled after Fianna Fáil's 1969 election victory, following Labour's anti-coalition campaign. FitzGerald saw the only hope of defeating the government party in an inter-party arrangement with Labour. But senior figures in that party told him this was not on while Cosgrave was the Fine Gael leader. FitzGerald finally decided to put this unpalatable news to his leader. Clearly it was not an overture which endeared him to Cosgrave.

Relations continued downhill thereafter. When Cosgrave dismissed certain elements in Fine Gael as 'mongrel foxes' at the party árd fheis, FitzGerald had no doubt that he was one of the people in mind. Indeed, he considered walking off the platform.

But the most serious showdown between them occurred in December 1972. Fianna Fáil had legislation before the Dáil to amend and strengthen the Offences against the State Act to combat growing IRA terrorism. Fine Gael decided to oppose it, and FitzGerald and Paddy Cooney, their Justice spokesman, led the opposition at a crucial party meeting. But Cosgrave stubbornly defied his party colleagues, and a major party split loomed. FitzGerald accused his leader of 'having neither led, nor been led' on the issue.

11

But then two bombs exploded in Dublin on the same night that Fine Gael were agonising over the bill. Two bus workers were killed. The party panicked and supported Cosgrave's line: they endorsed the Fianna Fáil bill.

Three months later, in March 1973, Cosgrave was in power as Taoiseach of a National Coalition government. In the February general election of that year, he had been the largest personal vote-getter in the country, ahead of both Jack Lynch and Charles Haughey. But he showed his magnanimity, and appointed FitzGerald to Foreign Affairs. FitzGerald had been opposition spokesman on Finance, and would have preferred that portfolio. But he was too radical, both for Cosgrave and for many of his party colleagues.

Cosgrave supporters in his 1973 government later surmised that FitzGerald had been given Foreign Affairs to keep him out of the country! They believed that FitzGerald hated flying, and reckoned that being confined to boats and trains, he would spend most of his time travelling to EEC and other meetings, well away from Government Buildings! In fact, although FitzGerald had not travelled by air since 1958, he had no fear of flying. But his wife Joan had. And she had prevailed on her husband not to fly either. However, having to resort to boat and train proved quite impossible after becoming Foreign Minister and, from October 1973, he persuaded his wife to resume air travel with him. FitzGerald did not know if this was the reason he was made Foreign Minister, but readily accepted that he would not have suited Cosgrave at Finance.

Indeed, the bulk of his Fine Gael colleagues in cabinet with him between 1973 and 1977 did not really like FitzGerald. They perceived him as too radical, too close to Labour; the man who canvassed for Justin Keating to get the Irish EEC Commissionership in 1976. Many of them later cited loyalty as the only condition demanded by Cosgrave, who otherwise let his ministers get on with their jobs. Some, like Ryan, Dick Burke and Paddy Cooney, saw their Foreign Affairs colleague as less than loyal to his team-mates at all times, and also wanting to meddle in other ministers' portfolios. For his part, FitzGerald regarded Ryan, Clinton and Donegan, in particular, as constituting a cabal around Cosgrave.

12

There was, therefore, plenty of animosity towards FitzGerald at the top of Fine Gael when he set out to woo a clear majority of them on 23 June 1977. An initial obstacle was Richie Ryan's absence in Washington. FitzGerald, Peter Barry and some other outgoing ministers agreed that there would be no formal canvassing until Ryan was back in the country. Ryan, however, could not get back until the weekend, not that that stopped FitzGerald's campaign being effectively launched. The White/Collins/Crotty/Griffin/Donnellan room became the centre of his campaign, and some of these deputies were allocated a quota of deputies and senators to be canvassed on behalf of FitzGerald. Paddy Harte and Gerry L'Estrange were also actively involved in the FitzGerald campaign.

That night, Cosgrave's decision to quit was the dominant news. In RTE, a radio current affairs programme presented by Maurice Manning did a hasty analysis of the leadership contest. But the only Fine Gael TD who could be contacted was Paddy Harte, and he went on air unequivocally supporting FitzGerald. The following night, an RTE television programme interviewed Harte, Donal Creed, Fergus O'Brien and John Boland, but Harte was the only one boldly to declare for FitzGerald. As he put it later, he was the first, and the second, to declare for Garret!

On this same Friday night, most of the TDs actively canvassing for FitzGerald gathered in his Rathmines home. His wife Joan and Alexis FitzGerald were also there. The tallies were looking very good. Not everyone in the party was going to support him, of course. Some of the Cork deputies, together with Tom O'Donnell, Joan Burke and others, had told FitzGerald's canvassers that they were backing Barry; Donegan and Cosgrave would be backing Ryan, as would be some other outgoing ministers. But no one in the FitzGerald camp doubted that their man would win comfortably.

Over the weekend, the canvassing continued, but it was early the following week before a meeting could be set up between FitzGerald, Barry and Ryan. Reluctantly, Ryan had decided not to enter the race. He accepted that the time was wrong for him: he was seen as the progenitor of both the wealth tax and farmer taxation and this, in the minds of many

13

party supporters, was too great a handicap.

It was now formally a straight fight beween FitzGerald and Barry. There was no animosity between them. In fact, in the few days remaining before the vote, they met regularly in Leinster House and compared tallies. Barry soon came to accept that FitzGerald had the greater support, but he was confident that he would muster a respectable total. Of the sixty-six TDs and Senators eligible to vote on the leadership, FitzGerald reckoned that he would get over fifty. Barry's camp reckoned the Cork man would get about twenty-five votes.

Barry was also very much aware that the Fine Gael grass-roots in the country were eager to support a new style of leadership, and wanted FitzGerald. The writing was on the wall for him, and he readily accepted it. Like Ryan, he withdrew from the contest, leaving the way clear for his rival.

At the very brief parliamentary party meeting on Friday, 1 July, the recollection of Fine Gael's humiliation in the general election was raw and vivid. A significant rump in the party might dislike or not really know FitzGerald, but their plight was desperate. FitzGerald was already a darling with the media, and a statesman with an international reputation. Most important of all, he wanted the job. The party desperately needed a leader with energy, skill and charisma. FitzGerald might not be festooned with All-Ireland medals, like Jack Lynch. But he was intelligent and charming, a celebrated economist and a formidable television performer, whose trouncing of George Colley in the 1973 election debate was still vividly recalled.

The doubters would have to hold their tongues, and make the best of things. Peter Barry proposed FitzGerald as the new party leader. Kieran Crotty, from Kilkenny, seconded him and the proposition was agreed unanimously. The new leader was fifty-one.

On the night of his election, he was interviewed on RTE. He issued an open invitation to people to join Fine Gael, and to write to him personally if they did not know whom to contact locally. It was a vintage FitzGerald gesture, signalling and symbolising an open approach; getting ordinary people involved, making them feel welcome. Equally im-

14

portant, the new leader was making expert use of television.

There was little doubt the party had made the right decision. The Cosgrave era was over, and had been replaced — at the helm, at least — by a new philosophy and a new style.

2

Ousting the Quota Squatters

The first task the new party leader set himself in July 1977 was to revitalise the organisation, democratise it, and take it out of the maw of the local sitting deputies. Before him, Liam Cosgrave had also been aware of this terrible paralysing grip by the TDs who, in the interests of their own political survival, ensured that a single-seat mentality pervaded the organisation. It was summed up in a remark to the ambitious new deputy, Michael Keating, on one of his first visits to Leinster House after winning a seat in Dublin North-Central in 1977. A full-time politician who believed that any TD's primary ambition should be to get into government, he was greatly taken aback when an older party colleague sought to assure him that 'It's far easier being in opposition.' In 'A message to the Fine Gael organisation' on 4 July, FitzGerald announced that he would visit every constituency that winter, and hold public meetings to attract new members. He called for better links between the organisation and the leadership, and renewed his invitation to people to write directly to him if they wanted to get involved with Fine Gael.

The party which FitzGerald inherited was dominated by business and professional people and larger farmers. Twenty-six of the deputies recently returned to Leinster House were in these categories, with nine of them farmers. Fine Gael had only one TD in thirty-three of the forty-two constituencies; two deputies in five, and none in the other four. The single-seat holders were especially wary of any encroachment which threatened their supremacy.

The party had the bedrock support of a mere quarter of the electorate. This ranged from 15 per cent unskilled working class backing to 46 per cent by larger farmers, as measured by

16

an RTE 'Survey' programme analysis of party support, by occupational class, in September 1976. Its middle class support exactly matched its overall standing with the electorate, at 25 per cent.

One of the new leader's first acts was to commission a comprehensive poll by MRBI of the 1977 general election result. He wanted to know what aspects of Fianna Fáil's policies had won most approval and to find out who had voted for Fine Gael and — more importantly — who had not.

The national survey of 2,000 voters provided grim findings. Only 23 per cent of men and 22 per cent of women had voted Fine Gael, to 47 per cent and 49 per cent respectively for Fianna Fáil. To make matters worse, Fine Gael's main support came from older people (35 per cent in the 55-64 age category), whereas only 19 per cent of men and 16 per cent of women aged from 19 to 26 voted Fine Gael. In the next category, those aged 27 to 39, only 23 per cent of men and 21 per cent of women voted for the party.

In each election since 1957, Fine Gael had gradually improved its overall share of the national vote, growing to 35 per cent in 1973. But all that progress was reversed in 1977. Its 30.5 per cent share was its worst performance since 1957, when it took 26.6 per cent.

The poll underlined the enormous uphill task faced by FitzGerald as he set out to make Fine Gael a popular party, one that could ultimately rival Fianna Fáil. The positive aspect of the 1977 reversal however, was that it was so total and traumatic that it allowed for no half measures. As they all realised at the time: they had either to shape up or throw their hat at it. To that extent, FitzGerald's unanimous selection had been an opting by Fine Gael for radical remedial action.

As many of his colleagues set off for a break in the summer of 1977, FitzGerald was busy setting his re-organisation drive in motion. He needed an able general secretary, and a party publicity officer. He did not regard the then general secretary, Jim Sanfey, who was fifty-five and a Cosgrave loyalist, as the man for the job. Sanfey, a former army captain, had been in the job for ten years. FitzGerald made a redundancy settlement with him, and advertised for a new man.

17

An interview board consisting of Peter Barry, Richie Ryan, Tom Fitzpatrick — chairman of the national executive — and FitzGerald himself met about fourteen of the candidates. The real choice was with FitzGerald, since his parliamentary colleagues recognised that the person chosen must be able to get along with the leader.

FitzGerald chose Peter Prendergast, a 38-year-old marketing consultant, whose biggest business marketing coup had been to turn the Irish nation on to Yoghurt. He had secured the Yoplait franchise for Waterford Co-op. But he was no slouch either when it came to politics. He had joined Fine Gael in 1969, having already been involved with Tom O'Higgins' very successful presidential election campaign in 1966. In the 1973 campaign, he worked with Garret FitzGerald, and they were both centrally involved in the limited use of opinion polling on behalf of the party.

He was also a running-mate of FitzGerald in that election. He had gone along to supervise the selection convention, but they were short a candidate, and to his surprise he was nominated. It was a grim comment on the lack of preparation even in FitzGerald's own consituency. Prendergast secured 1,300 votes and helped elect Fergus O'Brien.

Between 1973 and 1977, Prendergast ran most of FitzGerald's constituency clinics, and again in 1977 he ran in Dublin South-East. But again he failed to win, securing the same 1,300 votes. Along the way he had also served for some years on the national executive and national council, and was very aware of the party's organisational deficiencies. In September 1977, three months after his second election defeat, Prendergast suddenly found himself at the heart of a political new departure as Fine Gael's new general secretary and national director of organisation. His brief was to shake and transform the party so that it would out do even the fabled Fianna Fáil organisation as a vehicle for capturing votes and winning elections.

In August, FitzGerald had persuaded Ted Nealon to take on the job of Director of Press and Information Services. A household television personality after twelve years current affairs broadcasting with RTE, the 48-year-old Co. Sligo man had been head of the Government Information Bureau from 1975 to 1977. In the recent general election, he had been imposed as a candidate in Dublin Clontarf by the national executive. This had led to open warfare between his supporters and those of aspiring local councillor, Michael Joe Cosgrave. Cosgrave won the Fine Gael seat, with Nealon bowing out on the ninth count, having got a respectable 2,800 first-preference votes. Amidst much public controversy, he resumed his GIB job in the dying days of the coalition government, and incurred the inevitable sack when Fianna Fáil took over on 5 July. He declined a certain Seanad nomination from Liam Cosgrave because he planned to return to his first love, journalism. But he eventually succumbed to FitzGerald's pleas to stay with the party.

Here was the trio — FitzGerald, Prendergast and Nealon — who set out on 19 September 1977 to Cork, to commence a nationwide tour of constituencies. Everywhere the routine was the same: meetings with local Fine Gael public representatives; visits to local institutions; meeting the constituency officer board and the local media; and finally a public meeting. These meetings were deliberately structured as question and answer sessions, and FitzGerald made a huge impression with his openness, dynamism and charisma.

Between then and March 1978, he addressed forty-five such meetings and met over 20,000 people. Prendergast recalls that time:

> Garret talked about getting into power inside eight years, and the slogan became to make Fine Gael the largest party in the country. And everyone laughed up their sleeves and laughed openly.
>
> We licensed young people to get involved. To have the guts to stand up and tell us what was wrong. The strategy was to broaden the party, widen its appeal and achieve that target of power. Everything that was done after that was in keeping with that strategy.

In the winter of 1977, as Fianna Fáil's manifesto began to deliver on the removal of car tax and domestic rates, dispensing £1,000 grants for first-time housebuyers, and creating 20,000 jobs a year, the general public hardly noticed FitzGerald's forlorn-looking odyssey.

Along the way he had been working on the draft of a new party constitution. Many of the long journeys around the country were whiled away on this task. Only days after becoming leader FitzGerald had talked with Jim Dooge about this, and the need for a greater role for rank-and-file members. It was also something repeatedly highlighted in the tour of constituencies.

In Mid-Cork, a young vocational teacher, Finbarr Fitzpatrick, had only one question for the new leader: 'How do you get rid of office holders who have been there forever?' Locally, Fitzpatrick had recently become district executive secretary, succeeding a man who had been in the post for twenty-nine years. He had also been proposing resolutions for annual árd fheiseanna urging that public representatives should not hold constituency office, and that all party officers should vacate their positions after three years. In 1982, Fitzpatrick would succeed Prendergast as national general secretary.

Until now each Fine Gael constituency organisation was a creature of the local deputy. Local councillor friends of his held down the main posts; the TD selected the director of elections, and effectively chose his own running mates through deploying his own supporters' block of votes in subsequent counts. In the sixties, Jim Dooge once presided at a selection convention where the election literature was available at the end of the meeting. It was all so predictable that the literature had been printed in advance of the convention!

In Kilkenny one evening, Prendergast found himself at a meeting stating that the problem with the party as he saw it was that 'there were ould fellas there for bloody years, and as far as I am concerned I have to get rid of them.' Sitting at the top table was a man, Sean McKenna, who had been constituency secretary for thirty-seven years, and who was a close friend of Deputy Kieran Crotty.

Prendergast and FitzGerald were determined to smash the one-seat mentality, and the cosiness and lack of political drive that went with it, and between them they were de-

20

vising a constitution that would achieve that end. But it was a real high-wire strategy because it literally meant putting every existing Fine Gael seat at risk. Prendergast summed it up: 'If you have only one out of three seats, you cannot ever hope to win two without putting that one at risk.'

Their draft constitution was circulated to all affiliated branches in the spring of 1978, and formally considered at the árd fheis in May. By this time, FitzGerald was convinced that 'a party run by TDs would never get anywhere'. He wanted to see ordinary party members, with no ambition to hold public office, being able to aspire to senior posts in the party. He faced some opposition to his proposals in the parliamentary party. But he held all the aces. He was the one who had travelled the country and he knew that this was what the party faithful wanted. In some instances, though, he moderated his proposals to get them through the parliamentary party, but without compromising his principal objectives of loosening the TDs' grip on the organisation and shifting power to party headquarters and independent local structures.

FitzGerald turned to his friend, the lucid and concise Jim Dooge, to pilot the draft constitution through the árd fheis. Giving power to the party faithful was most dramatically symbolised by the proposal that the annual conference elect eight members to the national executive, the party's ruling body. Not enough, the delegates decided! They amended it to provide twelve members. Moreover, they rejected another proposal that the parliamentary party should elect twelve to the national executive: this figure was cut to nine.

The draft also provided that at least one of the party's four vice-presidents, and one of the two honorary secretaries, would not be members of the parliamentary party. TDs and senators traditionally held all these posts, and they had their last hurrah at that árd fheis. Deputies Donal Creed, Paddy Donegan, Tom Fitzpatrick and Senator Charlie McDonald were the vice-presidents, and Deputies Eddie Collins and Gerry L'Estrange were elected honorary secretaries.

A truly revolutionary innovation was the new voting system to select Dáil candidates and constituency executives. This became known as the 'model system', and was based on the very complex Seanad voting method. Under this, general election convention delegates vote only once, on a PR basis, for all the candidates. Gone were the days of the TD or local party officers being returned by acclamation; of the outgoing TD shifting his block of votes in second and succeeding counts in order to guarantee running mates of his choice.

Complimenting all this was a radical revision of the branch structure. Until then, each branch sent three delegates to selection conventions, whether they represented a large town or a mere village. The result was that Fine Gael was chronically weak in the larger towns, and rural-based candidates predominated. For instance, although the Louth constituency had two-thirds of its 60,000 electors in the towns of Drogheda and Dundalk, it was simply impossible to reflect this in the line-up of the party's candidates. Candidates from more rural parts of the constituency predominated.

From now on, branches would be reorganised so that their functional area would reflect precise blocks of voters on the electoral register, and have proportionate delegate status. Each branch with up to 500 electors could send three delegates to a convention or annual general meeting; each additional 250 electors in the branch's functional area entitled it to an extra delegate. Thus some larger urban branches could have twenty-five or more delegates, as against a rural branch having five or six.

Registration of branches with headquarters was tightened up and made more expensive. Until then a branch could be registered for £3, and stories abounded of outgoing TDs registering rafts of 'paper' branches in the run-up to a convention, each of which carried three delegates. Now the cost, including at least nine paid-up members, went to nearly £40.

However, as late as 1985, it was clear that the 'paper' branches had not disappeared entirely. In Dublin especially, it still made sense for certain TDs to register new branches, especially given the larger number of delegates it afforded. The problem was that party headquarters did not have the resources to check that all the registered names actually were voluntary members of Fine Gael, or whether they had simply been signed on by their enterprising local deputy or councillor. However, the computerisation of all registered party members in early 1986 made the formation of 'paper branches' a more risky undertaking.

The new constitution also formally ratified one of the most contentious of the reforms. Henceforth, there were to be two new positions filled in every constituency in the country; those of constituency organiser and PRO. In fact, Prendergast was already filling such positions before the formal árd fheis endorsement. Nothing signalled more clearly the determination of the new regime to break the stranglehold of the local deputy, for whom the organiser was often to become a figure of hatred in subsequent years. His appointment had to be approved by the general secretary and he was the key local liaison man for party headquarters. A veritable spy in the camp was how many deputies saw their local organiser, running off to Dublin to tell all and in turn being used as a hatchet man locally by headquarters.

The organiser and PRO were also very strong potential rivals for TDs and local councillors. FitzGerald would not have got the proposal through the parliamentary party at all but for agreeing that these new officers could not be candidates for upcoming local, Dáil or Euro elections.

The National Executive acquired the power to amend the list of candidates chosen for local or national elections. Further key refinements, to deal with situations where selected candidates might threaten to withdraw, and to order that geographic factors be taken into account in selecting candidates, came in later years, and were based on the lessons learned from the general elections in 1981-82.

Interestingly, a three-year rule restricting branch, district and executive officers from serving a fourth successive year only came in 1982.

FitzGerald demonstrated commendable prescience in the case of two other innovations in the 1978 constitution. One subjected a Fine Gael leader to an automatic vote of confidence, by secret ballot, within two months of a general election — unless the party was forming a government. One has only to recall the Byzantine scheming and plotting in Fianna Fáil against Charles Haughey in 1982-3 to realise that, if that party had had such a rule, a lot of the ensuing bitterness and division could have been avoided.

The other new rule had to do with the automatic expulsion from the parliamentary party of any Oireachtas member who breached the party pledge. This was taken by each candidate *before* a selection convention, and bound the member to vote for the party. The rule did away with the prospect of divisive party meetings where motions calling for the expulsion of members who had defied the party whip would have to be debated, with all the potential for acrimony which that entailed.

The constitution also gave official status to the party's trade union group, and to the new youth movement, Young Fine Gael. FitzGerald was determined to get that age profile of party support corrected. During his constituency tour, FitzGerald had promoted the youth movement idea, urging that at least one branch be set up for each district executive in the country, with one per constituency in urban areas. In April 1978, 28 year-old Dan Egan, a former RTE reporter from Claremorris, Co. Mayo, was appointed Assistant Organiser (Youth). He had been one of the candidates interviewed when the party was choosing a general secretary the previous year.

By the time the 1978 árd fheis had come round, there were nearly a hundred branches of Young Fine Gael already in existence. This organisation also had power to send delegates to selection conventions and other meetings of the senior party. Just like the constituency organisers and the PROs, Young Fine Gael was destined to get up the noses of the parliamentary party.

The new constitution marked a radical change in Fine Gael. The party was totally restructured. The TD, who had hitherto been a kind of feudal lord, now had to pay homage to the local organisation. He had to present himself for re-selection like any other aspiring candidate. Given the controversy this regulation caused in the British Labour Party in the early eighties, its significance can be fully appreciated.

Moreover, good candidates were being given a real chance to succeed at selection conventions, and rank-and-file followers could aspire to the party vice-presidency. Fine Gael was being democratised. Of course, democratic structures of themselves would not ensure a vibrant party. They would only be as effective as the calibre and commitment of the people in the party made them. But they were an essential prerequisite, and FitzGerald had them in place a year after taking over. It was a major achievement.

Ironically, very little attention was paid to the new constitution in the media coverage of the 1978 árd fheis. This was due not only to its technical nature, but also the fact that the real popular focus was on FitzGerald's first annual conference, and the fact that it had moved from the Mansion House to the cavernous main hall of the RDS in Ballsbridge. It was all part of FitzGerald's and Prendergast's ambition to shake off Fine Gael's minority, second division, amateur status. Previously the árd fheis was a two-day affair in the Round Room of the Mansion House, peaking on Saturday night with about 2,000 people for the party leader's address, and dwindling to a couple of hundred on Sunday. Accountant Seán Murray recalled having a whiparound of other members of the party's fund-raising Capital Branch in the late sixties to pay for the Mansion House.

Prendergast encountered a lot of nervousness when he proposed the move to the RDS. A half-empty hall would require some explaining! It turned out an enormous success. It was the party's biggest árd fheis in its history. It was also a huge personal triumph for FitzGerald. About 4,000 people were present for his keynote address, and afterwards he was carried triumphantly through the main hall on the delegates' shoulders. At last, Fine Gael had their own answer to Jack Lynch.

A mere eleven months at the helm, FitzGerald was able to report remarkable progress to the delegates. The party had also moved from its poky headquarters in Dublin's Hume St to a five-storey house on Mount St, right across the road from Fianna Fáil. They might have only half the number of deputies, but they were certainly thinking big!

No. 51 Mount St was officially opened on 4 May by the vice-president of the European People's Party, to which Fine Gael was affiliated in the European Parliament. It cost about £90,000 to purchase, and a further £50,000 to renovate. Even after the sale of the Hume St office, it left a major repayment headache. Prendergast, ever the marketing man, devised a scheme called 'Buy a Brick for 51', which party members could do by donating a fiver.

In fact, one of FitzGerald's pleas at the árd fheis was for more money from the organisation. Already, the party was costing three times what it cost to run in 1976. Fine Gael, he told the delegates, had never really mastered the art of efficient organisation. They now had a professional team at the helm. He urged greater participation by rank-and-file. But, he assured them, 'we are launched'. And he went on to promise that over the following three years they would become a truly formidable party, 'with the capacity to take Fianna Fáil on frontally, and displace them from top place in the political league'. He made it clear that the immediate task ahead was the June 1979 European and local government elections. Again he reiterated his concern for 'the role of women in Irish society and of the younger generation'. Here were two constituencies — hitherto electoral wastelands for Fine Gael — that were to be very assiduously wooed.

But the magnificently stage-managed conference could not disguise the persistent evidence of a ramshackle party organisation that still had massive deficiencies. And still needed massive surgery. In their report to the conference, the joint secretaries, Gerry L'Estrange and Eddie Collins, revealed the stark state of affairs:

> In a number of constituencies, executives have either been non-existent, or had not met for some years past. This is now being put right, but both constituency executives and other units of the organisation — district executives and branches — have an uneven record in relation to the holding of meetings.

Only two-thirds of branches in good standing had affiliated for the árd fheis. Only a third of constituency executives had responded to a request for information on the number and names of their branches and their financial situation. And only a quarter of district executives had come up with similar information.

Little wonder then that Prendergast was in such a blunt, aggressive mood in the following month, June 1978, in the party's newspaper. Despite the contrywide campaign by

FitzGerald, and the organisation of a superb árd fheis, there was still a long slog ahead:

> Anyone who believes that we in Fine Gael will win the next general election based on our present organisation is living in cloud cuckooland. Twelve months after our defeat in the general election we are still pathetically weak at branch, district and constituency level.

That paper, *National Democrat*, was a direct response to the requests FitzGerald received all over the country for Fine Gael to have its own journal. Edited by Ted Nealon, it made its first appearance in April 1978, and was used by FitzGerald and Prendergast as a major vehicle for the political education of party members. In its early monthly editions, especially, it had a Penny Cathecism flavour to it. It spelled out simple, direct answers to such questions as how to organise a party branch; conduct meetings; affiliate with headquarters. It explained the basics of the new constitution, party rules, the role of constituency organisers and PROs. And it introduced local constituency officers. In its first couple of years the paper sought to evoke a pioneering, exciting togetherness between party activists from all parts of the country.

In FitzGerald's hectic first year at the helm, the entire focus was on reorganising the party. For the present he was stuck with the parliamentary party he inherited. Many were uneasy about FitzGerald and his social democratic leanings. Others simply disliked the man for a mixture of reasons.

Immediately on becoming leader on 1 July 1977, FitzGerald announced that his outgoing ministerial colleagues would be his interim frontbench. They were Richie Ryan, Tom O'Donnell, Peter Barry, Paddy Donegan, Oliver Flanagan and Tom Fitzpatrick. The notable omission was Mark Clinton, who refused to serve under FitzGerald and retired to the backbenches with Liam Cosgrave. In fact, FitzGerald had been anxious to get Clinton as deputy leader. The man who had brought back the Euro-bonanzas for Irish farmers in the buoyant first years of EEC membership after 1973 would be the perfect complement to the new leader. Town and country would be wedded together in the pair; the economic guru and the farmers' champion. But Clinton had not got on well with the new leader in government. He had no reason to believe that things would change in the future. Moreover, any deputy leader must have the prospect of taking over at some stage. That was not feasible for him because of his age: he was then 62. Nor was he enamoured of the idea of an older deputy to a younger leader. In short, he felt the offer amounted to his being used. Clinton also believed at the time that Fine Gael would not be back in government for a long time, certainly not after the next election.

For all these reasons, he declined the offer. FitzGerald decided at this stage not to appoint any deputy leader, although many saw Peter Barry as the natural choice given that he had been the effective runner-up in the leadership contest.

In the autumn of 1977, FitzGerald appointed a full shadow cabinet. He retained Northern Ireland as part of his own brief, but formally shared it with Donegal's Paddy Harte, who was also spokesman on security.

The other portfolios went as follows:

Peter Barry	*Economic Affairs and Public Service*
Michael Begley	*Gaeltacht*
John Boland	*Health and Social Welfare*
John Bruton	*Agriculture*
Eddie Collins	*Education*
Austin Deasy	*Fisheries*
Tom Fitzpatrick	*Environment*
John Kelly	*Industry and Commerce*
Jim Mitchell	*Labour*
Tom O'Donnell	*Transport and Communications*
Jim O'Keeffe	*Law Reform and Human Rights*
Richie Ryan	*Foreign Affairs*
Jim White	*Defence*
Donal Creed	*Chief Whip*
Pat Cooney	*Leader of the Seanad*
Alexis FitzGerald	*Deputy Leader of the Seanad*
Joe McCartin	*Seanad Leas Cathaoirleach*

Other non-front bench appointments were:

Michael Darcy	*Agricultural Structures*
John Donnellan	*Public Works*
Tom Enright	*Tourism*
Michael Keating	*Urban Affairs*
Enda Kenny	*Youth Affairs and Sport*
Paddy O'Toole	*Consumer Affairs*

Four members of the shadow cabinet were new deputies — Boland, Deasy, Mitchell and O'Keeffe. The average age of the frontbenchers was 44.

It was scarcely a front bench of all the talents, and there was not a single woman included. Fine Gael's only woman deputy Joan Burke, was still recovering from a serious road accident and declined a post. Indeed the paucity of talent in the parliamentary party became very clear in late 1978 when FitzGerald started to draw up a team of candidates for the first direct elections to the European Parliament in 1979.

The European and local government elections gave Fine Gael a chance to identify able and dynamic candidates who could then be re-run at the next general election. The quota squatters were going to be challenged on all fronts!

3

A Face is Born

GFG or FG? The gradual subsuming of Fine Gael into the persona of Garret FitzGerald reached the first completed stage of development in June 1979. That was the month of the crucial European Parliament and local government elections. The cult of FitzGerald, leader extraordinaire, dominated the entire Fine Gael effort in those elections. A face was born.

It was a phenomenon that would grow and grow in succeeding years, as the party leader remained their greatest electoral asset. Its emergence in 1979 was for precisely this reason. Two months before the elections, a nationwide opinion poll for Fine Gael showed FitzGerald running 12 per cent ahead of his party. Jack Lynch trailed Fianna Fáil by 6 per cent. 'Vote for Garret's Team' became the main electoral slogan for Europe, and variations used included 'Get going with Garret', and 'Team FitzGerald'. The basic party badge was 'I'm for Garret', with the letters FG highlighted in different colours.

FitzGerald and Prendergast placed enormous importance on a good performance in these electoral contests, the party's first under their leadership and management. For a full year beforehand, the plans were being laid. The local government elections especially were targeted as a source of new blood, and a reflection of Fine Gael's new emphasis on women and youth. And where any old fogeys might stand in the way, they had to be ousted.

FitzGerald spelled out the message bluntly in the *National Democrat* in June 1978, a full year before the elections. Highlighting how important it would be to choose the right candidates, he went on:

Councillors who have not been active on behalf of their constituents . . . *must stand down, or be stood down* by their convention, in favour of energetic people willing to give their time and their dedication to the work of local government.

The leadership also used qualitative research and opinion polling as key guidelines on the conduct of the Euro election campaign, a practice which would be intensified in the run up to the next general election. In the autumn of 1978 Prendergast commissioned some qualitative research, based on group-guided discussions around the country, to discover what characteristics people wanted in their European representatives. The discussion groups generally opted not just for candidates with experience, but also with the expertise and ability suited to battling for national interests in the Common Market. At some of these discussions, Prendergast sat behind a screen, out of sight, making his own assessment of what the guinea-pig electors wanted.

This helped to guide FitzGerald's search for suitable candidates, the difficulty of which was compounded by a huge dearth of talent in Fine Gael. In fact, the eventual Euro line-up, and the need to deploy some candidates outside their own constituencies, really illustrates the deficiencies of the party he inherited. Prendergast's research had shown, however, that people were conscious of the need for Euro candidates to possess a degree of intelligence and expertise greater than they expected in an average Dáil deputy. FitzGerald was shrewd enough to act on this when he went headhunting for Euro candidates.

In the autumn of 1978, while on a trip to Brussels, he sought out a former economics student of his from UCD. Alan Dukes had gone on to be chief economist with the IFA in the early seventies and head of their EEC lobby centre in Brussels. He was now a member of Commissioner Dick Burke's cabinet. FitzGerald suggested he offer himself as a candidate at the Munster selection convention. (He had already sought unsuccessfully to persuade Mark Clinton to stand in this key farming province.) Dukes spent the Christmas holidays mulling over the proposal, and finally decided to

have a go. At the convention on 4 February, he was duly selected, along with former Gaeltacht Minister, Tom O'Donnell,
Deputy Jim O'Keeffe, from Cork South-West, and Cork
city alderman, John Blair. Dukes' farming expertise was to be
his selling-point.

In Leinster the party ran into difficulties when Councillor
Patsy Lawlor, from Naas, withdrew at the convention because
of a ruling from the national executive that Euro candidates
could not contest local authority seats as well. Consequently
no vote was necessary, with the two other candidates, Mark
Clinton and Senator Charles McDonald, from Laois-Offaly
being automatically selected. But the party ticket now had
no specific urban or women's appeal. The leadership had
a problem.

They decided to turn to Monica Barnes, a well-known
women's rights campaigner. She was administrator of the
Council for the Status of Women, and a leading member of
the Women's Political Association, a lobby group which
transcended party lines and sought greater involvement by
women in public life. A long-standing member of Fine Gael,
she had mounted a cheeky challenge for a nomination in her
Dun Laoghaire constituency in the 1977 general election.
But the Liam Cosgrave loyalists squashed her, and his running
mates were true, old mould Fine Gaelers, Percy Dockrell and
Sam Carroll.

With the accession of FitzGerald, Barnes was brought in
from the cold. He sent her to represent Fine Gael at the
women's conference of the European People's Party, and she
returned as its secretary-general. For much of 1978, Barnes
canvassed the party's Dublin organisation extensively, laying
the ground for a Euro nomination in the capital. She was
fairly sure of succeeding. But she agreed to her leader's
request to transfer to Leinster, although she knew she was
sacrificing her best chance of a seat.

The national executive duly ratified her addition to the
Clinton-McDonald ticket. This led to a fresh quest for a suitable women's candidate for Dublin. Prendergast had the
answer. Nuala Fennell was *the* leading women's rights campaigner, and was founder of a number of vital support groups,
like AIM in 1972, ADAPT in 1973, and the Women's Aid

hostel for battered women in 1975. Also a well-known journalist, she had stood as an Independent in the 1977 election in Dublin South County and polled very well, pulling just under 3,500 votes. She agreed to run for Fine Gael in the European election.

The other candidates in the capital were Richie Ryan, an outgoing member of the non-elected European Parliament, and Maurice Manning, a UCD politics lecturer. Manning had been a member of Fine Gael in the mid-sixties but played no role while Cosgrave was at the helm. When his friend and former colleague FitzGerald became leader, Manning wrote to him offering any help he wanted.

In Connacht-Ulster, the eventual line-up comprised three senators: Joe McCartin, from Leitrim; Myles Staunton, from Mayo; and the best known, Pat Cooney, from Longford-Westmeath. He had been Minister for Justice in Cosgrave's government and was one of the shock losers in 1977. However, his major handicap was that he was regarded as a blow-in to Connacht. A turbulent campaign ensued in this constituency, which led to complaints at the parliamentary party later.

Overall, Fine Gael's team was very uneven in terms of its calibre and public profile, and woefully lopsided geographically. In Dublin, there was no north-side candidate; nor any identifiable candidate for south Leinster. In Connacht-Ulster, there was neither an Ulster (Donegal) candidate nor one from Co. Galway; two of the three came from the middle of the constituency, and the third from a base outside the constituency altogether. On the other hand, in Munster there was a surfeit of runners. Three rather than four should have been the ticket.

In the approach to the elections, FitzGerald sought to make a virtue of his problems. 'No other party has put forward such a distinguished team, nor has any other party gone outside its own ranks to secure a high standard of representation.' The first claim was untrue; the second was enforced.

The party's MRBI poll in April 1979 was interesting. Asked which party was perceived as best for Europe, the findings were: Fianna Fáil, 50 per cent; Fine Gael, 40 per cent; Labour, 7 per cent, and Others, 3 per cent. But asked who would be the best leader for Europe, FitzGerald came out tops: 52 per cent, as against 44 per cent for Lynch. The poll also reflected very good support for Tom O'Donnell in Munster and for Mark Clinton in Leinster. But on a worrying note, it also indicated a good showing by the two Labour candidates in Dublin, Michael O'Leary and John O'Connell.

Although the poll signalled major criticism of the Fianna Fáil government — too many strikes, price rises, tax levels, not keeping their Manifesto promises etc. — support for them still looked remarkably good. Asked how they would vote in a general election, the poll sample indicated 51 per cent backing for Fianna Fáil, 35 per cent for Fine Gael, and 10 per cent for Labour.

A mere 4½ per cent recovery on the disastrous 1977 general election result did not augur well. Nor was Fine Gael able to mount a very elaborate campaign due to a shortage of finance. Fund-raising efforts were compounded by a marathon postal strike. Essentially each Euro-constituency was left to fend for itself.

Moreover, the virtual imposition of non-party people went down very badly. In Dublin, especially, the organisation did not take kindly to the arrival of Manning and Fennell, with the latter being seen as far too radical by Fine Gael's more conservative followers. But when an initial poll revealed that the party would not win even one of the four Dublin seats, it so shocked the Dublin party that it quickly pulled itself together and really got down to business under the leadership of the constituency director of elections, Mayo-born Enda Marren.

A well-known Dublin-based solicitor, Marren had been involved with Fine Gael since the sixties. In 1977, he was one of a group of Ted Nealon's friends, which also included Joe Jennings, Pat Heneghan and Bill O'Herlihy, who helped the former GIB boss in his bid to win a seat in Dublin Clontarf. Jennings, Heneghan and O'Herlihy were all professional public relations people. They were joined by Shane Molloy, a marketing expert with the Unilever Group. Marren's team faced a number of difficulties. Not only was there little public interest in the Euro elections, but their candidates had no electoral presence. The campaign needed to be livened up and the candidates hyped. The marketing men's box-of-tricks was used to discover those aspects of the three candidates which could most readily be sold to the punters. This resulted in a 'Richie was Right' slogan, highlighting the former Finance Minister's criticism of Fianna Fáil's giveaway manifesto.

The team projected Fennell as a fighter for women's rights. 'Back Your Woman' was the slick advertising slogan. Manning, the most difficult to retail, was presented as an expert on Europe. The campaign also employed a Euro-bus, T-shirts and stickers to boost both the Fine Gael team and public awareness of the election. It would all work extremely well, and Marren's boys would go on to greater challenges and successes.

But Fine Gael's real hopes of success were pinned on FitzGerald. On Monday 14 May, along with his wife, Joan, he set out on a gruelling 21-day, non-stop nationwide tour of the Euro and local constituencies. There were over a hundred stops at towns, large and small, and it ended in Wicklow on Sunday 3 June — four days before polling. It consolidated FitzGerald's standing with the party's grassroots, and emulated his winter 1977-78 odyssey. In an eve-of poll forecast, he predicted that Fine Gael would win a 'certain' five of the fifteen seats, and possibly up to seven.

There was little doubt that the party's fortunes had improved since the April poll. But the main reason for this was growing public dissatisfaction with Fianna Fáil. Quite simply, the government's extravagant 1977 manifesto was coming asunder. The essential exchequer retrenchment, following the massive growth in public spending to fund the creation of 20,000 jobs annually, was coinciding with the arrival of the second world oil crisis. May and June brought petrol shortages and long, impatient queues at filling stations. Moreover, pay settlements were exceeding government guidelines but there was still industrial unrest, particularly in the Post Office where a nationwide strike had been causing chaos since February. In Dublin, an unofficial refuse collection dispute in June meant that voters had to negotiate mounds of uncollected rubbish on their way to the polling stations.

The electorate duly poured their wrath on the government, both in the Euro and local elections. But Fine Gael was not the beneficiary. The results were a major disappointment for the party, and for FitzGerald and Prendergast in particular. Fianna Fáil's vote in the Euros plummeted from the 50.6 per cent they commanded in June 1977 to 34.6 per cent. But Fine Gael's national vote was only 33.1 per cent, less than a 3 per cent gain on 1977. The new leadership still had it all to do in order to win over the voters. The real winners in the Euro contest were the Labour Party.

Like Fine Gael, they took four seats. Fianna Fáil won five, and the remaining two went to Independents, Neil Blaney and T. J. Maher. Of course, Labour's performance was a freak outturn; they got the same number of seats as Fine Gael although their respective shares of the poll were 14.4 per cent and 33.1 per cent.

Fine Gael provided two poll-toppers. In the Dublin four-seater, Richie Ryan held this distinction, and was eventually elected, along with the Labour pair, O'Connell and O'Leary, and Síle de Valera for Fianna Fáil. Nuala Fennell also did very well. She only lost the final seat to O'Leary by 4,200 votes in a poll of 295,000.

In Leinster, Mark Clinton topped the poll, but the overall weakness of the party's team was reflected in the 8 per cent vote for McDonald and Barnes's 7 per cent. A similar fate hit Fine Gael in Connacht-Ulster where Cooney and Staunton cancelled each other out. But McCartin polled well, coming second on the first count. Here the spectacular performance was Neil Blaney's, taking 26 per cent of the overall poll.

Munster had been Fine Gael's best chance for a second seat in any constituency. But these hopes were destroyed by the intervention of the former IFA leader, T. J. Maher. He only emerged as a candidate on the very hour that nominations closed. With that, Alan Dukes kissed goodbye to any chance of a seat. In the event, Maher destroyed the field, taking 20 per cent, which compared with 26.8 per cent for the four Fine Gael candidates combined. His campaigners included many local Fine Gael party officials. This matter was subsequently raised at the parliamentary party, but they decided not to take any disciplinary action. Tom O'Donnell took the Munster seat, but Dukes ended up with a paltry 5 per cent for his months of weekend plane dashes from Brussels.

The outcome of the local elections provided some comfort for Fine Gael, however. They were defending a strong position, arising from the results of the 1974 contests, when the Cosgrave government were still dispensing EEC largesse, and the party did quite well. In the key Co. Council and Co. Borough Council elections, Fine Gael then took 33.7 per cent of the vote to Fianna Fáil's 39.8 per cent.

Now, in June 1979, the comparable figures were: Fine Gael, 35.2 per cent, Fianna Fáil, 39 per cent. The government party declined fractionally from an unaccustomedly poor position, while Fine Gael slightly improved what had been, for them, an exceptionally good position. But the real significance of the local election result only became apparent later. It was the emergence of a raft of very able new councillors, who would go on in 1981-82 to win Dáil seats. These were the younger generation that FitzGerald and Prendergast were seeking to woo to Fine Gael, and for whom they were making the going rough on the old guard.

Among the party's new councillors were Gay Mitchell, Richard Bruton, Mary Flaherty, George Birmingham, Hugh Coveney, Bernard Allen, Madeline Taylor, Ivan Yates, Brendan McGahon, Avril Doyle, Nora Owen and Alan Shatter. All were winning office for the first time, and would go on to win Dáil seats.

Prendergast's recruitment of Shatter, a leading advocate of family law reform, to run in the Whitechurch district of Dublin Co. Council led to uproar within the local organisation. It was very conservative, and had its fair quota of Knights of Columbanus. Shatter was seen as being pro-divorce and, therefore, anathema. He failed to get through the convention, but Prendergast had the national executive add him. It was only one example among many of the new regime's determination to have its way, even if it meant blood on the carpet.

———

Following the elections, FitzGerald reshuffled his front bench on 12 June to take account of three of its members, Ryan, Clinton and McCartin, being elected to Europe. They were dropped, but it rankled with Ryan and O'Donnell that they were not informed beforehand. They were in Brussels when they learned of the changes. The other major development was FitzGerald's designation of Peter Barry as deputy leader, as well as being spokesman on Finance and Public Service. Promoted to the front bench were Michael Keating (Law Reform and Human Rights); Paddy O'Toole (Industry and Commerce) and Gerry L'Estrange (Chief Whip). The new junior spokesmen were Paddy Hegarty and Fergus O'Brien.

After two years in charge, FitzGerald could claim qualified success. The decline of the party had been stemmed. It had improved on its very good 1974 local elections result, and in the process thrown up some very good general election candidates. But the Euro elections had betrayed the inherent lack of talent in depth in Fine Gael.

The glaring omission, however, still remained any real attention to policy formation. In the local elections, policy was a hotch-potch of vague ideas. For instance, it was proposed that local authorities be given power to put down questions to government departments regarding local projects, and have them answered like parliamentary questions! On the central question of how local government might be financed, now that domestic rates had disappeared, the party settled for presenting a series of options for consideration. A major policy document on local government reform was promised before the next general election.

In February 1979, four months before the local elections, a comprehensive Northern Ireland policy had been launched in Belfast by FitzGerald and Paddy Harte, and simultaneously by Prendergast in Dublin and Ted Nealon in London. This reiterated the party's existing commitment to Irish unity only by consent, which FitzGerald and Harte had been instrumental in formulating in 1969. It also indicated a preference for a federal/confederal approach. The previous month the party had approved a local radio policy, favouring a mix of public and private enterprise community stations.

Otherwise, the party's basic policy stance had been relentless criticism of Fianna Fáil. There was a marked absence of credible alternatives. This contrasted sharply with the more aggressive stance of the embryonic Young Fine Gael organisation. At its first annual conference in Liberty Hall in January

1979, it passed a series of resolutions that attacked the government's proposed family planning bill as inadequate; called for the repeal of the law against homosexuality, the abolition of the status of illegitimacy, a ban on the building of single-sex schools, and control of the price of building land.

The junior organisation had been given unique powers of freedom and representation in FitzGerald's constitution. It had two members on the national executive, and there was a youth officer on each constituency executive. At the 1979 árd fheis Young Fine Gael came of age within the party when national executive delegate, Madeline Taylor (27), a daughter of Clare's deputy Frank Taylor, was elected one of the two honorary secretaries of the party. The non-parliamentary party vice-president elected was Councillor Charlie Kelly, a Swinford solicitor. That árd fheis also marked the first election of twelve national executive members from among the delegates, none of whom could be public representatives. In June, Taylor and another Young Fine Gael executive member, Mary Flaherty, won seats in the local elections.

The June polls underlined the amount of ground that Fine Gael had yet to make up to pose a serious threat to Fianna Fáil. The conventional political wisdom, shared by FitzGerald and Prendergast, was that they still had at least two years to prepare. But in the autumn of '79, there followed the most dramatic political developments which transformed the whole situation.

During the summer, two Cork TDs, Fianna Fáil's Seán Brosnan and Labour's Pat Kerrigan, died. This meant two by-elections after the Dáil resumed in October. Long before then, however, Prendergast was immersed in a plan of campaign to ensure the best possible Fine Gael performance. Notwithstanding the enormous unpopularity of the government, Fianna Fáil were overwhelming odds-on favourites to win both contests. After all, the Kerrigan by-election would be in Jack Lynch's own Cork City constituency, where, in 1977, Fianna Fáil took 58.6 per cent of the vote to Fine Gael's 25 per cent and Labour's 10.2 per cent. In Cork North-East, where the Brosnan by-election would be fought, the statistics were not quite as grim for Fine Gael — in '77, Fianna Fáil had 48 per cent to their 33.2 per cent — but it was still a daunting gap.

In the second week of September, Prendergast ordered exhaustive opinion polls to be conducted in both constituencies in order to provide Fine Gael with the 'informational framework which would enable the party to maximise the prospects of success in the election'. It set out to measure every relevant piece of data: how the government were doing overall; the ratings of Lynch and FitzGerald; voting intentions in a general election; the issues the government should be tackling; issues a local TD should tackle; whether the by-elections were an opportunity to give a verdict on the government; was it good or bad for Fianna Fáil to have so many seats; how had people voted in 1977 and in the Euro-election; and how they proposed voting in the by-election.

The most significant finding was the very high level of undecided voters in both constituencies: 28 per cent in Cork City, and 26 per cent in Cork North-East. Otherwise, the Fine Gael showing was not encouraging. In Cork City, Fianna Fáil led by 32 per cent to Fine Gael's 19 per cent. In North-East the comparable figures were 35 per cent and 21 per cent. The only hope was to win over the uncommitted. That needed attractive policies and convincing candidates. But Prendergast, with the marketing man's ability to read the polls accurately, realised that the other research data held the key that might unlock the door to success.

The people were unhappy with the government over prices, taxation, unemployment, Northern Ireland, security, strikes and inadequate pensions. In that order. There was also a discernible feeling that Fianna Fáil was too large and complacent. The by-elections were seen as a chance to 'give a verdict' on them. A further refinement was that in Cork city people felt a local deputy should be concerned primarily about housing; they saw this, however, as only ninth in a list of priorities for the government.

It was the attention to candidate selection, which underscored Fine Gael's new professional approach. The poll aimed not only to assess their own possible candidates, but also those for Fianna Fáil! Now this was before either party had even selected their candidates. In Cork City, Fine Gael had a choice of five possibles: the former Euro candidate, John Blair; Lord Mayor, Jim Corr; and three aldermen, Bernard

Allen, Hugh Coveney and Liam Burke. In the poll, Burke pipped Blair on name-identification, with Coveney last. Burke also topped the party list on who would best represent Cork.

It had to be Burke. Then a member of the Seanad, he had been a TD from 1969 to 1977, and his outperforming of Blair was particularly significant. The latter had just had massive exposure as a Euro candidate. Prendergast made sure that, when the selection convention came round on 5 October, there were no foul-ups. Burke got the nomination.

In Cork North-East, the leading contenders for the Fine Gael nomination were Councillor Michael Broderick of Buttevant, and Tommy Sheahan. Broderick had been the party's unsuccessful candidate in a 1974 by-election. Sheahan was a former president of Macra na Feirme and was very well known in farming circles. However, Prendergast was anxious to see how Myra Barry, the 22-year-old daughter of their veteran local deputy, Dick Barry, would come across with those polled. She had already been active in Young Fine Gael, and was the first chairman of their Dublin Finglas constituency branch, while a student teacher at St Patrick's Training College. She was now teaching locally, at Bartlemy school. Myra only got to hear of Prendergast's move because one of her brothers, Pat, was among those polled. He told the MRBI researcher that he did not think Myra Barry would be a suitable candidate!

Nevertheless, Barry came a close second to Broderick in the various criteria used by the pollsters, with Sheahan trailing third. Prendergast reckoned that if she could show up so well without even being an aspiring candidate, then she was their best chance. Another consideration was that Broderick had been a two-time loser: in the 1974 by-election and in the 1977 general election. Moreover, Barry's father, who had represented the constituency since 1953, had already made a public statement indicating that he would not be contesting the next general election. After twenty-six years in the Dáil, the 59-year-old Fermoy auctioneer, publican and farmer wanted to make way for a younger person.

Armed with the findings from the opinion poll, Prendergast set out for Cork. His first task was to convince Myra Barry that she should stand at all. Fortuitously, he arrived at the

Barry home when Myra's parents were out at a funeral. She was very reluctant but finally, after further discussion with them, she agreed to go forward. But she felt she had no chance of winning. 'Just look at the figures', was her attitude. It was a view echoed by everyone else, and Prendergast was faced with a lot of scepticism among senior members of the party. 'How can you get a young blonde girl elected?' That was the question.

Prendergast left nothing to chance. At the beginning of October, he moved base from Mount St to Fermoy, in the heart of Cork North-East and within easy driving distance of the city. 'I wanted to prove to the organisation that you can do anything that you set out to do. According to Irish political mythology, you could not get Myra Barry elected. We had to get people thinking in terms of managing things.'

He also had to persuade the party's other deputy in Cork North-East, Paddy Hegarty, to throw his forces behind the elect-Barry campaign. Tensions had always run high between the two camps at election time, but the fact that Dick Barry would be standing down at the next election, and that Hegarty would be facing only one Barry then, was the clincher in winning his support.

The entire manpower and resources of Fine Gael were thrown into the by-elections. Voting day was finally fixed for Wednesday 7 November. FitzGerald played a major role, walking virtually every street and road of the two constituencies in the final three weeks. Fianna Fáil were on the defensive. Their economic plans and targets were in tatters and the budget deficit was out of control. Lynch, who spent little time in his home constituency, blamed a 40 per cent increase in oil prices that year for their woes. At the end of October, there were nationwide power cuts due to an ESB dispute. The lights were also going out for the government.

Nevertheless, on the eve of the by-elections, the Fianna Fáil general secretary, Seamus Brennan, confidently predicted that they would win both contests. The bookies agreed. Cork bookie Liam Cashman was offering 14 to 1 against Fine Gael winning both. Prendergast took the odds and placed his bet.

On Thursday, 8 November, when the counting stopped, the politically impossible had happened. Fine Gael had won both seats. Jack Lynch had been humiliated in his own back-yard. Fianna Fail's 33 per cent margin in Cork City and their 15 per cent margin in Cork North-East, had both been wiped out.

In Cork City, Burke won on the third count. The first preference shareout was 35.9 per cent for Fianna Fáil's John Dennehy; 33.2 per cent for Burke, and 22.6 per cent for Labour's Toddie O'Sullivan. The government's vote was down an incredible 22 per cent on the general election.

In Cork North-East, Myra Barry won on the second count. The first-preference vote was 38.6 per cent for Fine Gael; 36.3 per cent for Fianna Fáil's 'unbeatable' John Brosnan (son of the late deputy), and 22.8 per cent for Joe Sherlock of the Workers' Party.

A remarkable feature of the two results was the accuracy of Fine Gael's mid-September opinion poll on the size of Fianna Fáil's vote. That had put their Cork City vote at 32 per cent, and at 35 per cent in North-East. Clearly, Fine Gael's consummate planning had worked. They had managed, through judicious candidate selection and a good campaign, to win over a sufficient number of the uncommitted. They had pushed up their 1977 performance in the city from 25 per cent to 33 per cent, and in Cork North-East from 33 per cent to 38.6 per cent. Clearly many voters had been won over, but the really decisive factor was high abstentions among government supporters.

Fine Gael were ecstatic. It was FitzGerald's finest hour yet. And Prendergast had proved to the organisation that the impossible could be achieved electorally — provided it was properly managed!

FitzGerald made it clear in his subsequent comments that he did not foresee the real contest, a general election, for another two years. But they were nicely on course. Even half the swing to Fine Gael in Cork City would make them the largest party, if it were repeated nationally at the next election. When Burke and Barry took their seats in the Dáil on Tuesday, 13 November, pushing Fine Gael's strength to forty-five deputies, the party's joy was unconfined. There were many words of commendation for the two directors of elections, Austin Deasy and Fergus O'Brien. But the real hero was

FitzGerald. Clearly, Fine Gael had backed a winner in him, and in his scalpel, Prendergast, who was by now back at Mount St cutting away.

For Fianna Fáil the by-elections were a disaster. Jack Lynch had left for a scheduled visit to the United States before the results materialised. He was shaken by the outcome, and described it as a serious mid-term rebuff. He promised a government reshuffle in the new year. But many of his backbenchers were not prepared to wait that long. The heave against Jack was on.

4

Enter the National Handlers!

On the afternoon of 11 December 1979, Charles J. Haughey reached the top of the greasy pole. He was the political bene-ficiary of the Fianna Fáil backbench revolt against Jack Lynch. Following the Cork by-elections, fears for their own electoral survival drove government backbenchers to desert the man who had pulled off the triumph of 1977. They turned instead to Haughey, who thus achieved the greatest comeback in the history of Irish politics. Now, on 11 Decem-ber, came the formal Dáil debate on his nomination as Taoiseach. With the huge Fianna Fáil majority, he could not possibly lose: the whole business was a formality. But it was an important formality for the new Taoiseach. After all those years in the wilderness, this was to be the apotheosis of Charlie Haughey.

Garret FitzGerald did not regard the debate as a mere for-mality. He had a deep distrust of Haughey and genuinely felt that he was not fit to be Taoiseach. Moreover, he believed that some Fianna Fáil deputies had been intimidated into supporting Haughey against George Colley in the recent leadership election. All this so coloured his view of the new Fianna Fáil boss that he stayed up until 5 a.m. on the morning of the debate in order to finalise his speech.

Nearly twelve hours later, he rose in the Dáil. He began by saying that he had known Haughey for thirty-five years. 'I have never suffered insult or injury from him, nor exchanged with him bitter words at any time.' That was all about to change. FitzGerald was bracing himself 'to do my duty, regardless of these personal considerations'.

The remarks that followed were important for two reasons. First, they permanently soured the personal relationship of

45

the two men who were to dominate Irish politics in the first half of the eighties. Second, they damaged FitzGerald's reputation as the Irish politician who was uniquely above that sort of vulgar, personal abuse which is so common in Irish political life.

FitzGerald declared that Haughey was coming before the Dáil for ratification 'with a flawed pedigree. His motives can be judged ultimately only by God.' He was in no doubt that Haughey wanted to dominate, to own the state rather than to serve it. Nor did he believe that Haughey commanded 'the genuine confidence of even one-third of this House, never mind one-half. No previous Taoiseach has been elected in similar circumstances. . . . The feet that will go through that lobby to support his election will include many that will drag. The hearts of many who will climb those stairs before turning aside to vote will be heavy.' He called out the names of the 'genuine patriots' in the Fianna Fáil party, Deputies Colley, O'Malley, O'Donoghue, Wilson, Faulkner, Gallagher, Molloy and Woods, and declared that Haughey had not got his majority from them.

Haughey, he asserted, had had the backing of the self-interested and the fatally misguided nationalists of his party. He saw dangers to the state 'that lie almost inexorably and fatally embedded in the nomination now before us'. He forecast that 'the mixture of men and motives artificially concocted to create a formal majority for Deputy Haughey when this debate ends must be frail and fragile. It cannot survive indefinitely the pressures on it imposed by his — I must say it — flawed character'.

FitzGerald said the new Fianna Fáil leader had for nine years following the Arms Trial refused to utter one word of condemnation of the IRA. He would be a barrier to Irish unity by agreement. His contraception bill had been a piece of blatant hypocrisy. And his election would be 'an uncovenanted bonus' to Fine Gael, since it would bring them many Fianna Fáil voters.

Haughey listened in silence to all this. His wife, mother and other family members were in the public gallery. Much of what FitzGerald said actually proved quite prophetic: Haughey's leadership was a source of persistent and bitter division in Fianna Fáil. And he did prove to be one of Fine Gael's greatest electoral assets. But FitzGerald's speech was a bad miscalculation. It was both unctuous and pompous, and it flung the most serious charges at Haughey in general terms without any specific proof or support adduced for them.

Both in the immediate aftermath of the speech and later, FitzGerald showed a marked reluctance to be drawn further on it. Although he did explain that the 'flawed pedigree' was a reference to the arms trial and was never intended to refer to Haughey's private life, he conceded that it had been a stupid phrase to use. He also regretted the whole affair on account of the presence of Haughey's family in the Dáil that day, and further acknowledged that many Fine Gael supporters had been unhappy with parts of it.

Whatever about these considerations, the vote in the Dáil was unaffected. At the end of the day, Charles J. Haughey was the new Taoiseach.

Peter Barry was aghast. Charlie Haughey was stealing Fine Gael's clothes. Telling the Irish nation that they were living beyond their means, that the good times were over. There was going to have to be some austerity. But those were all Fine Gael lines! What was Haughey up to? Barry was torn between fears for what it would bode for his party, and the realisation that the Haughey prescription was what the country needed.

It was Wednesday, 9 January, 1980. Haughey was just a month in power. He had made his reputation as a strong, decisive Minister for Finance in the sixties. Many people, not only in Fianna Fáil, now looked to him to cure the contagion of strikes, spiralling prices, soaring unemployment, and looming national bankruptcy. And here he was, at the beginning of the new year, in a special televised broadcast, telling the nation what it wanted to hear. Government spending was too high, and had to be cut. Exchequer borrowing was excessive. There had to be industrial peace. The country had to live within its means. He was effectively disowning the politics of the 1977 manifesto and the policies of the previous three and a half years. Just as Fine Gael had been doing for all that period. No wonder Peter Barry was concerned.

He was not the only influential figure in Fine Gael with similar fears. Brendan Dowling, the economist who briefed FitzGerald and Barry on financial matters, was also watching and listening. He felt that Haughey's message would be more appealing to Fine Gael voters than Fianna Fáil followers.

It all led to a great fear inside the top ranks of Fine Gael. What if Haughey was to go to the country now? He could plausibly look for a personal mandate on a platform which stressed financial rectitude. Just as Fine Gael were planning to do . . . but not for about two years yet.

Haughey was a very different political animal to Lynch. Fine Gael needed to review their strategy. It was time for another opinion poll, this time based on a nationwide sample of 600 electors. It revealed a dramatic upsurge in support for Fianna Fáil since the change of leadership. Polls taken before Lynch stood down indicated that likely Fianna Fáil support in a general election had slumped below 40 per cent, and that a Fine Gael-Labour coalition would probably win an election. Fine Gael itself was only 5 per cent behind the government. Now, only a few weeks later, the party's own poll revealed that when the 'don't knows' were excluded Fianna Fáil would get 52 per cent; Fine Gael 34 per cent; Labour 9 per cent; Sinn Féin, 3 per cent, and others, 2 per cent.

Under various categories, those polled indicated a high regard for Haughey, and held high hopes for his leadership. How would the Fianna Fáil government do under him? Quite well, to very well, said 63 per cent. Even 45 per cent of Fine Gael people queried held these views. Only 29 per cent of those polled reckoned the government would do badly or not well under Haughey.

However, some glimmer of light for Fine Gael came from the response to another query. Should the Haughey government be held responsible for the 1977 manifesto? Seventy-three per cent said yes. The most important issues identified for the government to tackle were taxation, inflation, housing, strikes, Northern Ireland and the level of welfare benefits.

Fianna Fáil scored best in the ratings on which party cared most about farmers, employees, business and the under-privileged. Only on farmers did Fine Gael seriously challenge.

Asked to rate Haughey as Fianna Fáil leader, 35 per cent put him in the excellent/very good categories; a further 44 per cent rated him as good/fair; 58 per cent of all *Fine Gael* supporters were in these categories. Only 5 per cent of those polled rated Haughey a 'poor' Fianna Fáil leader.

And what were the main qualities perceived in the country's new leader? Twenty per cent saw him as strong, dynamic and positive, while 11 per cent reckoned he had good leadership qualities. The gun-running/Arms Trial affair led the list of negative qualities associated with him. But only 15 per cent of those polled cited it. Opposite him, FitzGerald's good points showed 17 per cent regarding him as a good man to be in charge, while 15 per cent rated him honest and straight. His biggest fault was that he criticised too much. That was the view of 10 per cent. Compared to Haughey's impressive showing, it did not add up to much of a profile.

Fine Gael also wanted to see whom the electorate rated as the best person to handle various key issues. Haughey was tops on energy requirements, unemployment, inflation, social welfare, the economy/public spending, industrial relations and women's issues. FitzGerald headed only four categories: education, security of the state, Northern Ireland and youth problems.

In January 1980 then it was clear that the public's concern was focused on the economy, and their hopes on the prospect of Haughey living up to his reputation as a financial wizard. His Northern policy was not then an issue. All this was clear from Fine Gael's poll, and the party leadership was terrified that the new Taoiseach might go to the country. Prendergast worried about whether Fianna Fáil would see their opportunity. He recalled later that 'if Haughey had gone for his own mandate, he would have won by a landslide'.

The front bench decided therefore, as a quite deliberate strategy, to go easy on the government, lest they give them any possible pretext to call an election! Meantime it was essential to redouble their own preparations for an election that was now possibly round the next corner. Thus was born the Fine Gael General Election Communications Committee. In charge was Ted Nealon, and he gathered around him a group of expert strategists to commence formal preparations for an election.

The nucleus of the group were personal friends who had worked for him in the 1977 general election: Enda Marren, Bill O'Herlihy, Pat Heneghan, Joe Jennings and Shane Molloy. They had also come together under Marren during the Dublin Euro campaign the previous year. Other occasional contributors included Des Benson, Vincent Hunter, John Blair, John Donegan, Bill Butler, John Kerry Keane, Paddy Jennings, and Dan Egan.

The committee covered all aspects of an election campaign, except for the party's policy. They ranged from election posters (samples from ten countries were studied), literature, advertising, gimmicks and a leader's tour, to special proposals for Dublin, equipment and staffing for an election press centre, music, and special youth campaigns.

Separate sub-committees were delegated to look after each issue. By March, Nealon's group were looking for a blueprint for a nationwide campaign tour. Another committee member, Cork-based PR man, Seán Power, who had been press officer on FitzGerald's Euro-tour suggested a rail safari of the country at the start of the election campaign.

Power waxed lyrical on the subject. A rail safari had not been done since Truman did it in the 1948 US presidential contest. He pointed out in a document to his colleagues that Truman had won. Moreover, a train blitz of the country would enable Fine Gael to seize the initiative, and would be certain to command extensive media coverage. He also advised small, relaxed, informal press conferences for FitzGerald, not sterile gatherings in large rooms. He illustrated the usefulness of 'press image and publicity' with two exemplary tales from the 1979 Euro tour. 'For instance, press reports that we had (a) telephone links on the bus (which we hadn't) and (b) cocktail facilities (which we hadn't) helped to whet many an appetite.' The message was: it pays to massage the hacks!

Haughey, however, showed no signs of going for that snap

election. The February budget was utterly irreconcilable with the January television address. But it did little to reassure Fine Gael: so acute was their election paranoia that they feared that Haughey was talking tough and acting soft, so as really to scoop the pool at an early general election.

FitzGerald underlined the new political uncertainty in the January issue of the *National Democrat*. 'We cannot know just how long the present unhappy alliance of Haugheyite and anti-Haugheyite Fianna Fáil will last. . . . From this moment onwards, we must be ready for a contest at any time, while continuing our preparations for a long haul to an end-of-1981 or early-1982 election.'

He summed up the party's requirements as (1) the perfection of the organisation; (2) 'the raising of finance on the scale necessary to a national party preparing to seek a mandate to govern the country', and (3) the formulation of policies. (Fine Gael, however, was unaware of the internal party constraints on Haughey. Colley had a veto on the incumbents at Justice and Defence and Haughey also had to pay off some of the backbench rump that brought him to power with junior ministries. The new Taoiseach couldn't just dash to the country.)

In February, Ted Nealon was assuring the Fine Gael faithful, through the party paper also, that policies on agriculture, health, education, social welfare, family and human rights were now well advanced. They were being considered at front bench and parliamentary party level.

The party had also approved a major document on Dáil reform by John Bruton at the end of 1979. But despite this sudden flurry of policy activity, there was a marked reluctance by Fine Gael to take up clear-cut positions on difficult policy issues. This was a hangover from the 1977 election. The conventional wisdom in the party was that a key reason for that trouncing was the introduction of farmer taxation and the wealth tax by the Cosgrave government.

We have seen the policy lacuna that persisted in June 1979 at the local government elections. What was happening was that FitzGerald was attempting a unique balancing act. He was seeking to attract younger people and women, which required innovative, sometimes radical, policies. But at the same time he did not want to alienate his bedrock support of 25 per cent of the electorate. Unfortunately, this largely comprised the solidly conservative farming and business sectors. By definition, the bulk of the party's Dáil deputies returned in 1977 would reflect their concerns. Neither they, nor their electorate, were social democratic or radical innovators. The party leader had to take account of these constraints.

Neither FitzGerald nor any other deputy, for instance, sought to defend the Wealth Tax when Fianna Fáil abolished it in 1978. Happily they were spared their blushes at having to take any formal stance on it. The guillotining of that year's Finance Bill precluded a specific vote on it. In 1979, the party eventually came down against the government's 2 per cent sales levy on farmers. That July, FitzGerald said that farming should be taxed on accounts, like any other business.

The most glaring evidence of the party's failure to come to terms with contentious issues was their response to Haughey's Family Planning Bill of 1979. It sought to confine non-medical contraceptives to married couples only, on a doctor's prescription. In March the Fine Gael Parliamentary Party decided, after very conflicting views were expressed, to oppose the bill. But they failed to put down any amendments whatsoever to it. 'Because we were too cowardly' was the reason bluntly stated by Deputy Michael Keating in an interview later that year.

An interview with John Bruton in the *Irish Times* in October 1979 also revealed much about the true nature of the party. Olivia O'Leary wanted to know if Bruton saw his party leader as too liberal. Bruton, a wealthy Co. Meath farmer, and then just 32, replied: 'There is no fear of FitzGerald, but there is fear of capital taxation as such.'

In the wake of the 1979 Euro elections, and especially the performance of T. J. Maher in Munster, Fine Gael were fearful of a Farmers' Party emerging. Some of their own local organisation people had campaigned for Maher. Fine Gael, and that included FitzGerald, would do nothing to ruffle the farmers.

Fortunately for Fine Gael, none of this really mattered. In 1980, as the party leader set out in quest of policies that would woo the voters, there was really only a single burning issue: income tax reform. The PAYE sector had exploded with anger into some of the largest street demonstrations the country had ever seen. The issues were the structure and spread of taxation, which taxpayers saw as not only oppressive, but biased against them. In March 1980, Haughey's government sought to solve the problem by setting up a high-powered Commission on Taxation. This was to examine the entire system, and make proposals to reform it and make it fairer.

FitzGerald had no doubt that a comprehensive tax reform programme, significantly easing the burden on the PAYE sector, would be a surefire election winner. He turned to economist Brendan Dowling for help. Aged 33, he had been a student of FitzGerald's in UCD. Later, in 1975, Dowling became his economic adviser when he was Minister for Foreign Affairs. Since 1977, he had been informally advising FitzGerald and Peter Barry on financial issues arising in the Dáil. Even better, he had special expertise on the tax issue. He was the author of a recent major report on taxation and social welfare for the National Economic and Social Council.

From early 1980, FitzGerald and Dowling began intensive examination of a tax reform programme. Nobody else was involved. None of the party's frontbenchers contributed, not even Finance spokesman, Peter Barry. Yet this was going to be the cornerstone of their election policy.

Meanwhile, the party — or, more accurately, FitzGerald — was having continued success in wooing young people and women. Young Fine Gael marked its further development with its second annual conference in Dublin in January 1980. And through them, the party leader continued to appeal to the younger generation, which as he told the conference, constituted one-third of the entire electorate.

He also made clear his commitment to letting them have their head 'despite the genuine doubts and qualms of some who sincerely feared that your free debates and uninhibited declarations might, in some circumstances, embarrass the party at national level.' They took him at his word. The conference decided to launch a nationwide campaign to abolish illegitimacy. A round of countrywide meetings was held, and 100,000 signatures collected.

A Women's Group in the party was also formally launched in February, at a meeting in the Royal Dublin Hotel. Already in the 1979 local elections, the number of Fine Gael women councillors had gone up by seventeen to fifty-two. The new group also doubled as the Women's Group of the European People's Party, to which Fine Gael was affiliated. FitzGerald addressed their first general meeting on 3 May and he urged women to aspire to all decision-making levels in the party. Already at that year's árd fheis, in March, two of them had made their mark. Madeline Taylor retained her honorary secretaryship and Monica Barnes, who topped the poll, became one of the four vice-presidents. In the process, she defeated a number of the party's TDs.

The woman that Liam Cosgrave had kept out in Dun Laoghaire in 1977 was now a senior officer of the party. Fine Gael was surely changing, although the winner of the other three vice-presidential posts reflected the more traditional, conservative face of Fine Gael. They were Mid-Cork deputy, Donal Creed, a 55-year-old Macroom farmer; Ted Russell, a 62-year-old Limerick businessman and company director; and Senator Charles McDonald, a 44-year-old Portlaoise farm-owner.

However, Barnes's achievement was significant. This was further borne out by the fact that one of the losers in the vice-presidential contest was the former government minister, Tom Fitzpatrick.

So far, so good for FitzGerald's Fine Gael. By fudging contentious policy issues on the one hand, and also sweet-talking young people and women, he was staying on the tightrope, and facing two ways at once.

———————

The internal party restructuring posed more direct difficulties. Prendergast continued to be the scalpel, and his incisions into various constituency organisations incurred the wrath of the sitting deputies and their supporters. This conflict was exacerbated in 1980 by his urgent quest for suitable candidates for that feared snap election. Later he described part of this role in those difficult 1977-81 years as being 'to dig holes to bury certain people'.

The constituency organisers were his storm troopers. 'My people', as Prendergast termed them, came to Mount St for regular briefings and missions. They were coached on canvassing and research, and the importance of securing later transfers from people voting for other parties. Prendergast pointed out that only 16 per cent of the TDs elected in 1977 won on the first count; all the others relied on transfers. His was a gruelling job. A continual cycle of meetings from Bantry to Glenties and back at his desk in Dublin the following morning. He observed later that he was closer to the constituency organisers than their own wives!

There were occasional summonses to the parliamentary party to explain his actions to angry TDs. In April 1980, Eddie Collins of Waterford complained bitterly about headquarters communicating with non-elected people in constituencies concerning their local TD, the local organisation, and party affairs generally. This was being done behind deputies' backs and he insisted that henceforth copies of all correspondence from Mount St should go to the local deputy. Other colleagues supported Collins's complaints, and the party decided that Prendergast and Ted Nealon should attend their next meeting.

When they duly turned up, they faced a torrent of allegations. Collins complained about leaks to the media of his earlier remarks, and said that the person responsible should be expelled from the party. He and Senators Patrick Cooney and Ger Lynch said that Prendergast was dealing with people locally behind their backs. The constituency organisers were biased in some cases, Cooney said. Deputy Joan Burke spoke of meetings in her Roscommon constituency that she was never notified about. Michael Begley complained about the activities of Young Fine Gael in South Kerry.

Prendergast said as little as possible. He denied that he had a low opinion of public representatives, or that he was trying to manipulate them in certain cases. FitzGerald said there would be no going behind people's backs and he invited any TDs or senators with fears to come and discuss them with him.

Such clashes recurred frequently during the remainder of 1980. Various TDs, including Begley and Kieran Crotty from Carlow-Kilkenny, accused Prendergast of approaching certain people to stand as Fine Gael candidates without the sitting TDs being consulted. Many others told similar stories.

———————

By August 1980, a comprehensive election campaign strategy had been drawn up by Nealon and his bevy of PR and marketing men. Standardised posters for the party leader (with the legend 'Garret for Taoiseach') and the forty-one constituencies 'Garret's Team') were devised. There would be 137,000 FitzGerald posters: a third would be mounted when the election was called. The second third would accompany the candidate posters. The final third would be retained for the leader's tour, polling day, and special campaign functions.

Nealon's committee attached immense importance to a nationwide leader's tour. They reckoned the election would be a presidential-style campaign between FitzGerald and Haughey. It would attract extensive media coverage and would be a major morale-boost to the local organisation. Seán Power's curtain-raising train tour was also adopted, and built into the schedule.

The August draft report also addressed the problem of campaigning in Dublin, where electoral apathy would be greatest. This required a special impact and unique gimmicks. A seaside 'topless' bus was one measure proposed. Another possible gimmick was an airship balloon, which would be hoisted each day over whatever town or city FitzGerald would be visiting during the campaign.

Nealon's people were also well aware of Fine Gael's dual focus by this time. They advised an election advertising campaign that would 'reassure the main body of our existing support', while at the same time 'going after the particular sections of the electorate where we think we can gain most new support.'

But there were a couple of question-marks posed in their blueprint. What would be the election policies, and the prevailing economic conditions? And what about the style of the campaign. 'For instance, will it be centred mainly on the leader?', Nealon asked. The Communications Committee therefore urged two things: a qualitative research programme on political attitudes, and talks with FitzGerald, and the Strategy Committee, to clarify the major elements of the campaign.

This latter committee had also been set up by FitzGerald to help prepare for the election. One of its primary functions became sorting out where outgoing TDs would stand in view of the revision of constituencies laid down that April by the first-ever Independent Commission. That review reduced the number of constituencies by one to forty-one; increased the number of Dáil seats by eighteen, and created fifteen five-seaters. Previously there had only been six. The strategy committee also wanted to identify other suitable candidates.

FitzGerald chaired it. However, one of the problems it faced was whether Richie Ryan should stand with the party leader in the revamped Dublin South-East. Most of Ryan's Rathmines/Rathgar base had been annexed to South-East, and he was adamant that he should. FitzGerald was opposed to this, but Ryan had his way. Because of his personal involvement with the work of the committee, FitzGerald yielded the chair to Dooge. The other members were Mayo solicitor Charlie Kelly, who advised on the Western situation, Seán O'Leary, Prendergast and Peter Barry.

The other crucial item to be addressed in the election preparations was fund-raising. In the 1977 election, party headquarters had spent £200,000. But most of this very sizeable sum went on newspaper advertising. After FitzGerald became party leader, the party's financial problems escalated as the organisation grew at their costly new headquarters in Mount St. FitzGerald was also paid a salary as leader; on his own suggestion it equated with a ministerial salary. Altogether, by 1978, head office was costing about £150,000.

By 1980, the party had run seriously into the red. The long-standing Capital Branch, which existed primarily to underwrite deficits, had ceased to function on a regular basis after 1977. It was time to shake it up. Under a re-organisation instigated by FitzGerald, Vincent Ferguson, a director of Fitzwilton, became chairman, and a nucleus of about a dozen active members were appointed around him. The most significant was accountant Seán Murray. Other businessmen giving of their time to boost the party coffers, through subscriptions from their own community, including James Barton, Enda Marren and Sylvester Muldowney (a veteran member of the Capital Branch). It was a very secretive affair, and they operated virtually anonymously. Only the party trustees, nominated by the leader, were entitled to view Capital Branch files. In 1980, they were Muldowney, Richie Ryan and Peter Barry.

In a message to the party in April 1980, Barry set a target of half a million pounds for a general election fighting fund. In addition to the Capital Branch's efforts, the national executive and parliamentary party agreed to levy the constituencies for nearly £300,000 of that. A levy of £2,000 per Dáil seat was set; thus a three-seat constituency would have to raise £6,000 for headquarters; a five seater, £10,000.

By the autumn of the year, Fine Gael were extremely advanced in their election preparations. Nealon's committee had drawn up a precise blueprint covering everything except the proposed manifesto. Capital Branch was sending begging letters to businesses, large and small, looking for donations. And Prendergast was beavering away, with the aid of the Strategy Committee, to identify the best possible candidate line-up.

Inevitably, he continued to incur the hostility of the parliamentary party. Along with FitzGerald, he was keen to get selection conventions going so that the chosen candidates could proceed campaigning unofficially. But this was a red rag to the parliamentary party bull. The last thing a deputy wanted was constituency rivals for his seat — officially licensed by the party to campaign — while he was tied down in Dáil Éireann for three days a week.

In mid-November, they made their position crystal clear and the parliamentary party discussed the whole question. FitzGerald sought to assure them that there was nothing sinister in the idea of early conventions. They were not impressed. Paddy Donegan, and Jim White proposed that no candidate be selected. The motion was passed unanimously! That was the end of that nonsense. Prendergast, however, had other ideas.

This setback for FitzGerald at the hands of the Oireachtas Party came on top of an even more dramatic reverse. Confident that they had Haughey and the government on the run, and that they were well advanced in their own election preparations, Fine Gael had faced into a by-election contest in Donegal on 6 November in a swaggering, confident mood.

Things had been going from bad to worse for Fianna Fáil. Having missed the chance of a sweeping endorsement by the electorate earlier in the year, Haughey's image as a tough, decisive man of action was proving false. Unemployment, which was 89,000 when he took office, was headed for 122,000 at the end of 1980. Inflation was soaring from 13 per cent at the end of 1979 to 18 per cent at the end of 1980.

In his celebrated January television broadcast, Haughey had described the 1979 budget deficit of £520 million and the capital programme, which brought total borrowing that year to over a billion pounds, as 'something that cannot possibly continue'. His own government's 1980 current budget deficit was set at £353 million. By November, it was overrunning massively. It would end up at £547 million — nearly £200 million out! Public service pay was out of control. The new Taoiseach was securing industrial peace alright, but by extravagant settlements with every sectoral group.

As if all these problems were not enough, agriculture, the country's primary industry, was gripped by an unparalled post-war recession. Clearly it was no time to fight an election; not even a by-election. But that is what Fianna Fáil had to do after the Dáil resumed in October. The Ceann Comhairle, Joe Brennan, had died in the summer. The battle for his Donegal seat was fixed for 6 November.

Fine Gael put down a motion of no confidence in the government to focus their onslaught on its economic failures. It was defeated on 21 October. There was no question of Fianna Fáil being defeated, but it was good by-election propaganda.

FitzGerald was in a bullish mood. Re-echoing his árd fheis address of that year, he painted horror pictures of the government's economic performance. He raised the spectre of the

International Monetary Fund having to intervene. He taunted Haughey to call an election 'and get the agony over'. He had no doubt that the verdict of the Donegal electorate would force the government to call a general election. He was confident that out of that contest a Fine Gael government would emerge.

For Fianna Fáil, and Haughey especially, everything was on the line in Donegal. It was his first electoral test since becoming leader. If he lost, would the backbenchers dump him, as they had Jack Lynch? And smouldering on the sidelines were Lynch loyalists, like Des O'Malley, George Colley and Martin O'Donoghue, ready to pounce.

Fine Gael sensed only one outcome. Victory! Intoxicated still with the heady wine of the Cork victories just a year before, anything else would be a disaster.

The opinion polls were reflecting the government's abysmal performance. The September *Irish Times*/MRBI poll had support for them at only 36 per cent. However, the disconcerting thing for Fine Gael (and Labour) was that the persistent fall-off in Fianna Fáil support was not switching to them. In that poll, the main opposition parties stood at just 24 per cent and 10 per cent. The remarkable factor was that 26 per cent of the people, according to the poll, were undecided how they would vote in a general election. The lesson for Fine Gael should have been obvious. Government bashing was not enough. They needed to demonstrate that they had credible alternatives.

More bad news for Fine Gael had come from a private opinion poll they commissioned in Donegal in October. While just over half those polled felt it would be a bad thing for Fianna Fáil to win, they were plainly not prepared to vote Fine Gael. When the undecideds were excluded the forecast was: Fianna Fáil, 45 per cent; Independent Fianna Fáil (Neal Blaney), 25 per cent, and Fine Gael, 20 per cent. Prendergast also found that their candidate, Bunbeg national school teacher Denis McGinley, was unknown in many parts of the sprawling county.

Nevertheless, Fine Gael confidently went about the campaign. Fianna Fáil's response indicated they were taking nothing for granted either. For the three weeks before voting, the entire government decamped to furthest Donegal. Haughey spent five weekends there, and vote-catching promises were flung about the county like snuff at a wake.

A further drawback for Fine Gael was that whereas McGinley was facing his first electoral contest, Fianna Fáil were fielding a well-known councillor, Clem Coughlan who was eight years on Donegal Co. Council, and was a former county footballer. Although this factor alone, not to mention the inescapable poll findings, should have cautioned a very restrained Fine Gael stance, the opposite was the case. In addition to his confident assertion on the outcome during the Dáil no-confidence debate, FitzGerald boldly predicted on the eve of the by-election that McGinley would win.

Not only did the poll rule this out. The party's two local deputies, Paddy Harte and Jim White, both front bench colleagues of FitzGerald, told their leader it was not on. True, Fine Gael had matched Fianna Fáil in 1977, with 36 per cent of the vote. But Blaney's organisation had taken 22 per cent. His candidate, Paddy Kelly, would be bound to transfer to Fianna Fáil. In other words, the ultimate Fianna Fáil vote was really well over 50 per cent. Harte and White wanted the party to take the line that they did not expect to win the seat, that they were primarily grooming McGinley for the general election. FitzGerald did not do this.

And when the boxes of votes were opened on Friday, 7 November, FitzGerald and Fine Gael were humiliated. It was Haughey who had come up trumps against the national economic odds. All day long, in the Isaac Butt Memorial Hall in Ballybofey, the Fine Gael leader was a slow-motion picture of agony as the count proceeded to its inevitable conclusion.

The first count outcome had Coughlan ahead, at 23,456, McGinley got 20,022, and Kelly 14,198. The Fianna Fáil vote was actually *up* over a thousand on 1977, and Fine Gael's was *down* 2,000! The subsequent counts merely prolonged the agony, as Coughlan went on to take the seat on the third. All the while, FitzGerald stood there, at times ashen-faced, with his little calculator in his hand, trying to figure it out.

Fianna Fáil were cock-a-hoop. Their director of elections, Ray McSharry declared: 'We are now ready to have a general election if the Taoiseach decided to call one. Fianna Fáil have turned the tide after last year's by-election defeats.' The following morning's main story in all the newspapers was Haughey triumphant, and likely to opt for an early general election.

For Fine Gael there was only despair. Prendergast would claim later that the hyping of McGinley as a winner in the last ten days of the campaign had been necessary to get him known. Perhaps it helped move the party's vote from the 20 per cent in the October poll to its eventual 33 per cent. But he and the party's other key strategist, FitzGerald, had got it wrong. Plainly there was never any chance of winning a by-election in Donegal.

FitzGerald claimed subsequently he had been misled into believing they could win. He agreed that his confident prediction made the resultant defeat more damaging, and accepted that he had blundered.

The party trundled back to Dublin dejected. People who had been talking of winning an overall majority at the general election had been brought down to earth with a bang. They had got used to winning, and FitzGerald had acquired an aura of invincibility. Now there were mutterings of discontent with his leadership. Haughey's economic policies might be a shambles, but he would prove a doughty opponent.

And the general election which Fine Gael had dreaded at the beginning of 1980, and subsequently came to relish and invite, now looked to be upon them. But the odds had changed dramatically. Suddenly the party realised that it was not half ready. It had still to convince the electorate that it represented a more credible government option than Fianna Fáil.

The strategists would have to revise their plans, and think it all out again!

5

The Politics of Fudge

Fine Gael was traumatised by the Donegal defeat. For the first time, since he became leader, FitzGerald faced serious internal party criticism. Going into the by-election many had been talking of emerging from the next general election as the largest party. Now the bubble of expectation and complacency had burst. Five years later, despite two bruising periods in government, senior politicians and backroom people alike, would consistently cite that as being the lowest point in their fortunes.

But it was not only the Donegal humiliation which rattled Fine Gael. Charles Haughey was concluding his first year as Taoiseach. Not everything had gone well for him. He had paid a recklessly high price for industrial peace. In the case of teachers, he had conceded more than an independent arbitration board recommended. The full cost would only emerge later. But there were other, more real and dramatic successes. A month after the by-election, on 8 December, a major breakthrough in Anglo-Irish relations was marked by an historic summit at Dublin Castle. There the British delegation not only included the Prime Minister, Mrs Thatcher, but also her Foreign Secretary, Chancellor and Northern Secretary. It broke new ground in the quest for peace in Northern Ireland. The agreed communiqué was full of dramatic terms that promised much: 'totality of relationships'; 'joint studies', 'institutional structures', and more. Haughey was making headway on the national question.

Meanwhile, a seven-man hunger strike had begun in the North on 27 October in support of political status. But, happily for the government, it was suspended on 18 December, without any loss of life. It added to Haughey's stature. His

63

government had also broken the stalemate in a long-running petrol dispute in October by sending in the army to drive the tankers. Petrol was back at the forecourts again; Haughey had got the country moving. And in the Dáil, Fine Gael and Labour were adjudged by all political commentators to have put up lamentable opposition to Fianna Fáil.

Fine Gael was getting panicky. At the December meeting of the party's representative national council, there were calls to bring back the old guard of Ryan, Clinton and O'Donnell, all MEPs, to the front bench. Some backroom figures were concerned that not only was the party losing the battle in the Dáil chamber, it was being eclipsed in the much more important venue of television debate. Peter Barry, in particular, was a disappointing Finance spokesman: he was consistently outshone, especially on television, by Martin O'Donoghue, to the point where his status within Fine Gael was actually threatened.

It took FitzGerald a couple of weeks to get over the shock of Donegal. He was rarely seen around in Leinster House during that time. He was pondering his problems. Fianna Fáil were gearing up for a general election which the by-election showed they would most probably win, and his own party organisation and personnel were no assurance of scoring a dramatic upset. Along with Prendergast, he undertook a major strategy revision. Having so woefully misread popular opinion in Donegal, the party leader now sought to establish what the people *really* wanted. Once again, it was time to do a little market research. But this time blunt-instrument opinion polls, posing options, would not suffice. Instead, Fine Gael embarked on a qualitative research survey on 'voter attitudes and voter propensities in order to assist the strategic objectives of Fine Gael'. A nationwide round of informal talk-ins with representative groups of people was planned for January 1981.

FitzGerald also decided it was necessary to sharpen his various committees working on different aspects of election preparation. They were too unco-ordinated. It was time for a single, integrated outfit that would cover all the strategic requirements, ranging from PR to policy. He turned to a personal friend, Derry Hussey, who had been chairman of his own Dublin South-East constituency executive. Hussey (46) was the financial director of the Jones Group of companies, and had done a little work in Dun Laoghaire during the 1979 Euro-campaign, but was really unknown politically in Fine Gael. Nevertheless, FitzGerald wanted him to head up a new 'Election Committee'. His wife, Gemma, was an independent senator since 1977.

Other people brought together for the first meeting of this new body in Christmas week at Mount Street including Seán Murray, Ted Nealon, Enda Marren, Peter Sutherland, Jim Dooge and Prendergast. A two-day session pored over what was wrong with the party, and what was required in the looming election battle. In the following weeks, the committee took final shape. Soon it would become popularly known as the Strategy Committee. This was the vehicle that would transform Fine Gael as a fighting force at election time, and play a pivotal role in the three general elections of 1981-82. As an electoral force the party was changing from well-intentioned amateurs to consummate professionals. A revolution was at hand.

One innovation FitzGerald and Prendergast decided upon was to ask Seán O'Leary to be national director of elections. Until then this key post was filled by a senior politician in the party. But FitzGerald wanted somebody who could give his undivided attention to the task. The ideal choice might have been Prendergast, but he had alienated too many people in the party. By contrast, O'Leary had been politically inactive for over three years, and had no enemies.

Like Prendergast and Nealon, O'Leary (39) had been an unsuccessful general election candidate. No less than four times, 1965, 1969, 1973 and 1977, he had failed to get elected in his native Cork city. It did not augur well for successfully directing a national campaign. But FitzGerald saw him as the man to do just this.

Another key man on the new committee was Seán Murray, from the Capital Branch, who took charge of financial control. A former Longford footballer, Murray (36) was the driving force behind the re-organised Capital Branch. Other members included Jim Dooge, who had also been on the candidate selection committee. A veteran of the party, Dooge (58) had been a close mentor not only of FitzGerald, but of Liam Cosgrave before him. He was chairman of the Seanad from 1973 to 1977, and long envied Fianna Fáil's capacity to run strong second or third candidates with outgoing TDs, and to split the party's vote geographically between them.

Prendergast was naturally put in charge of organisation, and Enda Marren, who had run such a successful campaign in the Dublin area in the 1979 Euros, was made his regional organiser for the capital. Other regional organisers added later were Myles Staunton (Connacht), Peter Curran (Leinster) and Peter Kelliher (Munster). Nealon took charge of publicity on the new Strategy Committee, and other members from the outset were two Dublin barristers, John McMenamin, who looked after speech-writing, and Peter Sutherland, whose task was to co-ordinate policy statements with the front bench spokesmen for inclusion in the election manifesto.

To secure parliamentary party approval of this new organisation, FitzGerald turned to his deputy, Peter Barry. The party was bound to be resentful of the new body of non-elected people getting such a powerful role, especially in view of their continual clashes with Prendergast. Barry was the ideal man to liaise with the TDs and senators; to secure their approval for involving so many outsiders in matters sensitive to their electoral fate. He was trusted by them, and along with another senior deputy, Tom Fitzpatrick from Cavan, agreed to sit on the new committee. Barry's appointment was a vital bridge between the background boys and the Oireachtas members.

Planning a reshuffle was the other preoccupation for FitzGerald at the end of 1980. Many political commentators had now joined in the clamour from within the party to restore the MEPs to the front bench. Even Mark Clinton, who had retired to the backbenches on FitzGerald's accession, signalled in a *Sunday Tribune* interview on 14 December that he was considering a more active role again in domestic politics. But the leader did not want to have his old cabinet colleagues back.

There was mutual dislike and distrust, and FitzGerald was trying to steer Fine Gael in a more youthful and liberal direction. When Paddy Donegan stated in December that he would

Strategy Committee

Director of Elections: Sean O'Leary

Leader on Tour: FitzGerald

Chairman: Derry Hussey

Strategy: Jim Dooge

Speech Writing	*Publicity*	*Organisation*	*Policy*	*Financial Control*	*Fund Raising*
John McMenamin	Ted Nealon	Peter Prendergast	Peter Sutherland	Seán Murray	Vincent Ferguson

Under Organisation:

Regional Organisers
Enda Marren
Myles Staunton
Peter Curran
Peter Kelliher

Constituency Directors of Election

not be going forward at the next election, there were no pleas that he reconsider.

On 1 January 1981, FitzGerald was interviewed on the RTE Radio programme 'This Week'. He was asked about the recent slump in the party's fortunes, and the calls for the old guard's return. He sought to have it both ways. They had suffered in publicity terms for having so many former ministers in Europe, he said, and how only Barry, Fitzpatrick and himself of their previous government were on the front bench. 'We might wonder whether we were wise to put forward our best men for Europe.'

Richie Ryan and Tom O'Donnell were wondering too, and were not prepared to let FitzGerald away with this piece of deception. Ryan spelt it out later that day. 'Neither Tom O'Donnell nor I retired from the front bench. We were dismissed from the front bench when we went to Europe. Had we not been, we would have been more involved at home, as well as we could.' He added that they had both indicated that they were now available to return to the front bench, and that the offer had not been taken up. O'Donnell said that FitzGerald's comments had been a reflection of the wishes of the party that the MEPs return. The front bench needed a blend of youth and experience, he added. Clearly, FitzGerald had been hoisted with his own petard, and had talked himself into a trap.

He decided to bow to the pressure, and invited the MEPs to serve again on the front bench. However, Clinton had now made up his mind to opt fully for the European Parliament, and flatly refused to return. He also announced that he would not be contesting the next election, and he strongly advised Ryan and O'Donnell not to accept. He told them that they would be setting themselves up for a mighty fall if they expected FitzGerald to give them posts in any government. But they were not dissuaded.

On Saturday, 17 January the new front bench line-up was announced. Ryan was given Foreign Affairs, the post he had held from 1977 to the Euro elections, and O'Donnell also returned to his former portfolio, Telecommunications and Broadcasting. FitzGerald told the press conference announcing his new team that these appointments did not mean that either man would automatically get ministries if the government was defeated. If they did, they would have to resign their European seats, he added.

Peter Barry was duly dropped from the key Finance post and was given the grandiose title of Chairman of the Economic Group of frontbenchers and General Election co-ordinator. The other notable casualty was Paddy Harte. He had been spokesman for Security and Northern Ireland, sharing the latter with FitzGerald. Now he was moved to Social Welfare. Harte felt he was being punished for the Donegal by-election humiliation. John Bruton, one of the hardest working frontbenchers, got the plum job of spokesman on Finance. There was an irony in this appointment, as we shall see presently. The rest of the new line-up was: Labour and the Public Service, Jim Mitchell; Industry and Commerce, Paddy O'Toole; Environment, John Boland; Education, Eddie Collins; Defence, Donal Creed; Transport, Austin Deasy; Law Reform and Human Rights, Michael Keating; Security, Jim O'Keeffe; Fisheries, Jim White; and Tom Fitzpatrick, Leader of the House and Health.

The Junior spokespersons were augmented: Youth, Myra Barry; Public Works, John Donnellan; Consumer Affairs, Tom Enright; Tourism, Paddy Hegarty; Western Development, Enda Kenny; Urban Affairs, Fergus O'Brien; Arts and Culture, Brendan Griffin; and Women's Affairs, Gemma Hussey. This latter was a surprise development. Hussey had been an ordinary member of Fine Gael since the early seventies, but was an Independent member of the Seanad on the NUI panel. By appointing her to the job in question, FitzGerald was giving formal notice of his campaign to woo women voters to his party.

From the beginning of 1981, general election speculation was rampant. Fianna Fáil was clearly gearing up. The annual public capital programme, published on 12 January, was hyped as a major investment plan totalling £1,700 million for that year and, in the process, almost doubled. The budget at the end of the month was clearly geared at an early election. However, it bore no relationship to the true state of the country's finances, and gross under-provision for many departments would emerge later in the year.

Fianna Fáil were not the only party who were engaged in reckless pre-election number-crunching. Fine Gael had caught the virus, through no less a person than John Bruton, their new Finance spokesman and soon to be the high priest of financial rectitude. Only a month earlier, while he was still Agriculture spokesman, he had published a six-point farm aid package, costing £70 million. Farmers were in the midst of a serious crisis, with incomes back 40 per cent in just two years, and Fine Gael was determined to pose as their saviour. Bruton's was a very extravagant package of measures, which included the abolition of agricultural rates, abolition *and refund* of the Fianna Fáil resource tax, and an interest subsidy. Bruton had the gall to state that the government should find the money not by borrowing but 'in the context of its overall taxation and expenditure plans for 1981'. However, he failed to spell out what taxes should be levied, or what spending cuts made. This was real pre-election stuff.

Fine Gael was determined that the mistakes of 1973-77, so far as farmers were concerned, would not be repeated. That winter farmers took their demands for special aids onto the streets, with massive demonstrations in Limerick and Kilkenny. At the latter rally in January, Fine Gael planned to distribute thousands of leaflets outlining their rescue package, but the organisers, the Irish Farmers Association, refused to allow this. At the same time, the former IFA leader T. J. Maher was publicly toying with the possibility of forming a Farmers Party, and in newspaper interviews refused to indicate his precise intentions. In the end, of course, it came to nothing, which was just as well for Fine Gael. It could have been disastrous for them.

The tide seemed to be coming in for Haughey and things were now nicely on course for a spring election. An *Irish Times* IMS poll on 24 January showed the government with a slight lead over the combined Fine Gael-Labour parties, and a slight recovery in Haughey's standing, to 37 per cent, as choice for Taoiseach (up 4 per cent). By contrast, FitzGerald was losing his earlier lead, down from 41 per cent in September 1980 to 39 per cent. But the really significant finding was that a quarter, to a third, of those polled saw no difference in the capacity of the government or the opposition to tackle the country's problems.

Although Fine Gael may have been short on credible policy alternatives they were accelerating their election preparations. Prendergast had been determined to start their selection conventions, and the unanimous rejection by the parliamentary party of such a move in November 1980 had been a setback. However, he and FitzGerald had other ideas. They persuaded the national executive, now with a clear non-Oireachtas majority, to overrule the TDs and senators. On 11 January the conventions began in the forty-one constituencies. Outgoing deputies and senators would now have to take their chances under the more democratic provisions of the 1978 constitution. The first candidates in the field were chosen in Kildare, a process made easier by the fact that there was no sitting TD or senator in that constituency. Two county councillors were selected, Bernard Durkan and Patsy Lawlor.

The third candidate in this new five-seater was the former Munster Euro candidate, Alan Dukes. His job with Dick Burke had run out at the end of 1980. Approached by both FitzGerald and Prendergast, he agreed to go forward in Kildare, where his good farming credentials with the IFA helped secure him the third place.

On 14 January, Ted Nealon's Communications Committee produced a detailed election campaign blueprint, fully costed at £380,000. A 'merchandising sub-committee', run by Bill Blair from Cork and Bill Butler of Mullingar, outlined and costed a host of gimmick material, including a helium balloon at £7,400.

When the Fianna Fáil árd fheis came round on Friday 13 February, everybody accepted that it would be the unofficial launch of the general election campaign. Government ministers confirmed later that they had planned to go to the country in April. But late that night, after the conference had just opened in the RDS, tragedy struck on the north side of Dublin, in the heart of Charlie Haughey's own constituency. A huge fire at the Stardust disco in Artane claimed the lives of forty-eight young people. After the full extent of the tragedy unfolded early on Saturday, a shocked Haughey was tramping the ruins, rather than making ready for his nation-wide presidential address that night.

The árd fheis was postponed indefinitely. Fianna Fáil's plans were baulked, and Fine Gael had won precious extra time to press on with their preparations. That they desperately needed every extra day was dramatically underlined later that month, when Prendergast received the completed report from the marketing consultants, ICR Ltd, on the attitudes and intentions of voters, which he and FitzGerald had commissioned in the wake of the Donegal fiasco.

It was a masterly insight into the mind of the electorate. Representative groups had been interviewed at eight venues around the country, including two in Dublin, during January. The resultant report dealt first with the 'mood of the people'. It was deeply pessimistic. They believed the economic recession was getting worse, and that further price rises and unemployment were on the way. Inflation in 1980 had been 18 per cent compared with 13 per cent the previous year, and the jobless total had soared by over 30,000 in the year to 122,000.

There was concern at the level of government borrowing but, significantly, the people felt Fianna Fáil were not primarily to blame. The real culprit was the worldwide recession, and the rocketing price of oil.

There was a feeling that the country should be more self-reliant. Many cited the fact that even farm families were buying their vegetables in the local shop. The principal election issues were reckoned to be prices and inflation, jobs and PAYE tax levels. There was scepticism about election manifestoes, and many felt conned by the 1977 Fianna Fáil offering. References to the return of car tax abounded.

Most believed Fianna Fáil would win the next election because they were so much larger (they then had a nineteen-seat majority). There was no expectation that Fine Gael could become the largest party. Some believed it was possible that Fine Gael and Labour together might win more seats than Fianna Fáil. However, the ICR team of analysts did not see any merit in a pre-election pact with Labour; it would alienate some Fine Gael voters.

The people found it 'virtually impossible to find ideological

72

differences between the two main parties. They are both seen as conservative. They both stand for the same values.' Northern Ireland was the main point of difference, but it was not rated an important election issue.

Given this perceived lack of policy difference, attention focused on personalities. The people regarded Haughey as a professional politician, who had amassed a considerable personal fortune. He was ambitious, with few scruples. But he had 'the common touch', and was 'a man of the world'.

FitzGerald's image was more flattering in human terms, but not politically. 'FitzGerald is thought to be a man who believes in justice, is dedicated and doing his best for the country . . . in political terms, FitzGerald is not seen as the professional that Haughey is.'

But perhaps the most disturbing news was the poor impact made by other Fine Gael politicians. The report disclosed that 'Ryan, Kelly and Burke received the most mentions. Barry, Cooney and Donegan were also mentioned. Others included were Bruton, O'Donnell and Clinton.' It also said that some of the groups interviewed before Ryan's return to the front bench had expressed regret at his absence.

Aside from generalised impressions of FitzGerald, it was found that people really knew very little about the Fine Gael leader. Some thought him to be 'slightly left of his party's perceived right wing positioning.' None of the new front bench faces since 1977, Paddy O'Toole, Michael Keating, Jim O'Keeffe, Jim White, Paddy Harte, Austin Deasy, Jim Mitchell or John Boland, had registered with the people. No wonder the pollsters recommended that the presentation of Fine Gael, and FitzGerald, should be improved. They also noted that the leader's unruly hair had received considerable comment.

Nealon set about getting more exposure for FitzGerald, and soon secured a 'Late, Late Show' appearance for him.

In view of the insecurity and concern expressed about economic matters, the ICR team recommended that Fine Gael should offer the prospect of government 'which in broad terms could be described as austere and idealistic'. A positive stance was urged. No points scoring off Fianna Fáil: that would be negative and merely flattering to the opposition.

Themes like 'the power is in your hands', and 'it's your country' were suggested as challenging, to young people in particular.

With the election imminent, it was obvious that Fine Gael were a long way from being perceived as a credible alternative government. They had no distinctive policy image. FitzGerald was seen as a nice, sincere man but no match politically for Haughey. And his front bench colleagues were nowhere.

Clearly, distinctive and relevant policies were now an urgent priority. It was little wonder therefore in mid-March to find the new Strategy Committee expressing impatience at the absence of a policy programme. Peter Sutherland was instructed to get a resumé from each frontbencher, and in the absence of this, to proceed with any available material. They were calculating on an early election, and on 3 March, Seán Murray had presented a cash-flow projection for a May contest. That showed expenditure of £33,000 in March; £33,000 in April, and £267,000 in May, overall election cost of £333,000.

But things were now going badly for Haughey. Thrown off course by the Stardust tragedy, he faced intensifying economic problems. Another petrol strike; a relatively paltry £32 million farm aid package from the EEC, and a major row over neutrality. He had said that if there was a peaceful solution to the northern problem, the Republic would have to consider new defence arrangements. But most worrying of all, a new hunger strike had started in the North on 1 March.

All this led, inevitably, to a recovery in Fine Gael's electoral fortunes. A further opinion poll commissioned by Prendergast at the end of March held out the prospect of an election win with Labour. Voting intentions gave Fianna Fáil 42 per cent; Fine Gael 33 per cent, and Labour 11 per cent. However, Fianna Fáil were adjudged best for dealing with most of the major economic problems. It was only when the poll posed personal comparisons as between Haughey and FitzGerald, and governments led by both, that Fine Gael was perceived as being best. Clearly GFG, rather than FG, would pose the best challenge to the government in an election campaign.

The party's árd fheis on 27-29 March sought desperately to present a winning, professional image. There was much ridiculing of Fianna Fáil, with the witty, acerbic John Kelly doing a star turn. He derided Haughey as taking over like an economic Mussolini who had been pitifully exposed. Gene FitzGerald, who had succeeded Michael O'Kennedy as Minister for Finance the previous December, was Rommel, the Desert Goat. O'Kennedy had been appointed EEC Commissioner to succeed Dick Burke. Gene Fitzgerald was very much at sea with this key government portfolio. Brendan Dowling had said of him, in a memorable phrase, that such was his knowledge of economics that he thought Milton Friedman was a cutter with Louis Copeland.

The highlight of the conference naturally was the Saturday night presidential address. Warmed up with military music by the Artane Boys Band, the bulging attendance of up to 8,000 was in near-hysterical mood for FitzGerald. He was the man who, they believed, would lead them to the promised land. He gave them plenty of fighting, optimistic rhetoric. They loved it. 'Never have we been stronger, more united or more determined', he told them, and promised 'a resounding victory whenever Fianna Fáil has the guts to take us on.' He said that Fine Gael's task was to lead the country to economic recovery, prosperity and social progress. He promised radical tax reform, and the eradication of injustices and discrimination against women. But, significantly, no details of policy were disclosed. But if he was short on policies, he was long on self-projection. The lessons of all that qualitative research and opinion polling had been taken to heart. It was time unashamedly to plug himself and his reputation for honesty: 'I want to finish my address to you and to the Irish people with a promise. When we are elected to government, we will make sure that it is the country that wins. And I hope that when you come back here next year to hear me address you as Taoiseach, you will be able to say "Garret, you have kept your promise".'

Clearly, if the public was later to judge him by the sternest of yardsticks, FitzGerald could blame nobody. It was he who set the dizzy-high standards. The conference slogan was 'With Garret, the Country Wins.' The boys from ICR must have been pleased. And the people around the country who, in January, had such a lowly opinion of Fine Gael were certainly given plenty to ponder as they watched the party rally on television.

The árd fheis also marked spectacular progress by women and Young Fine Gael through the ranks of the party. Madeline Taylor, from Clare, and Nuala Murphy, from East Cork, were elected the two joint honorary secretaries. A twenty-year-old medical student, Maria Stack from Listowel, who was a member of the junior party, took one of the four vice-presidencies. She was making history.

Naturally, Ms Stack commanded much media comment for her precocious ascent of the Fine Gael ladder. The party of Dillon and Cosgrave was certainly changing. On Monday, 30 March, in an interview in the *Evening Herald*, she spelled out her views on many subjects – including abortion. 'If a woman wants to terminate an unwanted pregnancy, there is nothing the law can do to stop her', she was reported as saying. She went on: 'Many of those who oppose abortion do so without giving any thought to the problem. On medical grounds I would support the right of a woman to chose abortion as a last resort.'

This was against a background of growing popular clamour in the country against abortion, and moves to have the constitution amended specifically to outlaw it. Indeed, the árd fheis had carried an anti-abortion motion by a huge majority. Within days, Ms Stack was embroiled in a bitter controversy within Fine Gael, with a massive clamour coming from the parliamentary party for her expulsion.

The árd fheis had also underlined that Fine Gael was rapidly becoming a coalition of conservatives, liberals and radicals. Besides Stack winning a popular ballot for one of the top party posts, FitzGerald told the delegates that the former EEC Commissioner Dick Burke had agreed to become a member of the front bench as an adviser on European affairs. The announcement was greeted with rapturous applause. Yet in 1974, as a member of Cosgrave's government, Burke had joined his leader in voting against their own government's family planning bill. A party that had room for the likes of Stack and Burke together was attempting a dangerous ideological juggling act.

In appointing Burke, FitzGerald had been influenced by

the qualitative research poll and the high standing of the Cosgrave's ex-ministers. Burke had moved to Harvard to take up a fellowship of international affairs in January 1981. In March, FitzGerald rang and asked him to come home and fight a general election for them: the party needed him. Burke said no; he and his wife, Mary, were enjoying Harvard. FitzGerald rang again. He also got Enda Marren, a friend of the Burkes, to ring. Finally, Burke relented, and decided to come home at Easter, in mid-April. Putting someone on the front bench who was not an elected person was utterly unprecedented. Naturally, Burke assumed that FitzGerald prized his presence highly.

But it was not all plain sailing on the front bench. The return of Ryan and O'Donnell was resented by some colleagues. For his part, Ryan felt that the front bench was totally cowed by FitzGerald, who was prone to interrupt. Ryan would not take this. Such was the disarray that it was agreed that Senator Alexis FitzGerald, deputy leader of the Seanad, would chair meetings. The plain fact was that the party leader was a lousy chairman, always tending to dominate. This was often due to the fact that he knew more about colleagues' briefs than they did themselves. But it was not conducive to orderly meetings.

The resultant chaos had lighter moments. On one occasion, Michael Keating was trying to speak, but without success. Finally, in exasperation, he shouted: 'The place is like the Muppet Show.' FitzGerald was puzzled. 'What's the Muppet Show?', he asked. Besides his inability to preside, the other thing that annoyed many front bench colleagues was the frequent telephone interruptions from his wife, Joan, during meetings.

Nor was it all harmony either in the parliamentary party, where the onslaught on Prendergast's constituency designs continued unabated. From the beginning of 1981, many deputies objected to the selection conventions going ahead. Patrick Cooney, in particular, quizzed Prendergast about possible candidates being approached in his Longford-Westmeath constituency. Prendergast denied this. He also told the party that only one opinion poll, in a single constituency, was being done: such polls were intended to assess various candidates, and they caused apoplexy among outgoing TDs and senators.

One contemporary incident conveys the flavour of unease. Despite the rules debarring constituency organisers and PROs from standing, a motion reiterating this — proposed by John Boland and John Donnellan — was passed by the party in late February.

But also at this time, Mrs Joan Burke signalled her intention not to stand in the coming general election. She had topped the poll in Roscommon-Leitrim in both 1973 and 1977. Now she and her supporters were locked in a bitter battle with Prendergast. She felt that the general secretary saw her poll-topping performance as militating against a more balanced vote spread. She felt that Prendergast wanted her out. He denied this. The battle focused on whether an ambitious younger man, John Connor, from Frenchpark, could be a candidate.

He was the constituency PRO and, therefore, under the rules, was ineligible to run. But he claimed, and Prendergast agreed, that he was merely the acting PRO, and had never been formally ratified. Despite pleas from her colleagues in the parliamentary party, Mrs Burke decided to opt out. Her supporters sought to persuade her to run as an Independent. She decided against this, primarily because she was still suffering from the injuries incurred in a serious car accident in 1976.

The selection conventions continued. By the end of March, they were completed in eighteen constituencies. A month later, Prendergast planned to have about thirty done. He was delighted, as was FitzGerald, that many new, younger candidates, with no family pedigree as public representatives, were coming through.

As Prendergast put it at the time: members of the party now felt they belonged and had a real role. 'They are given an annual membership card, and their names, addresses and occupations are logged at headquarters. In the past, they were supporters, but now they are full members, and that has hardened their commitment.'

April 1981 came round, and Haughey was increasingly beleaguered. Most serious of all, the Long Kesh Prison hunger strike was continuing, and some of the prisoners were getting dangerously weak. There was increasing pressure on Haughey to deliver on his 'unique relationship' with Thatcher. But the British government would give no concessions.

Meantime, FitzGerald was continuing to promote his and Fine Gael's credibility as an alternative government. That month, in *Magill* magazine, he gave a major interview on the theme 'If I was Taoiseach.' He was careful not to alienate any of his more conservative followers. For instance, he said that redistribution of wealth could only come from the sharing of new wealth created in the future, not from existing wealth.

Most importantly, he wanted to address the country's growing economic problems. The current budget, i.e. day-to-day government spending, would have to be got into balance within three to four years. In recent years especially, there had been growing budget deficits. In other words, the government was spending more each day than it was recouping in taxes, and was financing the gap through domestic and foreign borrowing. In 1980, the budget had allowed for a deficit of £354 million: it ended up the year at £547 million. In 1981, Haughey's current budget deficit was targeted at £515 million. On top of that, there was further government borrowing for capital purposes, giving an overall Exchequer Borrowing Requirement (current plus capital) for the year of £1.29 billion, or 13 per cent of GNP. The country was living hopelessly beyond its means. This issue was to become the central issue of the next three general election campaigns.

FitzGerald, one of the country's leading economists, was adamant that if things did not improve, our economic independence would be forfeit. What's more, the International Monetary Fund would intervene to stop the rot. Identifying the problem was one thing however. Curing it was far more difficult, since it involved either raising taxes or cutting government spending.

FitzGerald sought to have it both ways: on the one hand, clearly identifying the problem, and urging its cure; on the other, funking the only real solution. 'The primary way we will seek to attain this objective' [removing the current budget deficit] he told Vincent Browne in the *Magill* interview, 'will be through buoyancy in the economy. Our next alternative will be to look towards the expenditure side. Increases in taxation ought to be the last resort in a year in which the burden of taxation has already been increased by one eighth.' Courting popularity on the eve of an election was the name of the game. This fanciful, painless solution was immediately scoffed at by nearly every leading economist in the country.

Another crucial issue FitzGerald skipped deftly around was possible coalition with Labour. While a majority Fine Gael government was obviously his preference, he saw no reason why the Coalition option would not work. But he was also anxious to reassure any party followers worried about contamination by Labour:

> I can state quite categorically that in the event of a coalition arrangement, there will be no abdication of Fine Gael policy.
>
> We are not going to barter away our approach to government and our policy simply to secure power. And I think that people who know me, perhaps even by repute, know that if I lead a government it will be led on the basis of policies that we've put forward, and that we will not be diverted into following other policies that are incompatible with the philosophies of Fine Gael.

FitzGerald was taking refuge behind his honest guy image. But time would tell.

The extent to which he was compromising on fundamental issues to maintain a catch-all appeal was spelled out in the same interview when the availability of artificial contraceptives was raised. Again, it was a case of wanting to have it both ways. Haughey's 1979 Act, confining them to married couples on a doctor's prescription, he dismissed as a 'nonsense'. But his own view was that 'there is no enthusiasm in any party to introduce any further legislation at the present time'. It was a breathtaking cop-out. It also said a lot about the conservative reality of the Fine Gael party, notwithstanding the emergence of Young Fine Gael, and the obvious progress of women within the party. The priority clearly was an attempt to be all things to all sectors of the electorate, as general election fever mounted.

On the other side of the divide, Haughey was being baulked in choosing his own time to go to the country. He was totally luckless. He was under increasing pressure from his back-benchers. They were unnerved by the fact that Fine Gael already had its campaign up and running, with its candidates selected in most constituencies. The hunger strike in the North was casting a pall of helplessness, and open violence, over the whole island. Haughey's much vaunted republican credentials were on the line. He desperately sought a solution, but the British would not listen. Then, on 5 May, the leader of the hunger strikers, Bobby Sands, died.

The economy was also deteriorating steadily. Haughey flung huge sums of money at problems in order to keep the electorate sweet. The phasing out of food subsidies was reversed in April. The same month, his government gave the go-ahead for the incredible: an international airport at Knock, Co. Mayo, despite outright opposition from the relevant Department experts.

Although his government had actually got another year to run, Haughey had actually run out of time. He had gambled with the government estimates for the year, and he lost the gamble, as the half-yearly exchequer returns would reveal. Most of the money provided for the full year would be spent by the end of June. To hang on longer would expose this fact, in turn necessitating a supplementary budget.

With no room for manoeuvre left, Haughey went to Árus an Uachtaráin on 21 May to seek the dissolution of the 21st Dáil by President Hillery. Voting was fixed for Thursday, 11 June. The moment of truth had arrived for FitzGerald's Fine Gael. The outgoing Dáil showed Fianna Fáil with a 38 seat advantage, 83 to 45. It was a formidable challenge.

The party also knew from its elaborate private research that it had a major credibility problem with the public. Fine Gael was not viewed as an alternative government, nor had it many distinctive policies. Just as vital, it was not perceived as matching Fianna Fáil in its capacity to fight an election. The árd fheis had been gloriously hyped and stage-managed to improve this image.

Prendergast had got his runners into the field. But it would all now depend on the merit of their election programme, and the strength of the campaign that the Strategy Committee and the revitalised constituency organisations could mount. FitzGerald's leadership, badly smudged in Donegal seven months earlier, was also on the line.

The times were not auspicious for either Haughey or FitzGerald. The country was in a deep financial and political crisis. In was draped in black flags. There was a sinister air of intimidation, as H-Block demonstrators blocked the main thoroughfares of Dublin at will, and with impunity. But the drama and hype of three weeks general election campaigning would obscure this.

6

The Show Hits the Road

A week before the election was called, Seán O'Leary packed
his bags and headed for Dublin. Like the other members of
the Strategy Committee, the director of elections was satisfied that the battle was finally at hand. Just a few constituency selection conventions remained. The organisation had
been at the ready for weeks, and now was really on the boil.
In an exact repeat of 1977, it was the opposition rather than
the government which was best prepared. But in party terms,
roles were dramatically reversed. This time Fine Gael would
take the initiative.

Once polling day was announced, the first task facing
FitzGerald was to get his secret election manifesto approved
at a hastily convened meeting of the parliamentary party. Its
centrepiece was a radical and imaginative tax reform package,
devised by himself and Brendan Dowling over the previous
year. However, a major weakness was that virtually nobody
else understood it. It had not been discussed at the front
bench. FitzGerald had become almost paranoid about keeping it under wraps, lest it leak to Fianna Fáil. On one occasion
he and Dowling were discussing aspects of the programme
with some of the frontbenchers. Dowling got a kick under
the table from FitzGerald when he talked too close to the
details.

Nor would they discuss it on the telephone. This was a
very sensible precaution by FitzGerald. It stemmed from an
incident in November 1980, when Prendergast had accident-
ally picked up on his phone a conversation between two
people who were obviously listening in on his line. He took
notes of what was said, including references to an earlier
conversation of his with Bruton. His conclusion was that his

home phone and the line to Mount Street were both tapped. Along with FitzGerald, he had a meeting with the Garda Commissioner, Patrick McLaughlin, to raise the matter. However, the gardaí were unable to give them an assurance that the phones were not tapped. It made all the senior people in the party very careful with their telephone conversations.

At previous meetings of the parliamentary party and the front bench, FitzGerald assured his colleagues that the election programme would contain imaginative and attractive proposals. He also assured them there would be no diminution of basic party policy. They had no option really but to trust Garret, the economic wizard. Moreover, they accepted the need to avoid the possibility of leaks. Now that the election was officially under way, the parliamentary party readily endorsed the programme, clearing the way for its printing, and formal launch on Friday, 22 May – the day after Haughey called the election. In fact, they were elated. Fine Gael was going to give the people a standard rate of tax of just 25 per cent.

It was a jaunty FitzGerald who launched the policy, 'Let the Country Win' (the strategic research certainly had been taken to heart), to a hungry press corps. A preface outlined the grave economic crisis besetting the country, and made a virtue of its alleged intention to spell out clearly how its tax reform and investment promises would be financed. It stated that the current budget deficit for 1981 was likely to be £800 million, rather than the £515 million Fianna Fáil target. Therefore, no political party could promise measures 'that are not matched by a clear statement of how the revenue to meet these commitments will be raised'.

It piled on the political virtue: 'Our people have been sickened by the politics of promise, and by the accumulation of an unsustainable level of borrowing which they and their children will have to repay.'

The programme committed Fine Gael to phasing out the current budget deficit over four years. This would be done by cutting public spending after 'buoyancy deriving from growth' had been taken into account. But the cuts were not spelled out. The analysis was fine, but the solution offered was pure fudge. 'In opposition, we cannot however assess the scale of this problem (the budget deficit), or the kind of measures that will be needed to deal with it.'

This point was, and would remain, of crucial importance. Balancing the government's books was a laudable, orthodox economic aim. But achieving it over four years required cuts in public spending of £200 million a year in 1981 terms. Neither then, nor later, did Fine Gael face up to how this might be achieved, or measure its impact in social and economic terms. Yet eliminating the deficit over four years was to remain its central policy dogma. Eventually it would become a major political liability.

'Let the Country Win' identified unemployment – then around 130,000 – and inflation as the central issues to be tackled. There were elaborate policies to tackle both. However, no job targets were set. Nor indeed was unemployment the terrible problem it would later become. At that time, bricklayers were being brought over from England for £400 a week. Fine Gael's primary focus was elsewhere; on the PAYE sector and farmers.

A spectacular tax reform programme was the real headline grabber. The standard tax band would be cut to 25 per cent, and applied to married couples earning up to £15,000. The top tax rate would be 55 per cent. Tax credits would replace tax allowances, to make them of equal value to all income earners. Half the credit, worth £9.60 per week, would go directly to the wife in the home. The monthly children's allowance was replaced by a weekly child benefit of £3 per child, rising to £4 for any sixth and subsequent children.

It was an audaciously expensive programme, costing over £263 million. This was to be paid for by increased social insurance levies, and an anodyne-sounding hike in expenditure taxes (VAT), which would boost the cost of living by 3.5 per cent. The programme did not spell out what the PRSI levy hikes would be, nor the price changes attendant on extracting £263 million extra in VAT. So much for that clear statement of how the revenue to meet commitments would be raised.

On top of all that, a further programme of spending totalling £101 million was promised. Nearly half, £49 million, was for concessions to farmers. Other sectoral attractions were increases in third-level education grants, and a 2 per cent cut in PRSI for the tourism and manufacturing sectors. The bulk of the cost was to be met from further increases in payroll taxes.

Fine Gael was taking no chances with the farming vote this time. An interest subsidy, effective abolition of rates, fertilisers and silage grants were all promised. The third-level grants move would appeal to student voters. The £9.60 for the stay-at-home wife was the carrot for the women of Ireland. Thus all the specific constituencies that failed Fine Gael in 1977 were being courted. Altogether the tax reform and special measures programme would cost £364 million. All this in a document which actually stated that 'our people have been sickened by the politics of promise'.

But the novelty and attractiveness of the manifesto ensured that from the very first day of the campaign, the main opposition party had seized the initiative. Clever presentation. which sought to make a virtue of costing it, without really doing anything of the sort, was the master-stroke.

It was not the only place Fine Gael took the lead. On the night of 21 May, within hours of Haughey calling the election, a postering campaign swung into action across the country, which was almost military in its precision. Stocks of the Garret posters, and the standard candidate posters, had been allocated to key party officials around each constituency weeks earlier. By the following morning, every main road in the country was postered, including the entire road from Naas to Cork. People would have to revise their impression of Fine Gael as a sleepy, amateur party.

The initiative was sustained over the first weekend with a truly brilliant publicity coup. It was Seán Power's rail safari. Some months earlier, Joe Jennings, CIE's press officer and a member of Ted Nealon's Communications Committee, had provisionally booked a train in the name of an international company. He did not want any work colleagues sympathetic to Fianna Fáil to get wind of what was afoot.

On Saturday morning, FitzGerald set off from Connolly Station in Dublin for a two-day provincial tour on the 'Garret Express'. On board were his wife, Joan, a full secretarial and PR team, and a contingent of news reporters. Almost all party candidates in the capital turned up on the platform to cheer their leader off. More accurately, they sought to bask in his reflected glory by making it into any of the television or newspaper picture frames.

The Saturday odyssey took Garret to Mullingar, Athlone, Castlebar, Galway and Limerick. The next day it was on to Cork, Waterford, Kilkenny, Carlow and back to the capital. Each venue had the local party faithful in attendance, and local candidates on their best behaviour. Garret hats, T-shirts and posters were everywhere. FitzGerald held press conferences on the train for the local media, explaining the party's programme, and ensuring invaluable print and picture publicity from the provincial newspapers.

As the train journeyed towards Mullingar, a red helicopter hovered low. It was filming the Garret Express for later party political broadcast films. Everywhere people were being assailed by the party's election song:

Fine Gael, Fine Gael,
A bright new future we hail.
Led by Garret, the man you know,
You wont be taking a chance. . . .

It was composed and sung by Limerick singer/songwriter, Denis Allen. The song and many of the other gimmicks were direct copies of the Jack Lynch election campaign in 1977. But in the vital business of electoral razzmatazz, Fine Gael had not just matched Fianna Fáil. They were eclipsing them.

At his various press conferences, FitzGerald stressed that his programme was no giveaway. Repeatedly, he put a cost of £101 million on it. This was misleading. The real interest was in the tax reform package, which cost an additional £263 million. He lectured the bemused journalists about the need to eliminate the budget deficit; gave his views on Northern Ireland, the death penalty . . . anything he was asked about. He was in his element; it might have been his tutorial room in UCD.

'We will be the largest party in the Dáil after the election', he declared. By Sunday evening, with Fianna Fáil trying to complete its conventions, that did not look so impossible. The country was talking about the tax plan; the party leader had blazed a trail across the land, and Garret and Fine Gael posters were everywhere. A revolution was occurring, and was being amply reflected in the media. The campaign was succeeding beyond the wildest dreams of the backroom strategists. Eighteen months of planning was reaping its bounty.

The Strategy Committee was so well prepared that Ted Nealon had been able to pull out some months earlier. He had his eye on a nomination and – hopefully – a seat in his native Sligo. Some, like Seán O'Leary, were unhappy with the departure of the key media liaison man. An eminent replacement was located, however, in Liam Hourican, formerly press officer in Dick Burke's EEC office, and prior to that a reporter with RTE. In the run-up to the election, a trio of PR and advertising experts, Bill O'Herlihy, Pat Heneghan and Shane Molloy, had also joined the strategy team. They had helped Marren with the 1979 Euro campaign in Dublin.

Each morning, the committee met at 8 o'clock in the Berkeley Court Hotel, where O'Leary, the director of elections, stayed. They devoured all the morning papers over their breakfast. Every twist and turn of the campaign was carefully assessed. On Tuesday, 26 May, FitzGerald commenced a major countrywide tour of the constituencies. A key feature of the morning inquests was liaising with him and his tour managers, and planning a schedule of speeches for all the frontbenchers.

The other backroom personnel who were particularly busy now were the key members of Capital Branch, notably Seán Murray and Vincent Ferguson. In the preceding months, they had launched an elaborate campaign to secure financial donations from the business and professional communities.

Drawing on various membership directories, and their own knowledge of the corporate sector, they had sent begging letters to thousands of people. The fact that some were noted Fianna Fáil backers did not dissuade them. The sales pitch was that a strong Fine Gael party was essential to the democratic process. It did not have any special funding to contest the election, and they wanted responsible people to help out. It met with only limited success, and with one wealthy group was a total failure. All American companies declined to contribute, stating that their rules forbade it.

But gradually a list of about 400 likely subscribers was built up, mainly over small private business lunches attended by FitzGerald or other senior politicians. Now that the election had arrived, Murray, Ferguson and other members of the Capital Branch divided up the names and began an intensive phone-around. It was time to cash in the commitments. Absolute anonymity was assured, and the money flowed in. Average donations were under £1,000 with a handful in the £5,000 range, and a few more up to £10,000. Any hints of IOUs being sought in return were rejected. After consultation between Murray and FitzGerald, one donation of £10,000 was sent back because the company was simultaneously seeking a government contract. It had not linked the issues but no chances were taken.

Capital Branch raised an incredible £500,000. In addition, nearly £30,000 came from the general public in pounds, fivers and tenners, following a newspaper appeal for funds. The £2,000 per seat levy on the constituencies was not so successful. They had their own financial demands. But they did contribute about another £100,000. This meant that instead of the £333,000 campaign originally planned, and later revised upwards to £400,000, Mount St enjoyed the luxury of being able to splash out £600,000. Each morning Murray told his Strategy Committee colleagues how the inflow of money was going, and expenditure on newspaper advertising, party political broadcasts, and other outgoings was reviewed.

The people at these daily meetings, chaired by Derry Hussey, included Prendergast, O'Leary, Jim Dooge, Hourican, Marren, O'Herlihy, Heneghan and Molloy. O'Leary was a brilliant strategist, with a consummate understanding of the constituencies. Prendergast, via his constituency organisers and his regional directors (Myles Staunton, Peter Kelliher and Peter Curran) was intimately aware of how canvassing and attempted vote splitting, was progressing in each of the forty-one constituencies. Marren was the expert on the eleven Dublin constituencies. O'Herlihy, Heneghan and Molloy were the advertising and marketing experts. It was just as well there was so much expertise around. From the outset, they came up against a major problem. Nobody understood the intricacies of the tax reform programme.

Tax credits and the £9.60 for women in the home were the real conundrums. What did they mean, how did they work, who was entitled to them? The queries poured into Mount Street from party officials around the country, and from the general public. But nobody knew, except O'Leary who had some understanding of them. He had been involved in some of the final policy sessions with FitzGerald and Dowling. The party leader was the author of the £9.60 plan, which was rapidly capturing the public's interest. And Dowling was the originator of the tax credit idea. However, FitzGerald was touring the highways and byways, and the other fellow had gone off on holidays.

The policy also posed terrible difficulties for Shane Molloy, whose job was to devise the newspaper advertisements. Molloy (37) was marketing director with Lever Brothers, and he wanted the ads to convey simple concepts, not these complicated novelties. He had to scrap many of his preconceived plans. For the first Sunday of the campaign, he chose a safe banner theme: 'Fine Gael puts more money in your pocket', accompanied by some of the headline items from the manifesto.

Thereafter, much of the advertising campaign in the newspapers, which cost almost £200,000, had to be devoted to explaining the tax credits, the £9.60, and the other tax switches. It was not what Molloy and his colleagues wanted to do. But they had no choice.

Seán O'Leary also had to prepare leaflets explaining the tax programme to his strategy colleagues and to the office staff manning the telephones. Around the country, FitzGerald faced the same task. His tour bus would arrive at the outskirts of any town, where the local candidates got on board. They dived on the leader like drowning men clinging to a raft. FitzGerald wanted to know how the campaign was going. But they wanted the tax plan explained to them. No problem at all: Garret would whip out a pen and paper, and happily commence totting and explaining. People on the streets were treated to similar impromptu lessons. It was some stroke. A political party campaigning on a policy that only two people fully understood. Within a week, however, the problem had receded. Everyone knew enough to get by.

FitzGerald was an uneasy glad-hander, but he set to it with a grim fervour. Soon he was more relaxed with people, but the stiff arm wave betrayed a basic unease. Propelled along by tour press officer, Seán Power, and manager, Dan Egan, he took his carefully packaged Fine Gael to two or three constituencies every day. The Nealon blueprint had it all worked out to a tee. The posters, hats, jingles, T-shirts and badges were everywhere. Only the helium balloon was missing. The committee feared somebody would take a pot-shot at it, and the idea was dropped.

The attention to detail was reflected in other novel schemes. An articulated truck brought a specially prepared trailer stage to each town for the setpiece night rallies where FitzGerald was the star attraction. No backs of lorries, or makeshift platforms for this new, slick Fine Gael. And Cork city businessman and councillor, Bill Nolan, moved around the country, staying a day ahead of FitzGerald on the same route. His function was to make last-minute checks with the local organisation to ensure that everything was ship-shape when the leader hit town.

No wonder Fianna Fáil were reeling. At the outset of the campaign, Haughey had sought a renewed mandate to deal with the Northern problem. But the economy quickly took precedence, and the Fine Gael and Labour emphasis on taxation, jobs and inflation predominated. Again, 1977 roles were reversed. This time Fianna Fáil were forced into a reactive campaign against the Fine Gael manifesto.

They claimed that the tax package would send the cost of living soaring. They were right! And they especially sought to shoot down the £9.60 plan. A cruel con trick, they dubbed it. 'Robbing Peter to pay Paula' was their clever newspaper ad. dismissing it. But the notion of a payment for the housewife who stayed at home had taken root, even if most people did not fully understand now it would be financed.

The Fianna Fáil claims that the Fine Gael package would drive up the cost on food, footwear, clothing and other essentials did get the strategy committee worried. They decided to counter some of the more damaging claims. An advertisement headlined 'Nail the Big Lie' sought to dismiss six specific ones. One of the rebuttals stated: 'Fine Gael will not put VAT on clothing and footwear.'

It was not the only hostage to political fortune offered up by Fine Gael in the campaign. Some of the others were truly outrageous. A special 'Programme for Dublin' was launched, and the bulk of the candidates in the capital turned up for the press launch. It promised a free bus service in the city centre; an electrified rail link from Heuston Station to Tallaght, and another on the western line as far as Clonsilla: 240 uncompleted housing estates around the capital would be taken over by the local authorities; new local community centres for Tallaght, Blanchardstown, and Lucan/Clondalkin; major relief roads on the north, west and south.

Meanwhile, off in the west of Ireland, where Fianna Fáil were plugging their Knock international airport, Paddy O'Toole was committing Fine Gael not only to retaining that project. For good measure, he insisted that an international sports complex would also be built at the site.

All this from the party that piously proclaimed that the people were sick of promises. In subsequent years, Fine Gael deputies, from FitzGerald down, would get very sheepish and shifty when these matters were raised.

Despite an otherwise brilliant campaign, there was no serious prospect of Fine Gael emerging after 11 June with enough seats to form a government. FitzGerald knew that. The very best he and other senior party figures hoped for was 70 seats which, of course, would be a remarkable achievement. The only real hope of ousting Fianna Fáil therefore lay in a possible Coalition arrangement with Labour. But both opposition parties were running separate campaigns. However, neither ruled out a possible pact and they supported interparty voting transfers. But there were key differences in policy between them. Fine Gael was committed to a major increase in indirect taxes to pay for its tax reduction programme.

Labour was emphasising inflation and jobs, and would be opposed to the inevitable inflationary thrust of the FitzGerald package.

Both parties minimised the differences during the campaign however. But the fact that there was a second opposition party posed other difficulties. Naturally, Labour looked for representation in the round of radio and television election programmes. This led to uneven, inconclusive three-way tussles, rather than a head-on clash between Fianna Fáil and Fine Gael which would have been more beneficial to the main opposition party. This was one bonus for Haughey. He needed it. Not only was he being challenged by a superb Fine Gael machine, but the Republican Movement were focusing their anger at the continuing H-Blocks hunger·strike on the outgoing government. There were H-Block candidates in Republican constituencies who were primarily taking votes from 'The Republican Party', Fianna Fáil.

The clear possibility of Fianna Fáil losing power was borne out by an *Irish Independent*/MRBI opinion poll, conducted at the beginning of June, and published on 8 June. It showed Fianna Fáil at 45 per cent; Fine Gael, 38 per cent and Labour 11 per cent, a 4 per cent advantage for a potential Coalition government. Given the predominance by Haughey and FitzGerald on their party campaigns, their personal ratings were also seen as crucial. The Fine Gael leader's campaign impressed 57 per cent but Haughey's rating was only 47 per cent.

With 166 seats in the new Dáil, making 84 a clear majority, the government would need 48 per cent of the vote to be assured of victory. On issues and with key electoral sectors, Fine Gael was also doing well. According to the poll, FitzGerald was ahead with younger voters, and the £9.60 was having a significant impact, in rural as well as urban constituencies.

Given the predominance of grey economic data in the campaign, much attention focused on the eve-of-poll television showdown between the party leaders. Fine Gael had no fears. Their man, the most popular politician in the country, was certain to win. The early indications from Fianna Fáil had hinted they too feared such an outcome. Personality contests were not what the people wanted, Haughey said in lofty dismissal of such an encounter.

Despite successive on-off twists to the story, a televised showdown was finally agreed for Monday, 8 June. Labour leader Frank Cluskey had insisted on being included, and this led to an unbalanced format. Haughey had supported his inclusion, which raised expectations that he was afraid of taking on FitzGerald directly. The outcome was a flop, with the impact being as dull as the format: each leader being interviewed separately by a panel of journalists.

However, the real shock for Fine Gael was that if there had to be a winner, it was Haughey. FitzGerald was hesitant and nervous, and got bogged down in statistics. Nor had he any clear answers on how he would reduce borrowing, inflation and unemployment all together. The Strategy Committee was shocked. FitzGerald was ten points ahead, and now his opponent had come out and won the final round.

It was one of very few lapses over the three weeks. Irrespective of the outcome on 11 June nobody would be in doubt that Fine Gael had arrived as a political organisation to rival Fianna Fáil. The poor-second-best image was buried. The credit for this lay with FitzGerald, Prendergast and Nealon, and the brilliant team of backroom strategists they had assembled. A revitalised and democratised constituency organisation complemented this headquarters revolution.

The face of the party returning to the 22nd Dáil was also certain to be much changed. Seven of the outgoing 45 Fine Gael TDs were not seeking re-election: former leader Liam Cosgrave, Dick Barry, Mark Clinton, Paddy Donegan, John Mannion, Frank Taylor and Joan Burke.

One of the great benefits of the early conventions, enforced by FitzGerald and Prendergast, was that when the campaign proper began, most of the local difficulties had been patched up. Peace reigned uneasily in most constituencies, and the strategy team were confident the party was on the threshold of a major leap forward. But in some constituencies it was not possible to keep the peace. Louth was such a case. Party headquarters had imposed Drogheda man, Dick Branigan, as a third candidate, much to the dislike of Bernard Markey from Ardee. And Paddy Donegan was disappointed that his son, Tommy, was not added. In fact, three candidates in this three seater (the fourth seat went automatically to outgoing Ceann Comhairle, Padraig Faulkner) was a mistake.

On the eve of polling, FitzGerald took his election tour to this border constituency. Division and disarray was everywhere. It was the low point of the entire campaign. More damagingly, it resulted in a bad press on the morning the people were going to cast their votes.

On 10 June, the final opinion poll, in the *Irish Times*, showed the outgoing government, and Fine Gael-Labour together, running neck and neck. The potential coalition partners were at 48 per cent, 1 per cent ahead of Fianna Fáil. The personal popularity ratings had FitzGerald also one point ahead of Haughey, at 44 per cent. The fieldwork for the IMS poll had been done before the television debate.

That night FitzGerald and some of his mentors had an end-of-campaign drink with party staff and journalists who accompanied him on his countrywide tour. He had plenty of reason to be satisfied, having masterminded a campaign that saw Fine Gael out-perform Fianna Fáil. Even if the outgoing government won, this much would still be true. But he hoped for victory, in the shape of enough seats to form a government with Labour. Throughout the previous three weeks, he always stressed the common ground with Labour. Such an eventuality would pose serious policy differences, although any discussion of this fact had been scrupulously avoided.

However, the real danger was that the election might throw up a hung Dáil. The balance of power could be held by a handful of Independents. Given the serious economic crisis, that would be the worst possible outcome for the country.

Yet, the opinion polls pointed clearly to such a possibility. Writing on the eve of the election, *Irish Independent* political correspondent, Chris Glennon, said it all: '. . . the new [poll] figures now suggest that the balance of power in the next Dáil could be held by a handful of Independents.' How right he was.

7

How to Lose Friends and Alienate People

All day the expectations see-sawed. In head office, the strategy boys paced around the improvised press room on the second floor. Up on the next floor, FitzGerald, a veritable human calculator, was devouring every tally return. With him were Prendergast, O'Leary and Dooge. The reports from the constituencies fluctuated wildly. Around midday, a beaming Prendergast skipped downstairs to tell the waiting journalists they were on course for over 70 seats. Incredible. Were Fine Gael really headed for a stunning victory? The early editions of the evening newspapers duly reported these claims. It was Friday, 12 June 1981, and all around the country the general election count was under way.

Elation swept through the room at Prendergast's forecast. But there was one fellow in the room who totally disagreed. 'Bullshit', said Frank Flannery dismissively. He, too, had been doing his calculations from the available tally information, and an intimate knowledge of the constituencies. Sixty-eight seats would be the best result they could hope to achieve, he declared. But few were taking any notice. Besides, Flannery was really an unknown: he had only begun to play a minor role on the Strategy Committee in recent days, helping Enda Marren.

By mid-afternoon, the first TDs were being elected and the overall picture was firming up. Yes, those early tallies were wrong. There would be no 80 seats. But nevertheless, Fine Gael was doing remarkably well. And Fianna Fáil was in serious trouble. There was no way they would get the magical 84 seats for an overall majority. Then as the count dragged into the night, and the early hours of Saturday morning, the government fought back. It was going to be a real cliffhanger.

The 5 a.m. editions of the newspapers had FitzGerald and Haughey disputing the final outcome. The forecasts were hardening around 79 seats for Fianna Fáil and possibly 66 for Fine Gael.

There had been notable casualties, including the Labour leader, Frank Cluskey. But there was a complicating factor nobody had foreseen. Prisoner H-Block candidates were doing remarkably well. They had taken two seats, in Louth and Cavan-Monaghan. In both cases, Fianna Fáil was the loser. As the destination of the final seats was awaited, only one thing was certain. The country was indeed headed for a hung Dáil, with the balance of power held by a handful of 'Others'.

When the remaining seats were eventually decided, Fianna Fáil were the real losers. They had 78 seats and 45 per cent of the vote. Fine Gael had pushed its vote up to 36.5 per cent and taken 65 seats. Labour had 15 seats, and 9.9 per cent of the vote. Clearly neither Fianna Fáil, nor even a Fine Gael-Labour coalition, were assured of power.

Despite this inconclusiveness, it was a remarkable result for Fine Gael. Consider their disarray six months earlier; their lack of impact with the public, the absence of distinctive policies. Their conservative, ageing profile. They had now won a record share of the vote as Fine Gael, exceeded only by their Cumann na nGaedhael predecessor in 1927. They had won 50 per cent more seats than they did in 1977. But to keep their performance in perspective, it should be noted that in 1973 they had taken 35.1 per cent of the vote, and 54 seats, in a smaller Dáil (144 seats).

Not only was the parliamentary party transformed in size, it was also a much more youthful and potentially liberal team. Twenty-six new Fine Gael TDs would be heading for Dáil Eireann for the first time. And many of them were very young. They were Bernard Allen (36), Seán Barrett (36), George Birmingham (27), Paul Connaughton (37), John Connor (37), Liam Cosgrave Jnr. (25), Hugh Coveney (45), Frank Crowley (42), Alan Dukes (36), Bernard Durkan ´36), John Farrelly (26), Brian Fleming (35), Joe McCartin (42), Bernard Markey (45), Gay Mitchell (29), David Molony (30), Ted Nealon (51), Michael Noonan (38), Alan Shatter (30), P. J. Sheehan (48), and Ivan Yates (21).

The party had also made dramatic headway in attracting women deputies. Of the eleven women elected to the new Dáil, six represented Fine Gael, and five – Nuala Fennell, Mary Flaherty, Alice Glenn, Nora Owen and Madeline Taylor – were new deputies. The sixth, Myra Barry, was being returned in a general election for the first time. FitzGerald's wooing of the women and youth electorates was paying handsome dividends. Three of the women deputies, Barry, Taylor and Flaherty, had first come to prominence in Young Fine Gael.

Two former Cosgrave ministers, Paddy Cooney and Dick Burke, were also returned, as was Des Governey, another former deputy. Only one outgoing TD, Luke Belton, had failed to make it back.

It was a truly formidable breakthrough by Fine Gael, and FitzGerald was entitled to take the credit. True, others like Prendergast and many on the Strategy Committee had played key roles. But FitzGerald was the man who picked most of them out. (It is a point worth emphasising, given that later he would be represented as some kind of puppet, utterly beholden to his advisers.) The party's appeal had been dramatically widened. It had a younger face, exuding a youthful and feminist appeal, although it still contained a significant conservative rump. At last Fine Gael was confirmed as a serious rival to Fianna Fáil's traditional pre-eminence.

Fine Gael had an economic policy. It was committed to getting the budget balanced in four years, lowering direct income tax, and shifting that burden to indirect levies. But it had devised no blueprint for implementing this; just the vaguest macro-economic notions. It had also to clarify its position on various divisive social issues which were now preoccupying Ireland. These included family planning, divorce and illegitimacy. In this respect Young Fine Gael was well ahead of the senior party.

However, in the immediate aftermath of the election, the understandable preoccupation was who would form a government when the Dáil assembled on 30 June. Aside from the three main parties, the remaining eight seats had gone to H-Blocks (Kieran Doherty and Paddy Agnew); Neil Blaney, Dr John O'Connell, Noel Browne, Seán Loftus, Joe Sherlock and Jim Kemmy. The H-Block deputies were ruled out not only by being in prison, but by being abstentionist. This effectively reduced the Dáil to 164 seats. If one of the remaining six was willing to take the Chair, that left 163. Therefore a working majority would be 82. That meant that Fianna Fáil were four short, and a Fine Gael-Labour coalition, just two. The H-Blocks intervention had screwed Haughey.

From the outset, therefore, the odds favoured a coalition. But not everyone in Fine Gael was satisfied they should try to go into government on such precarious terms. After all, the economy was in a mess, and required drastic surgery. Could any of the Others be relied on to back such a course? They had not really won. If Fine Gael did go into government, it would be at the pleasure of people who were antagonistic to what the party had set itself to do.

Derry Hussey was one who felt strongly that they should not seek to form a government. He felt that since Fianna Fáil had 13 seats more than them, the onus should be on Haughey to get the necessary minority support. Don't dilute your policies, and it won't be long before you get a chance to gain further seats: that was the clear message he spelled out to FitzGerald in the latter's home. Alexis FitzGerald agreed with Hussey.

But FitzGerald saw it differently. If Fianna Fáil got back in, the initiative would lie with them to call a snap election to appeal for the extra seats to govern alone. Besides, he believed that if he could secure a coalition arrangement with Labour, then they would have an effective mandate to govern. And FitzGerald and his parliamentary colleagues were ambitious. They wanted to get their hands on the levers of power.

The first obstacle was the leaderless Labour Party. Its fifteen deputies met the following Wednesday, and unanimously chose Michael O'Leary, who had been a minister in the Cosgrave government. He was pro-coalition now also, and got on well with FitzGerald. They held their first exploratory meeting that evening in the Fine Gael leader's house in Rathmines.

O'Leary was very concerned about the inflationary effects of the Fine Gael tax programme. With inflation at a horrendous

20 per cent, and wages chasing it, the Labour priority was to bring both down by curbing price rises and increasing food subsidies. In his view, trade unionists would simply pocket the Fine Gael tax concessions, and still look for pay increases to compensate them for the resultant price rises.

After some initial discussion, and an exchange of position papers, talks got down to serious detail that weekend. They were held in the home of a mutual friend of both leaders, Gabriel Hogan, in Sandymount. Assisting O'Leary were party general secretary, Seamus Scally and Sugar Company economist Willie Scally (no relation). FitzGerald was accompanied by Alexis FitzGerald and Jim Dooge. At later stages, the parties' deputy leaders, Peter Barry and Jim Tully, joined in.

The negotiations went on for a full week, concluding in agreement on Friday, 26 June — four days before the new Dáil was due to meet. Fine Gael's tax reform package was retained intact, but with one addition. Reflecting Labour's concern, the £9.60 weekly allowance for wives in the home would also go to low-income families who did not have a tax liability.

The consequent indirect price rises were given the go-ahead, subject to Labour constraints. Basic foodstuffs, bread, flour, milk, butter and margarine, were to be subsidised so that they would not rise in price by more than 6 per cent a year. They also agreed that while the 3.5 per cent hike in consumer prices could go ahead to help pay for the tax package, no additional taxation would be imposed on 'food, electricity and coal, or clothing and footwear'. This would be one worth watching. The agreed programme stated that nine out of ten taxpayers would be in the new 25 per cent band.

Labour had to make major concessions to its capital taxation demands, settling for a total yield of £65 million in 1983 under this heading. But the precise Fine Gael commitment to eliminating the current budget deficit was now amended to a vaguer time scale called 'a planned basis'. After much haggling, Labour secured a commitment to a National Development Corporation. But Fine Gael nobbled it by also making it a holding company for the existing semi-state companies.

Labour's Youth Employment Agency was adopted, to provide training and work experience for up to 20,000 young people. It would be funded from a 1 per cent on all incomes. The parties also agreed to draw up a four-year national plan, and to establish agreed pay norms between government, employers and trade unions to bring down inflation.

But both sides were committed to getting agreement, and there were no major crisis points. Dooge was the man who drafted much of the compromise. It finally emerged as a massive fifty-page document, ambitously entitled 'Programme for Government, 1981-1986'.

During the week, meanwhile, FitzGerald had talks with Jim Kemmy and Noel Browne about possible support from them, and some Fine Gael people toyed with the idea of offering the post of Ceann Comhairle to Seán Loftus. Haughey was also wooing these deputies. But he was only assured of Blaney, though he also held high hopes of winning over John O'Connell. Loftus was also approached by him.

A sign of the dilemma facing these deputies was O'Connell's decision to place an advertisement in the evening papers inviting his supporters to give him their views. There were to be no early declarations from him, or the others. The weekend before the Dáil assembled the outcome was still clouded in uncertainty.

By Sunday evening, 28 June, following the pro-coalition vote at the Labour Party special delegate conference, FitzGerald and O'Leary had moved much closer to heading up the next government. The following morning they resumed their efforts to agree the division of cabinet and junior ministerial posts. The Labour boss set out looking for five senior and junior posts; FitzGerald offered three of each. The final agreement was that Labour would get four cabinet posts, and three juniors. Many Fine Gaelers would later feel Labour had been dearly bought; half their TDs were getting government jobs.

With agreement on coalition secured, FitzGerald was now confident he would be the next Taoiseach. He could be reasonably confident of the backing of Kemmy and Browne. Both were trenchant critics of Haughey's Northern Ireland policy. It was time to get down to cabinet making. He consulted Alexis FitzGerald, Dooge, Peter Barry and Prendergast, and he also discussed the matter with O'Leary. But ultimately, the decisions were his. It was not an easy task. There was a rash of new, younger deputies around. They reflected the kind of Fine Gael he wanted to create. And there were the old guard, conservative and experienced, led by former ministerial colleagues from the Cosgrave government: Cooney, Ryan, O'Donnell, Burke and Flanagan.

Tuesday, 30 June, dawned. The twenty-second Dáil was assembling for the first time at 3 p.m. There was still no certainty about the outcome. From early morning Leinster House was agog with rumour and speculation. It seemed that everyone wanted to be there: the deputies, their families, party supporters. By early afternoon the place was crammed.

Unknown to most, the coalition-in-waiting had achieved a notable breakthrough. Jim Tully persuaded his former Labour colleague, John O'Connell, to become Ceann Comhairle. When the Dáil convened, the time-consuming listing of the writs for the forty-one constituencies, and the reading of individual election returns from them prolonged the tension and drama. Then came nominations for Ceann Comhairle. Peter Barry proposed O'Connell, and Tully seconded him. Fianna Fáil did not nominate anyone. The Dublin doctor took the chair without a division. He then called for nominations for Taoiseach. George Colley and Brian Lenihan proposed Haughey. Oliver Flanagan and Ivan Yates, the Father of the House and its youngest member, proposed FitzGerald.

Noel Browne then rose and asked the Chair for permission to speak. He strongly criticised Haughey, but was also scathing of Fine Gael's commitment to the capitalist system. He would vote against Haughey, and abstain on FitzGerald's nomination. The packed public and press galleries saw all kinds of stalemate possibilities opening up. The other Independents took their cues from Browne and all spoke. Kemmy committed himself to FitzGerald. Seán Loftus made a long rambling speech: he was to abstain on both votes. Joe Sherlock of Sinn Féin the Workers Party came down against Fianna Fáil and said he would abstain on FitzGerald, since he did not support coalition. Blaney was dismissive of both government options.

All these interventions meant that the eventual vote on Haughey's nomination did not take place until 4.30 p.m. It was defeated by 83 votes to 79. Browne, Kemmy and Sherlock voted with Fine Gael and Labour, while Blaney backed Fianna Fáil.

Then the Ceann Comhairle put the motion: 'That Dáil Éireann nominate Deputy Garret FitzGerald for appointment by the President to be Taoiseach.' Long before the result emerged from the lobbies, the outcome was clear. Gerry L'Estrange the chief whip, handed the result to Dr O'Connell. Tá, 81, Níl, 78. Precisely four years after he had become Fine Gael leader, Garret FitzGerald was Taoiseach.

After the vote, FitzGerald rose and thanked the House for the great honour conferred on him. He proposed that they adjourn until 7.30 p.m. when he would present his government for approval. He was now going to Árus an Uachtaráin to receive his seal of office as Taoiseach. It was 5.05 p.m. That left precious little time to get to the Phoenix Park and back, and confer with his ministerial appointees. What was more, he also planned to appoint his Junior Ministers as well, and . . . hold a press conference! Even for a fast talker like FitzGerald, it was expecting a lot.

FitzGerald had already agreed with O'Leary that Labour would get Health and Social Welfare (Eileen Desmond); Defence (Jim Tully); Labour and the Public Service (Liam Kavanagh) and Industry and Energy (O'Leary, who also became Tánaiste).

After FitzGerald left for the Park, Gerry L'Estrange set off with two lists. One contained the names of the nine Fine Gael TDs to be offered cabinet posts. The other had nine names for Ministers of State and one for Leas Ceann Comhairle. L'Estrange wanted the ministers-to-be in Garret's third office at 6 o'clock, and the junior brigade there half an hour later. But he had a dreadful time trying to find his people. Every corner of Leinster House, and the bars especially, were jammed with people.

All 64 Fine Gael deputies harboured varying levels of expectation. The party spokesmen in the previous Dáil expected something, a junior post at least. Former Ministers Burke, Ryan and O'Donnell were especially hopeful. They had been restored to the front bench earlier in the year, amidst cries for more experience on the Fine Gael team. 'The country needs men like Dick', FitzGerald had told Mary Burke when he rang them in Harvard in March. For the previous couple of days, Burke had expected a call from the leader. None had come. But he was still hopeful. That morning on RTE Radio, he made it plain that he expected to be appointed to Foreign Affairs. As he saw it, FitzGerald had prevailed on him to return from the States, asked him to serve on the front bench, although he held no elective office, and honoured him with a special presentation at the March árd fheis. Surely he was not going to be offered a relatively junior ministry like Fisheries. Imagine Fianna Fáil doing something like that to another ex-EEC Commissioner, Paddy Hillery.

So he waited in Leinster House, hopeful, yet fearful. His thoughts went back to the evening of the count. After his exhaustive campaign in Dublin West, he had won on the twelfth count, crowning a smashing victory for Fine Gael, taking a third seat for them in that five-seater. He was elated, and on his way home decided to call into the Mount St headquarters. There he accepted a whiskey in the press-room, and inquired where Garret was. He sauntered upstairs to see his boss, his former colleague. But he was virtually ignored. He even received a mild rebuke for having brought drink up to the room. Still, that kind of behaviour could be explained by the tension of the occasion. But surely he was not going to be ignored now.

Others were fearing the worst. In the Dáil chamber in the afternoon, O'Donnell sought out Richie Ryan. Any word? No. Ryan urged his colleague to stop hoping; they weren't going to be appointed. Still O'Donnell said they were bound to get something.

Now, with the Dáil adjourned until 7.30 p.m. and everyone milling around, waiting and hoping, some solid news began to emerge. Ryan bumped into Michael O'Leary. The Labour man commiserated with him. The former Minister for Finance and one-time leadership aspirant now knew he was out.

Soon the word was also out that there was a list, and that Jim Dooge was going to be Minister for Foreign Affairs. Burke heard this. He was absolutely stunned. Dooge had not been a member of the Oireachtas since 1977, and then only as a senator. He was never a TD: no foot-slogging and door-knocking for him. Burke could not believe it. Imagine an expert in hydrology being preferred over an ex-EEC Commissioner, a man who was first elected to the Dáil in 1969, who had been in charge of taxation and transport policy for the entire EEC. A man who had been decorated by King Baudouin of the Belgians!

When FitzGerald returned from the Park, he went to the Taoiseach's office on the first floor. Peter Barry, who was one of those assembled in the third floor office, told the other ministers-to-be to go down to him. Besides Dooge and Barry, the others were Tom Fitzpatrick, John Bruton, Pat Cooney, John Kelly, John Boland, Paddy O'Toole, Jim Mitchell and Alan Dukes. FitzGerald knew he was going to be desperately caught for time. In 1973, Cosgrave had seen all his appointees together. Now he thought of this. But he decided to speak with each of his would-be cabinet colleagues separately. The reason for this was that he wanted to make sure none of them were Knights of Columbanus, or members of any other secretive organisation.

'Are you a member of any organisation, the membership of which is not publicly known', he asked each of them. Two of them confessed to being in the Knights, but undertook to resign their membership. FitzGerald, who was concerned with what he saw as undue influence by the Knights in the party in his earlier days, accepted the undertakings, and proceeded with his appointments.

Jim Dooge knew he was on board from the previous week. He was FitzGerald's closest political confidant after Alexis FitzGerald. Now aged 58, he had presumed his representative political career was finished in 1977, when he decided not to go forward again for the Seanad. But FitzGerald was very impressed with his intellectual capacity and political judgment. Dooge was completely surprised when he was offered Foreign Affairs, and asked for some time to consider it. He also told his leader that it would cause problems in the party. But with FitzGerald adamant that he was the man for the job, Dooge was happy to accept.

Another man who knew of his position in advance was

Peter Barry. He could virtually nominate his department, even Finance. But he was not carried away with the notion that this was the most important job, especially in such straitened economic times. And he was also alive to the probability that FitzGerald would find it impossible not to interfere. Barry chose Environment, a powerful department whose influence reached into every parish in the country.

Bruton virtually chose himself for Finance, given that he had been one of the most active and able frontbenchers in the previous Dáil. But Alan Dukes was a controversial choice. The rural side of the party was initially aghast at a Dubliner getting charge of Agriculture, whatever about his IFA and EEC experience. It was his first day in the Dáil, and he had only won the fifth and final seat in Kildare. But he still resided in Drimnagh. Dukes joined the select band of deputies made cabinet members on their first day, alongside Noel Browne, Kevin Boland and Martin O'Donoghue.

Some of the remaining ministerial allocations were logical enough. John Kelly had 'shadowed' on Economic Planning and now he was given Industry, Commerce and Tourism. It had been agreed with O'Leary that the Labour Party would get Industry, and in August a departmental revision altered Kelly's Department to Trade, Commerce and Tourism.

At Education, John Boland was a surprise choice. Eddie Collins had been spokesman since 1977, surviving the June 1979 and January 1981 reshuffles at that post. Jim Mitchell's appointment to Justice was equally remarkable. Since June 1979, another Dublin deputy, Michael Keating, had covered this area, under the description Law Reform and Human Rights. He, too, had been one of the most active frontbenchers in opposition. Tom Fitzpatrick was an important link for FitzGerald since 1977 with the more conservative wing of the party. He backed all the reforms, and at the same time reassured the old guard. He was duly honoured, getting the Department of Fisheries and Forestry.

That left two. The Gaeltacht was an obvious choice for an Irish speaker, and a western deputy. Or Tom O'Donnell, the man who had made a household name for himself there from 1973 to 1977. FitzGerald opted for Mayo's Paddy O'Toole. The final place went to Paddy Cooney, at Transport and Posts and Telegraphs. Originally, FitzGerald was not going to appoint him at all. He saw Cooney as deeply conservative. The Longford-Westmeath man had also been one of the strong critics of Prendergast's re-organisation drive in 1980-81. However, Peter Barry and O'Leary argued strongly for Cooney's inclusion. Thus for the second time, he made it to the cabinet table by a whisker: in 1973, Cosgrave only decided at the last minute to include him.

When FitzGerald had completed his cabinet appointments it was nearly 7 o'clock. He could have postponed the junior appointments to another day, or he could have delayed the resumption of the Dáil by consultation with the Ceann Comhairle. But that would raise speculation that there were problems with the formation of the government. And putting off the appointments would increase the pressure and representations from those who were now being omitted. He decided to plough on. But instead of seeing the Ministers for State in his new office, the new Taoiseach decided to dash upstairs to his old office where they were waiting.

With his list in his hand, he decided he would appoint them all together. Having checked they were all there, he charged on. First, Paddy Harte, Leas Ceann Comhairle. 'Jesus Christ', muttered Harte. What was wrong, FitzGerald asked. 'Nobody has been thrown out of the House more often that me,' Harte wailed. Three times in one term, he added. But that was it. The Taoiseach moved on.

The others on the list were Eddie Collins, Fergus O'Brien, Donal Creed, Mary Flaherty, Michael Begley, Michael Keating, Michael D'Arcy, Ted Nealon and Jim O'Keeffe. Collins, Harte and Keating were sorely disappointed at not being full members of the cabinet. Now the brusque doling out of junior posts was adding insult to injury. FitzGerald was behaving as if the whole thing was an irritant.

'Eddie Collins, Overseas Development', he announced. 'I don't want that', Collins interjected. 'I want something in industry.' FitzGerald just ignored him and ploughed on. When he announced that Jim O'Keeffe was to have Industry and Energy, O'Keeffe turned to his Waterford colleague.

'Listen, Eddie, I'm willing to swap with you.' Eddie Collins was unsure. He turned to the Taoiseach, who was well down the list by now and galloping hard.

'Excuse me, Garret, is it OK if I swap with Jim?' FitzGerald looked up. The penny dropped.

'Oh yes. That's all right.' And that was that. By this neat piece of barter, a small matter of state was settled to the satisfaction of all concerned.

In another few minutes the Taoiseach had finished his list and was gone. In his first couple of hours at the top, Garret FitzGerald was rushing about breathlessly, leaving bruised egos in his wake.

The new junior ministers were stunned by it all. One of them said afterwards the whole episode made him feel unclean. There were only a few who could be really satisfied. Mary Flaherty was totally surprised at her elevation on her first day in the Dáil. She would have been quite satisfied simply to get used to Leinster House and to come to terms with the role of a backbencher. Ted Nealon was also getting a job on his first day in the Dáil.

Someone else who was pleasantly surprised was Fergus O'Brien. Although he had been a junior spokesman in opposition, he was seen as a Cosgraveite, close to the Beltons on Dublin Corporation, and not one of FitzGerald's set. When the Dáil had adjourned at 5.30 p.m., O'Brien, who was the Lord Mayor of Dublin at the time, slipped out of Leinster House and across the road to Paddy Belton's pub, Hunters, for a pint. He was *that* certain that nobody would be looking for him to go and see Garret. But he was wrong. Eventually Gerry L'Estrange tracked him down: the new Minister of State choked down the rest of his pint and was back in Leinster House like a shot.

Among the frontbenchers who got nothing were Austin Deasy and Jim White. White had been one of the main campaigners for FitzGerald in 1977, and was sure he would get something. Indeed all five in his room had strongly backed the man who was now Taoiseach: Kieran Crotty, Collins, John Donnellan, Brendan Griffin and himself. Collins was the only one to get anything, and at that it was only a junior ministry. After that Tuesday night, it was a very bitter room. Jim White, in particular, felt utterly humiliated: if only FitzGerald had explained that he could not find a place for him. . . . He resolved there and then to get out of politics. Donnellan, another who had campaigned for FitzGerald in 1977, was also bitterly disappointed.

The new Taoiseach had faced an unenviable task. With four departments and three junior posts pre-empted by Labour, there were bound to be Fine Gael deputies disappointed. But he grossly compounded the difficulties through a number of factors, some of them gross errors. He never had any intention of appointing the old guard of Burke, Ryan, O'Donnell and Flanagan. The party he was seeking to build would be more radical, in the social democratic mould. He did not believe his old Cosgraveite colleagues would fit in. He wanted his cabinet to reflect a younger generation. But having brought back Ryan, O'Donnell and Burke to the front bench just a couple of months earlier, it was natural that their expectations of office had been heightened. FitzGerald should have met them and explained, preferably before announcing his cabinet, that they would be getting nothing. It was not done, before or afterwards. The same courtesy should have been extended to the other deputies who held briefs in opposition. Deasy would make this point with devastating effect later.

In fact, FitzGerald was here betraying a trait not appropriate to a senior politician, an inability to convey bad news. Until June 1981, everything had gone relatively smoothly for him. His popularity rating, especially within Fine Gael, had gone on soaring. But a political leader has to be tough enough to defend the inevitable unpopular decisions. FitzGerald liked being Mr Nice Guy. He would later concede that he should have talked with any spokesmen who were not being appointed, and that his handling of the junior appointments was 'messy and unorthodox'.

The other factor that enflamed the party and many of its supporters was what were seen as out-of-turn appointments. Well-established seniority rights in the party suddenly seemed to count for little. Dukes, Flaherty and Nealon would be singled out for criticism because they had got preferment on their first day in the Dáil. But it was the appointment of Dooge that really sent passions soaring on the backbenches.

The surprise that greeted the new government line-up was palpable when FitzGerald led them into the Dáil chamber at 7.30 p.m. An animated buzz went around the press and public galleries. On the Fine Gael benches, the 43 deputies who had got nothing put a brave face on it as FitzGerald reeled off the names of his Ministers and Ministers of State.

He told the House that he would be appointing Professor James Dooge as Minister for Foreign Affairs in due course, and would be nominating him to the Seanad. He also announced that Mr Alexis FitzGerald would be retained as a special adviser to the government, yet another appointment which was bound further to wound the backbenchers. Indeed, things might have been even worse! FitzGerald had also toyed with including Senator Gemma Hussey, the party's spokesperson on Women's Affairs and a close personal friend of his own, in his cabinet! Hussey expected some appointment, but Michael O'Leary advised strongly against such a move. Even then, however, there were some indications that FitzGerald proposed to give her one of the two remaining junior ministries which he had left vacant (he had filled ten positions; the full Fine Gael quota was twelve). But such was the wave of bitterness and alienation that swept the party's backbenches in the wake of the botched appointments that even FitzGerald got the message. There was no job for Gemma.

There was a final twist to the appointments saga. When the Dáil duly approved the new government by 82 to 78 votes, it adjourned for a week. On its re-assembly on 7 July, it voted on the appointment of a Leas Ceann Comhairle.

Paddy Harte was duly proposed by FitzGerald, and Fianna Fáil nominated Jim Tunney. However, the first vote on Harte's nomination was tied at 80-80. L'Estrange, the Chief Whip, was not aware that Eileen Desmond was missing through illness. With the vote now tied, the new Ceann Comhairle, John O'Connell gave the first of many controversial decisions from the chair. 'I have decided that in the interests of fair play in this House, I will cast my vote against.' He declared the motion lost. It was totally against the tradition of the Dáil for the Chair to give his casting vote against the government of the day.

110

When the House moved on to vote on Tunney, the shock outcome was a one vote win for Fianna Fáil, 80 to 79. What had gone wrong? It transpired that Richie Ryan was missing from the government lobby. For years afterwards, many party deputies would claim that Ryan deliberately absented himself to get one back on FitzGerald. L'Estrange, who took quite a bit of criticism in the party for failing to deliver the goods in the lobbies, maintained that he had told every deputy not to leave the House that evening, and that included Ryan. The latter argued, then and subsequently, that his absence had been a genuine mistake.

It was a second humiliation for Harte. FitzGerald really had no choice but to appoint him to one of the remaining Junior Ministries. Two days later, Harte became a Minister for State at the Department of Posts and Telegraphs.

With that, the appointments were over, but the bitterness lingered on. It found occasional expression, as at a Parliamentary Party meeting later in 1981, when Mary Flaherty expressed irritation because some deputies were putting down so many questions to Social Welfare. (She was carrying the brunt of this routine work in the department because the minister, Eileen Desmond, was ill.) She asked them to be more selective. John Donnellan, who had been first elected to the Dáil in 1964, and who had over fifty questions down, was on his feet in a flash. It was fine for some people, just in the Dáil, with departmental staff to do the work for them. But what were deputies who were up to twenty years in the House to do, he asked angrily.

Above all else, the botched appointments reinforced the strange relationship between FitzGerald and many members of the parliamentary party. Neither then nor later, would many Fine Gael TDs feel very close to the leader. They realised he was their greatest electoral asset. They admired him. But very few of them felt real warmth and loyalty towards him. In a sense he intimidated them. Being engrossed so often in the really important affairs of state, he did not have time to work on developing the personal relationships necessary to leading a large party. He was, moreover, blissfully unaware of this character trait. To many backbenchers, rightly or wrongly, it smacked of disdain: it seemed to them as if they simply bored their leader.

111

There should have been yet another twist to this affair. FitzGerald never did fill the remaining junior vacancy. But in January 1982, there were indications that he was going to allocate it — to John Donnellan. However, the government fell before the decision was made.

8

'We are Doomed!'

Garret FitzGerald and John Bruton were horrified. It was their very first day in government, and they had a genuine economic crisis on their hands. They were at an emergency summit in the Department of Finance. The Secretary, Maurice Doyle, was spelling out the dreadful facts. Ninety per cent of the year's budget deficit was already spent, and it was only 1 July. It was plain that Fianna Fáil had grossly underprovided for various Departments in the 1981 estimates. Without more funds, various key government services would run out of money by September or October. In all, there was a shortfall of £115 million in the year's departmental estimates. A detailed Finance document spelled it out starkly. All the election campaign warnings by Fine Gael were real, and worse. The country faced a major financial crisis, which ultimately threatened its capacity to go on borrowing abroad for essential services.

On the previous evening, a senior government official had already apprised FitzGerald of the alarming situation before he led his Ministers into the Dáil for ratification. What he was told had so shaken him that he referred to it in the House.

> Even in the brief time [*since his appointment as Taoiseach*] I have learned something of the scale of the damage done. I have to say I am shocked to find the position is even worse than our most pessimistic [*interruptions from the Fianna Fáil benches drowned out his next words*].
>
> I do not say that without careful consideration. It is not a propagandist remark; it is a factual remark. When the facts are disclosed, they will validate what I have to

113

say. . . . The scale of the mess is beyond anything that had to be faced previously.

It meant there would be no honeymoon for the new minority government, not even a summer break after the exhausting general election campaign. The true state of the public finances cast an immediate question mark over the government's capacity to remain in office. It also compounded the problem of delivering on two of its main policies. Phasing out the budget deficit and — more importantly — implementing its £364 million manifesto.

Fine Gael's credibility, and especially FitzGerald's would be on the line. What was now clear was that the election manifesto had been over the top. FitzGerald confessed later that perhaps they should have adjusted their commitments downwards. But the electoral possibilities were too alluring. Looking back, Prendergast conceded that the manifesto had been 'too optimistic'.

In July, however, the immediate imperative was the state of the public finances. Reluctantly, the government decided they would have to act quickly, and bring in a supplementary budget. It was a brave decision, not the kind of thing any government, especially a minority one, would willingly opt to do within a month of winning power. Acting swiftly had two political advantages. It should lock the Independent TDs into support, since they would be most unlikely to cause another election a month after winning their costly seats. And it was a chance to put one over on Fianna Fáil, to nail Haughey to his profligacy.

Of course, the Department of Finance officials were more than happy with their new political masters: the advocates of financial rectitude. However, only a few weeks before, they had been endorsing the cavalier economics of the Haughey government. In early July FitzGerald discovered that the draft of the department's annual 'Review and Outlook' — drawn up in the dying days of the Fianna Fáil government — was painting a much more sanguine picture of the national finances than was the position being represented to him. Clearly, the Finance men's soothsaying depended on what the government of the day wanted to hear. The result was that

Brendan Dowling and another economist, John Blackwell, had to spend a weekend rewriting the document to reflect more accurately the parlous reality. It did not say much for the mandarins of Merrion Street.

The Dáil reconvened on 21 July for the supplementary budget, which Bruton stated was primarily concerned with ensuring that Ireland 'remains an independent economy'. The facts were staggering. At the end of June the current budget deficit was £457 million. Fianna Fáil had set it at £515 million for the full year. 'In the absence of corrective action, the current budget deficit would be nearly £950 million, equivalent to 9.5 per cent of GNP by the end of the year.' The highest previous level had been 7.25 per cent in 1979. Without corrective action, the opening deficit for 1982 would be £1,500 million, 'merely to maintain the present level of services'.

One of the major problems was the enormous growth in the public sector: 30,000 extra people had swollen the numbers to 300,000 over the previous four years. Without any further increase in 1981, public sector pay and pensions were set to rise 25 per cent in that year alone. Bruton imposed a recruitment embargo, and pleaded for pay moderation. But the really effective way of curbing public spending — cutting public service pay — was funked for obvious reasons of political survival and to avoid massive problems with the unions. But it totally contradicted FitzGerald's and Fine Gael's commitment to tackle the economic mess by cutting spending rather than by imposing additional tax. Public sector pay and pensions ended up costing £1,924 million in 1981 — £369 million more than the previous year. And as if all this was not enough, the FitzGerald government negotiated yet another inflationary pay deal with the public sector later in the year!

In his July budget, Bruton did the very thing that Fine Gael policy had ruled out. He hiked taxes to fund unsustainable levels of public spending. Up went the old reliables, drink, cigarettes and petrol. The standard VAT rate of 10 per cent was increased by 50 per cent. A 23 per cent rise in CIE charges, held over by Fianna Fáil for electoral reasons, had to go ahead also. It was, as the newspapers described it next day, a savage budget. It did, to be fair, have some effect in checking the careering national finances. The new deficit would be £787 million (8 per cent of GNP), £160 million less than it would otherwise have been.

Fianna Fáil's response was incredible and totally contradictory. Gene FitzGerald said that if corrective action was needed, it could wait until the 1982 budget. Haughey embraced what would become one of his stock terms, 'monetarism'. And yet he chided the government for doing so little to correct the finances. 'After all the preaching of doom and gloom, and all the drama, and the state of the nation broadcast, and around-the-clock cabinet sessions, what the government are engaged in here today is, from the point of government finances, a minimal exercise.' At the same time, he also attacked the Coalition for having an unfeeling obsession with balancing the books, at the expense of people's well-being. Haughey's power of logic and consistency were almost as feeble as his talent for financial management.

As a political gamble, the coalition's budget worked in the short term. Amidst renewed speculation on how the 'Others' would vote, and with Oliver Flanagan having to leave his hospital bed for the vote, the coalition survived. On the first crucial vote, at 7.30 p.m. that evening, Kemmy and Loftus backed them; Sherlock abstained; Blaney voted with Fianna Fáil and Noel Browne was absent. The result was 82 to 79, and margins of that order decided the other votes on the measure.

For Fine Gael, there were other serious implications, however. Their election manifesto was in tatters. For FitzGerald especially, 'the man you can trust', it looked grim. The supplementary budget would add 3 per cent to the cost of living. That was almost the full cost of the much-hailed tax reform programme. But nothing at all had been done on that front: Bruton said it was impossible in mid-year. Yet in his budget statement he promised: 'I will implement the government's tax reform proposals, including the £9.60 tax credit for spouses and the new, augmented child benefit, from the beginning of the next income tax year.'

Pre-election euphemisms for dealing with the budget deficit, like looking to buoyancy, were also having to take a very cold shower now that Fine Gael were in government. 'It would be unrealistic to expect, or to pretend, that the process of phasing down the current budget deficit of the present scale could be a painless experience for the community', Bruton said in his budget statement.

All in all, the first month in office had torpedoed the Fine Gael economic programme. The government was forced to abandon the policy on which it was elected. In its place there was nothing — except desperate day-to-day crisis management.

———————

FitzGerald's minority government encountered a second major crisis on coming to power. The unresolved H-Block hunger strike and the attendant lawlessness and anarchy fomented by Provisional Sinn Féin/IRA throughout the country. One of the Taoiseach's great passions in life was to resolve the Northern conflict, and he immediately threw himself into the quest for a solution.

He pressed the British government to deal directly with the hunger strikers. He called Margaret Thatcher on the phone. He sought to persuade her ambassador, Sir Leonard Figg. On one occasion he summoned him for talks at 2 a.m. On 8 July, Joe McDonnell became the fifth hunger striker to die. On 13 July Martin Hurson became the sixth. FitzGerald, increasingly alarmed, held meetings with anyone he thought could break the impasse. He had two meetings with relatives of the hunger strikers in Government Buildings, next door to the cabinet room. On the second occasion, some of the relatives refused to leave and staged a sit-in. FitzGerald began to realise that the IRA was manipulating the unfortunate relatives.

On Saturday, 18 July the National H-Blocks Committee staged a march from the centre of Dublin to the British Embassy in Ballsbridge. Gardaí blocked off the approach road, and were subjected to a ferocious barrage of missiles. Soon it was a full-scale riot, and the gardaí eventually counter-attacked. Many people were injured, and parts of Ballsbridge were left with the battleground appearance most Dubliners only saw on their television screens. The riot represented a

117

major security crisis for the government. Sympathy for the H-Block cause rapidly waned in the South. The Provisionals had overdone their emotional ransom stuff.

For his part, FitzGerald was accused of getting too emotionally involved in the crisis, and later he admitted that there was some truth in this. In July alone he had twenty-seven communications with the British government on the matter. But it was not FitzGerald's efforts that ended the H-Blocks hunger strikes. In the end, it was the pressure from the strikers' families which told, as they realised that there would be no concessions forthcoming. It was a peculiarly Northern tragedy, born of the awfulness of the republican ghettoes. No outsider could settle it. All the Southern government could do was to hold an Anglo-Irish summit when it was all over, in order to normalise relations between the two countries again.

In mid-August, after the Seanad election results emerged, FitzGerald nominated his eleven members to the Upper Chamber. Naturally, Jim Dooge was included, since this was how his appointment as Foreign Minister had to be facilitated. But he could not formally assume office until the Dáil ratified his appointment when it resumed in the autumn, on 21 October. Until then John Kelly doubled as Minister for Foreign Affairs. It was a messy set-up. Dooge could not attend cabinet meetings, but under a special cabinet minute he was provided with copies of all relevant papers. He did much of the work of the department, but when he went to London on business, Kelly had to accompany him. On EEC business, the junior minister, Jim O'Keeffe, went along.

It all heightened the awareness within Fine Gael that FitzGerald's buddy was getting special treatment. When Dooge was eventually ratified by the Dáil on 21 October, Haughey attacked the appointment as the height of cronyism. On the government backbenches, many deputies were of a like mind.

In the event, Dooge established an outstanding reputation at Foreign Affairs. FitzGerald had felt that it was an ideal department to be filled by a senator, given that there was so much overseas work. Despite all the criticism, the appointment was triumphantly vindicated by Dooge's performance.

FitzGerald also honoured another of the backroom strategy people when Seán O'Leary was nominated to the Seanad. Young Fine Gael was not forgotten either. Miriam Kearney (22), chairperson of its International Affairs Committee, was another Taoiseach's nominee, and in September, she became head of Young Fine Gael. Her predecessor, Dan Egan, moved over to the post of party press officer, filling the place of Liam Hourican, who had become Government Press Secretary. FitzGerald also offered a Seanad seat to Prendergast, the outstanding architect of his restructured party. But he refused it, mainly because he felt unable to sign the party pledge on voting in the Oireachtas. A true radical, he feared that on some social issues he would find himself at odds with the party position, and unable to vote with them.

From 1 July, Prendergast felt strongly that the government was living on borrowed time. He had no doubt as the weeks went on that it would never get a second budget through if it were to pursue the policies the country needed. 'We are doomed' was his verdict on the financial mess.

He and FitzGerald began to toy with the possibility of a snap election in the autumn. Already, George Birmingham, a young backbencher from Charlie Haughey's Dublin North-Central constituency, had written to his leader urging such a move, and saying that it would be valid for FitzGerald to appeal to the people for a clearer mandate. It would be reasonable to ask for a working majority.

Prendergast remained at his post in August and September making tentative preparations, and 5 October was pencilled in by him as the day to go to the country. FitzGerald discussed it informally with some cabinet colleagues, and an opinion poll was carried out. But, alas, it indicated that there was little chance of improving their Dáil strength. The plan was aborted.

The general secretary now began to consider his own future. He had already been invited by Bruton to join him in Finance as a special adviser. Finally, at the end of October, Prendergast decided to resign as general secretary and took up Bruton's offer. He paid a glowing tribute to FitzGerald.

'Without your clarity of purpose, courage, skill and stamina, it would not have been possible to make as much progress. Very few people gave us much chance in Autumn 1977 of being in a position to return to government in 1981.' And there was a special commendation for the constituency organisers and PROs, who had so upset the old guard. 'Our team of constituency organisers and PROs were extraordinarily good, and will be of great assistance to you in the years ahead.'

Meanwhile, Prendergast's new boss, John Bruton was finding the going tough. On top of having to bring in the emergency July budget, he was having difficulties convincing many of his cabinet colleagues about the true state of the finances. At times it was a case of Bruton and FitzGerald against the rest.

Bedevilling the government's efforts to address the economic crisis in the autumn of 1981 was the costly tax reform package. Obviously it would have helped if Brendan Dowling had joined the government. FitzGerald did, in fact, invite him to become his personal economic adviser. But Dowling had just become a partner with the stockbrokers, J & E Davy. He literally could not afford to move. And Bruton, the man now charged with implementing the party's policy, had not been involved at all in its formulation.

Dowling had been especially disappointed at the July budget's failure to make any start on the tax plan, while the cost of the tax plan had been exacted to fund additional government spending. He had come to see Bruton as a reluctant tax reformer.

However, despite the Minister's reservations about the scheme and the overall exchequer problems, the parliamentary party were naturally anxious to deliver on their promises. A meeting on 15 September saw them press the matter, and Bruton assured them that they were progressing with plans to introduce the tax plan, farm aids, and so forth. A public statement to this effect was issued after the meeting by the party's press office.

The reality, however, was that the plan was running into serious difficulties in the Department of Finance, whose officials plainly did not like it. They were opposed to the integration of the social welfare and income tax systems it required.

Dowling believed one reason for this was the implication that civil servants would end up paying the full rates of PRSI like other workers.

He was repeatedly called in to explain details of the package. There were many arguments about costings and implementation. Dowling felt that considerable efforts were being made to thwart his plan. But a further problem was that he and FitzGerald had actually got their sums wrong! They had started work on the plan in 1980, and some of their crucial tax projections were done for 1981-82. They should have calculated forward for 1982-83. In the election programme, the cost of the plan was put at £263 million. FitzGerald later said they had under-calculated the cost by about £60 million. However, the Finance officials put up a document to government claiming it would cost over £400 million to implement.

Dowling also found it impossible to get forward projections on tax from the Revenue Commissioners, as he strove to explain to Finance that the model worked. It appeared that both Revenue and Finance officials had closed minds to a scheme which would reduce the income tax yield. Of course, the Dowling-FitzGerald plan envisaged this being recouped in indirect taxes. But what the taxman had, he was reluctant to yield. Nor could Dowling secure projections for charging PRSI on total incomes, as the plan proposed: as things stood, PRSI was only charged on the first £8,500 of income.

In the end, the scheme was abandoned. It was not included in the January 1982 budget. FitzGerald would insist that the reason was the parlous public finances. Only the famous £9.60 for stay-at-home wives was introduced. On this also, Dowling had fundamental differences with Finance. He wanted it implemented automatically, with an opt-out clause. In other words, families who did not want to operate it could cancel out. But Finance maintained this was not feasible. What resulted was an opt-in scheme. Families had to apply for the £9.60 which was, after all, a deduction from the husband's earnings. Inevitably, only a highly motivated minority of women pursued it.

Nor was there joy on any other front for this beleaguered minority government. Every issue it embraced seemed to bring immense controversy. There was, for instance, the raising of the primary school entry age to four and a half. This proposition had been around for some years. It was raised in a 1979 Fianna Fáil white paper on education. It was also on a Department of Finance hit list to save money. The Minister for Education, John Boland, had been a member of Dublin County VEC, and was readily convinced of the educational merit of the proposal. Indeed, very many people saw the infant classes of the country's primary schools being turned into creches by working mothers.

In July, before he had properly warmed the ministerial seat, Boland took up the policy, and proceeded to plan its implementation for that October. But this brought the wrath of the Irish National Teachers' Organisation down on his head. They instantly saw job losses. A furious debate on the subject went on during the autumn of 1981, with arguments about the educational merits being met with claims that the measure was merely a crude, cost-cutting exercise.

Many deputies came to regard it as a very foolhardy undertaking, given their tenuous hold on government. Fianna Fáil went on the offensive when the Dáil resumed in October, and the issue culminated in what amounted to a confidence vote on the Coalition in Private Members' Time. When Boland stood up to defend the measure, the public gallery — packed with teachers — began to boo him. They cheered John Wilson, the opposition spokesman. The government had to thank Noel Browne and Jim Kemmy for their survival in a tense division on 10 November.

Boland was convinced about the merits of the issue. The correspondence reaching his department endorsed his view, showing about 60 per cent in favour. But in political terms, it appeared as if the government were courting self-destruction. The measure saved very little money, and they had to devise hasty financial proposals for pre-school playgroups to neutralise the criticism. Basically, it was no issue for a minority government to embrace, and betrayed political immaturity.

This time they got away with it. But a stark lesson should have been learned. The coalition held government at the pleasure of a handful of solo deputies: therefore, they would have to work really hard on securing their support in advance of future Dáil divisions. It should have been an elementary fact. Incredibly, the lesson was not learned . . . with disastrous consequences when the 1982 budget came round.

An air of crisis always hung over the first FitzGerald coalition. Years later, ministers and backbenchers alike would describe it as a harrowing time. They were simply stumbling from one crisis to another. Around the cabinet table there was constant tension, for Labour disagreed fundamentally with the policy thrust of their senior partners.

————————

Amidst all this crisis management, FitzGerald declared a bold initiative to 'desectarianise Southern society' in what was to become a famous RTE radio broadcast on Sunday, 27 September. He later maintained that it had all been thought out in advance by him. But he had not raised it with any ministerial colleagues or announced his intention in cabinet. In the previous week, there had been much debate in the newspapers following a statement by the Taoiseach that Articles 2 and 3 of the constitution, which enshrined the Republic's claim on the North, should not be there. Gerald Barry, the interviewer, now asked him if he proposed holding a referendum to have them deleted.

FitzGerald said he was passionately committed to a united Ireland on the principles enunciated by Tone and Davis. Growing up he had seen the partition enforced by the British being reinforced 'by constitutions and laws being passed here, which were alien to the people of Ireland as a whole'. One of the reasons he had entered politics was to do something about this,' and also to try to achieve social reforms, and to eliminate poverty from this country'. He was determined his government would tackle these issues.

He pointed out that his mother was a Northern Protestant, but that we had created a state that was unacceptable to her people. Asked what he proposed doing, FitzGerald said: 'I want to lead a crusade, a republican crusade, to make this a genuine Republic. . . . we expect the Northern Unionists to join a state, which in 1979, was bringing in laws based on the theology of one church. Now that has to change, and what I want to do is lead public opinion towards that change.'

In a little over a year, that commitment would become an embarrassing nightmare for him.

For now, though, he would do all he could to lead the people to endorse this approach. 'And if eventually it transpires the Irish people don't want this, if the people in this state want to remain fundamentally a 26-county state based on a majority ethos, and are not prepared to work with the people of Northern Ireland towards unity on a basis that could be common to both, well then I will accept defeat and leave politics at that stage, if necessary.' He would not put a referendum to the people to endorse a new constitution, however, until there was a real prospect of it succeeding. But he would continue working to that end.

FitzGerald was setting very lofty standards indeed by which he was to be judged in his subsequent political actions. Later he said he deliberately chose to launch his constitutional initiative on radio to achieve more direct contact with people. This was the radical FitzGerald, clearly willing to lead from the front, intent on breaking the conservative mould of Irish politics in dramatic fashion.

Expounding such lofty intentions in a studio in Donnybrook was one thing. However, taking the people of Ireland along his crusading road with him was entirely another matter. Could he even succeed in persuading his own parliamentary party to back such a vote?

9

The Patter of Tiny Feet

By the end of 1981, it was a matter of common gossip that Fine Gael might not be able to deliver their tax reform plan, and that there were difficulties over the possible abolition of food subsidies. The coalition government were agonising over the proposed budget provisions. Although ony six months in office, many cabinet ministers were exhausted and near despair.

Fine Gael had most to lose. Reforming the tax code and cutting public spending, had been their political passport to office. In particular, FitzGerald's reputation and credibility hung on delivery. It was one thing to have made no headway in the supplementary July budget: they had been less than a month in office, and had had to take emergency action. But that would not be a sufficient reason now for failing to make a start at least.

At 3 a.m. on Friday, 22 January 1982, Michael O'Leary, the Tánaiste, rang FitzGerald to tell him that Labour opposed outright the proposal to abolish food subsidies, a measure that had earlier been agreed in cabinet. Budget day was only a week away, and FitzGerald could have done without being woken in the middle of the night with this kind of news. (It was not unusual for the bachelor Labour leader to work with his staff, often over a meal, until that hour, although it did not make for the most punctual starts in the morning. 'Where is O'Leary?' had already become a refrain around government buildings.) When the cabinet finally came together later that morning, the party differences were signalled dramatically. The Fine Gael ministers gathered in the cabinet room, but the four Labour members — O'Leary, Jim Tully, Eileen Desmond and Liam Kavanagh — stayed together in the ante-room. The coalition had split.

125

The earlier budget package, which Labour was now abrogating, had proposed the abolition of food subsidies, to be compensated for by a record 25 per cent increase in social welfare payments. It had also been agreed that VAT at 10 per cent would go on footwear and clothing. Now this carefully designed package was in tatters. But soon the instinct for survival reasserted itself. If Fine Gael and Labour were to split irretrievably on a budget issue, it would be curtains for both of them. They would be swept from office. Rather than hang separately, they decided to hang together, and began to cobble together a new package. They started with changes in the food subsidy plans. The subsidies would remain on bread, flour and margarine; the butter subsidy would be cut by 8½p to 14p, and the milk subsidy would go entirely. But this left two anomalies: a gap in the projected finances, and the fact that the 25 per cent social welfare rise had only been agreed on the assumption that food subsidies were being abolished entirely. It was soon decided to raise the proposed 10 per cent VAT rate to 18 per cent (which was to be the new standard rate) in order to bridge the revenue gap. But inadvertently, the 25 per cent welfare rise was not altered. In the context of budgetary constraints, it was too great an increase. But the incident demonstrated the battle-weariness of the cabinet: they were so exhausted that they had simply overlooked it.

O'Leary later recalled that the compromise 'was greeted with relief as it resolved the government split. At that stage we were at the end of a desperately intensive period of panic and pressure. We were an exhausted government.'

On the same day that the new cabinet deal was done, FitzGerald had meetings with Jim Kemmy and Noel Browne. They were alarmed at reports that the food subsidies were to go, and they told the Taoiseach that they would be unable to vote for such a measure. FitzGerald listened, but gave no indication of his plans. He was quite obsessive about secrecy on the matter. That weekend, in a *Sunday Independent* interview, Kemmy publicly signalled that he would not vote for the budget the following Wednesday if the food subsidies were removed, or if there were further VAT increases. However, FitzGerald was not too concerned. He calculated that Kemmy would not desert because the subsidies were only being modified, and the 25 per cent welfare rise would offset the VAT rises for the less well-off.

That was basically the government frame of mind facing into the budget. The published estimates already made it very clear that it was going to be tough. The key indicator was that current spending was set to rise by 16 per cent, with over half that increase earmarked for higher public sector pay and pensions. This statistic alone signalled the failure of FitzGerald's government to deliver on its commitment to cut public spending.

As budget day loomed, there was much speculation on the voting intentions of Kemmy, Browne and the other Independents. But as John Bruton rose at 3 p.m. on Wednesday, 27 January, to deliver his financial statement, the conventional wisdom was that they would not precipitate an election. They would huff and puff, but in the end would not bring the Dáil down.

For the first time ever, the budget statement was broadcast live by RTE. It made grim listening. 'Regrettably, it is not possible to adopt the 25 per cent rate as the standard rate of tax immediately, because of the cost of the change, and the consequent increases in indirect taxation that would be required to pay for it', Bruton said. Both the IMF and the ESRI had so advised the government, 'because of the poor state of the public finances'.

The child benefit scheme would go ahead in April, however, though at a slightly lower rate than promised. So would the £9.60 for wives in the home, and tax credits would replace personal allowances, thus making them worth the same to everyone. But although the government was abandoning its 25 per cent income tax rate because it would entail huge increases in VAT, this did not mean that there would be no VAT increases in Bruton's budget. There were plenty, but they were imposed not to finance a tax reform plan but to pay for increased public spending. It was the public funeral of the election manifesto. The 'low' VAT rate, which had gone from 10 per cent to 15 per cent in July, was pushed up to 18 per cent. The standard VAT rate went from 25 per cent to 30 per cent. Bruton also outlined the reduction in food subsidies, the taxing of short-term social welfare benefits, and the abolition of tax relief on personal loans. A special tax allowance of £1,000, which had been an election carrot aimed at young flat-dwellers, was introduced — but only for those over sixty-five. The promised farm reliefs were not introduced in full: agricultural rates were only halved, with the remaining half not due to go until the following year. It all went to underline how extravagant that manifesto had been.

But one of the biggest shocks was the proposed extension of the new 18 per cent VAT rate to all footwear and clothing, which had been zero-rated. Bruton clearly anticipated a torrent of criticism, and set out a robust defence of the measure:

> Clothing and footwear are undeniably necessities of life. Yet this category covers everything from the most simple garments to the most expensive and ephemeral creations of fashion. Substantial expenditure on high-cost clothes should not be allowed to continue untaxed.

Moreover, most clothing and footwear was now imported. In 1975, he added, when the zero-rating was introduced, half of those goods were made in Ireland. He also anticipated criticism for including children's footwear and clothing in the net. He had considered exempting them: 'I am aware that it is done in the UK, but I am also aware of the major difficulties which it poses in practice, and on the anomalies it has created.'

He went on to pile further taxes on the old reliables — beer, spirits, cigarettes and petrol. Up, too, went road tax and colour televisions. The shopping exodus across the border could already be envisaged.

Bruton also demonstrated a timeless Fine Gael weakness for hectoring the great unwashed. He chided people for taking foreign holidays: it was 'a measure of the unreality of our living styles [given] the recession in the economy generally'. And with that he slapped a £10 tax on each aircraft seat booked! Children under two were mercifully excluded. It was not quite in the class of Ernest Blythe cutting the old age pension, but the mentality was the same.

Bruton was not, however, totally without the instinct for self-preservation. In announcing the increase from 25 per cent to 30 per cent in the standard VAT rate, he also transferred from this band various house furnishing items, including furniture, joinery and carpets, all thriving industries in Bruton's Meath constituency. They moved down to the 'low' 18 per cent rate.

But there were other biting impositions whose full impact would only emerge later. Employee PRSI was to rise from 3.75 per cent to 5.5 per cent; the income cut-off point for it went up £1,000 to £9,500, and there was a 1 per cent Youth Employment Levy on all incomes. When he finally sat down, after two hours, he had levied an extra £330 million in taxes on the community. This was to have been FitzGerald's last resort, after buoyancy and public spending cuts, to get the books balanced. But just as in July 1981, it was now the first, easier option. On the credit side, however, Bruton had at least succeeded in reintroducing the principles of good management into the state's finances, after the mad excesses of the Fianna Fáil years.

While the overall package was being greeted with horror around the country, many Fine Gael backbenchers were equally dismayed. Richie Ryan feared the 18 per cent tax on footwear and clothing would drastically depress retail sales. Paddy Harte thought about the crucial solo deputies whose support the government required in order to survive: if they back it, we're in for five years. But . . . already an ominous note, Jim Kemmy had left the chamber before Bruton finished. Outside, he made clear his strong opposition to the budget, and re-echoed it in an RTE interview. But he was not saying how he would vote. One seasoned Fine Gael deputy had no doubts about the outcome. Gerry L'Estrange was a former government chief whip, and was now a Junior Minister in the Department of Health. He went back to his office, and striding in the door called out to his secretary, Angela Edgehill: 'Start the campaign. We're gone. We're finished.'

But most backbenchers felt that surely the arithmetic had been done. Fergus O'Brien, the chief whip would have it squared. But he had done no such thing. The doctrine of budget secrecy meant that he could only pursue that task *after* the budget was disclosed publicly. He had already had his own premonition of failure. That morning, backbencher Nuala Fennell had asked him if she could go to a meeting in Trinity College that night. 'If the House falls before 7.30 p.m. you can go', he said jokingly, but wondered afterwards about the accuracy.

Michael O'Leary had been worried too. But when one of the ushers handed him a message from Senator Ruairi Quinn, listening and watching from the division lobby, he was buoyed up. Quinn's message congratulated him on a good budget, and the 25 per cent social welfare increase in particular.

Among those in the public gallery was Frank Flannery. He was now more actively involved in the Fine Gael backroom scene. He was a member of a communications committee which advised the government on policy presentation and public feedback. He was appalled as he listened to Bruton. The budget was badly crafted and negative in the extreme. Only a throwaway reference to the 25 per cent welfare rise, the largest in the history of the state! He, too, reckoned the government would have counted the heads, but he was so depressed that when Bruton sat down, he headed directly home.

O'Brien now set about tracking down Browne, Kemmy and Loftus, as the opposition began their reply to the budget. He first contacted Browne, and took him to FitzGerald's office. There the veteran radical argued his opposition to the footwear and clothing tax. FitzGerald held out the prospect of some amendment in that area. Browne said he would support the government, and he also promised to talk to Kemmy.

The Independent Limerick socialist was deeply upset. He had rung some of his close associates in Limerick, and they agreed with him that he could not support the budget. There was too little capital taxation; £47 million was being cut from the food subsidies; the footwear and clothing tax would exact £67 million in that year, and £106 million in a full year. Noel Browne called in and said that FitzGerald wanted to see him. Fergus O'Brien turned up with the same message, and Kemmy left with him to see the Taoiseach in his first floor room.

Kemmy made plain from the outset that he would not vote for the budget. Again FitzGerald suggested something

130

might be done on the footwear and clothing. He gave Kemmy some pages he had drawn up showing the impact of the budget measures on people with different incomes, showing how the less-well-off could benefit. Kemmy left with these and returned to his room. But he had not said he would be changing his mind. O'Brien became desperately worried. He was certain Kemmy was gone, and said as much to FitzGerald.

O'Brien next brought Seán 'Dublin Bay' Loftus to the Taoiseach. The Dublin Independent also focused on the footwear and clothing tax. It was after 7.30 p.m. by now, and the first of the crucial votes was coming at eight o'clock. Loftus was very agitated, and FitzGerald made little impression on him.

O'Brien now sought to impress on the Taoiseach the parlous situation that was looming. If Kemmy and Loftus deserted, the government were gone. They entertained no hope of winning over Joe Sherlock. FitzGerald was not so sure. 'Loftus won't vote against us, and he may vote for us', he said, seeking to reassure his chief whip. But O'Brien was not a bit happy.

As Seán Loftus was leaving the Taoiseach's room, he was buttonholed by the young Fine Gael backbencher, George Birmingham, a Dublin City Council colleague. He too sought to nail down Loftus's support, and they moved in to the nearby whip's office. Subsequently, Jim Mitchell, Peter Barry and O'Brien all joined in the effort. But Loftus felt awfully unhappy and told them so over and over again.

They were all still arguing when the division bells rang for the first vote. Soon the Chamber was filling up. Kemmy entered and went over to FitzGerald. He returned the document to him and repeated that he could not support the government. The division bells had now ceased, and the chamber doors were locked. The deputies began to troop up the steps to the division lobbies, Government supporters wheeling left at the top, opposition voters right.

In the flurry and flux of so many people moving about and leaving their seats, nobody really noticed FitzGerald as he headed across to Kemmy in the no-man's-land between the government and opposition benches. Now he was actually kneeling on the bench in front of the Limerick man, talking earnestly and low to him. It was the posture of a supplicant.

Suddenly the packed press gallery noticed it. Word was already out that Kemmy might not back the government. FitzGerald was pleading with him. He was shaking and distraught. But Kemmy had his mind made up. 'The die is cast', he said. It was too late for further argument. Fianna Fáil deputies had also noticed the extraordinary scene. They began jeering and catcalling at FitzGerald. He drew up hurriedly from his kneeling posture, backing away, like a child caught with his hand in the cookie jar. It was an ignominious, embarrassing exposure of the government's lack of political nous and professionalism.

FitzGerald now joined his colleagues in the fateful climb to the lobbies. For an eternity, it seemed deputies were filing from their seats. Now they were down to a trickle. Only Kemmy, Loftus and Sherlock remained. Browne had duly gone into the government lobby, Blaney into the Fianna Fáil one.

O'Brien stood on top of the steps watching the remaining trio. Kemmy was the first to move. Slowly he reached the top. All eyes were on him. They had all seen FitzGerald plead with him. Everyone realised the importance of what was happening. For the first time in a major division since he came into Leinster House seven months earlier, Kemmy turned right.

There was a gasp of excitement in the press gallery. Sherlock was now at the top of the steps. He too wheeled right, after Kemmy, into the opposition lobby. That left Loftus. He could still save the government. He had been contesting general elections unsuccessfully for twenty years and he had finally made it. Surely he would not risk it all after just seven months?

'Come on, Seán', his old City Council colleague, O'Brien, pleaded. But Loftus also turned right. 'We're fucked', the chief whip exclaimed aloud to anyone who was listening. Everyone knew the government were gone. But now that the incredible had happened, there was a shocked, dignified reaction. The finalising of the tallies went on. Journalists checked with one another to make sure their eyes were not playing tricks. Yes, that was Kemmy on the Fianna Fáil side; and also Loftus. 'Maybe I should have caught him by the arm', O'Brien thought.

Deputies were now scrambling back to their seats. The chief whips were totting up the votes. And it was the Fianna Fáil chief whip, Ray Burke, who popped down the steps with the slip of paper detailing the result. Before handing it to the Ceann Comhairle, he shook hands with his party leader.

Dr O'Connell rose to announce the result of the vote to increase the excise duty on beer from midnight. It was also a vote on the fate of the FitzGerald government: 'Tá, 81. Níl, 82'. Cheering and clapping erupted from the Fianna Fáil benches. It was just 8.15 p.m.

Now all eyes turned on FitzGerald, who looked shocked and pale. He rose and, in a calm voice, announced that he would go immediately to Árus an Uachtaráin to ask President Hillery to dissolve the 22nd Dáil. It was the first time in the history of the state that a government had fallen on its budget.

All the bright hopes of the expert election campaign of June 1981 lay shattered. Fine Gael would have to fight an election on the worst possible platform: defending a swingeing, hairshirt budget, having utterly failed to deliver on its own promises and facing a winter campaign, with party finances still in the red in many constituencies since the previous contest.

———————

Was it avoidable? That was the immediate question. Kemmy was bitter. He felt he had been taken for granted. The man who had backed the government in all crucial divisions had clearly outlined his breaking point over the previous days and weeks. The government pleaded budget secrecy. But FitzGerald and other ministers never believed that Kemmy would vote to put Haughey back in office. To that extent, they had certainly taken him for granted.

There should have been a more formal structure for dealing with the solo deputies, who were crucial to the government's survival. Indeed such a proposal had been put at the first Fine Gael parliamentary party meeting in July 1981, after the formation of the coalition. It was Mary Flaherty, one of the youngest new deputies, who called for these TDs to be briefed on all contentious business. The idea was never formalised, however.

In the scramble and excitement after the Dáil adjourned. Bruton was unrepentant about his abortive budget. He told journalists: 'We trimmed our sails as far as we could. But we are Fine Gael in government. We, with the Labour Party, went as far as we could to satisfy Independent demands.'

President Hillery was not immediately available to grant the dissolution, and it was after 11 o'clock before Dr FitzGerald got back to the Dáil. He said that the election would take place on 18 February, and the 23rd Dáil would convene on 9 March. During the intervening three-hour period, Haughey and other Fianna Fáil frontbenchers had sought in vain to speak with the President. The party was making itself available to form an alternative government without another election being held. After the defeat of the government, the opposition front bench had met, and Haughey issued a statement: 'It is a matter for the President to consider the situation which has arisen now that the Taoiseach has ceased to retain the support of the majority in Dáil Éireann. I am available for consultation by the President should he so wish.' But President Hillery decided to accede to FitzGerald's request for a dissolution. There really was no other course open to him, since the government had been defeated on a budget provision.

After the Dáil was dissolved, FitzGerald and his Ministers headed for a hasty convened parliamentary party meeting. Although many deputies felt they had gratuitously thrown power away, there was an instinct to close ranks. FitzGerald was given a standing ovation, as was Bruton. The parliamentary party then adjourned until the following day.

FitzGerald proceeded to hold a press conference. It was an unreal affair. He put too brave a face on the disaster: he was 'happy to face the electorate on this budget'. What was more, he said that the government had actually prepared for the possibility of losing the vote. (This was, of course, a total fiction.) He did not think anything would be changed. The issues in the campaign would be the state of the economy and Northern Ireland. He was 'exhilarated' about the election. But his colleagues sitting around him, including Peter Barry, looked far from exhilarated. They looked tired, fed-up and exasperated.

FitzGerald was questioned about the budget strategy. Why had they not exempted children's footwear and clothing at least? He gave a truly extraordinary reply. If they had done this, he said, the possibility would arise of women with small feet buying children's shoes. And they would evade the tax! The journalists thought they were hearing things. Some of them left the room seriously wondering if Garret had not suddenly lost his marbles. Later, FitzGerald maintained that it had been a joke. But nobody was laughing on the night of 27 January 1982.

This bizarre performance was one reflection of the panic that immediately enveloped Fine Gael. Nobody was ready for this catastrophe. Press officer Dan Egan was busy preparing a budget summary for overnight dispatch to branches around the country when the dramatic news arrived that the government was gone.

To make matters worse, at this point the party had no general secretary. Prendergast's successor had been selected, but he was not due to take up office until 24 February. The man, Finbarr Fitzpatrick (35), from Freemount, Charleville, Co. Cork, was an adult education organiser, and had been constituency organiser in Cork North-West. He had watched the collapse of the government from the public gallery and like Frank Flannery, felt that better efforts should have been made to secure the necessary Independents.

Now, suddenly, he found himself at the eye of the storm. He sat beside FitzGerald at his 'small feet' press conference, and after that he participated in an emergency strategy meeting. Soon, Fitzpatrick was surrounded by familiar faces, because all of a sudden, the handlers were needed again.

At around midnight Seán O'Leary, Derry Hussey, Enda Marren, Frank Flannery, Catherine Meehan, Fitzpatrick and some politicians, including FitzGerald, Tom Fitzpatrick and Peter Barry, had their inaugural campaign meeting. It was decided, there and then, that since the broad thrust of the budget was necessary, they would defend it aggressively. It was necessary for the country's economic survival: that would be the theme. It was also decided that O'Leary would again be director of elections. The other committee members would resume their former roles. There was no time to consider changes.

The following morning, the Parliamentary Party resumed its meeting. Many deputies were still shocked and deeply pessimistic. They would be battling for their seats with this awful budget around their necks. Some of the deputies gave vent to their anger and their fears, like P. J. Sheehan and the veteran Oliver J. Flanagan, who warned his colleagues that they would all be returning to the Dáil in a single taxi. But the survival instinct, and the need for credibility, dictated once more that they hang together. They agreed to stand by the budget. Only a few deputies disagreed. It was a Hobson's choice really. Had they walked away from it they would have been totally discredited.

But this was also the time for some of the humiliated deputies of June 1981 to cash in their chips. Jim White headed home to Donegal South-West and told his supporters that he was quitting. He was still disillusioned and bitter. It wasn't so much his exclusion in June but the absence of any explanation from FitzGerald. His supporters urged him to change his mind, but he was adamant.

Tom O'Donnell also wanted out. He was due to head for the European Parliament on the day after the budget and he had had his ticket bought. The scars of June were still fresh with him too. Twenty years a deputy, and a former minister, he had topped the poll in Limerick East and helped bring in Michael Noonan, the first time ever that there were two Fine Gael deputies in the constituency.

The June government was the first one in decades not to have a Limerick minister. 'Shame on you, Garret' was the banner headline on the *Limerick Echo*, decrying the omission of O'Donnell. Such was the furore in Fine Gael in the city that FitzGerald at one stage held out the prospect of a junior minstry to O'Donnell. But he did not take it up. The matter rested and was not revived by either of them. But the constituency executive in Limerick East contacted O'Donnell and urged him to stand again. Without him, they wouldn't have a chance of holding the two seats: Noonan was only seven months in the Dáil. Finally he agreed to cancel the Brussels trip and go back and campaign in Limerick.

Richie Ryan, another Euro-deputy, also decided it was time to bow out. He had been a running mate of FitzGerald's in June, insisting on standing in Dublin South-East because his Rathmines/Terenure base was added to it by the 1980 constituency commission. FitzGerald did not want him there, and Ryan claimed a last-minute invasion of his territory by FitzGerald supporters had been the reason he polled so badly in June. He got just 1,722 votes to the party leader's 13,794, and suffered the humiliation of taking the final seat without reaching the quota.

Although he was confident that he would greatly improve his vote, there were other considerations. He felt that he would be consigned to the backbenches for as long as FitzGerald was leader, so he decided to concentrate on Europe. He opted out of the Dáil, where he had been a member since 1959 and no one in headquarters asked him to change his mind.

Meanwhile, Finbarr Fitzpatrick was installing himself in Mount St to co-ordinate the conventions in the forty-one constituencies. He would not get home again until after the election was over. From the outset, the Strategy Committee decided that nothing less than national financial survival would be the central election theme. And the credibility of FitzGerald, as the man who was prepared to put country before party, power or office, would be foremost. These were the themes the advertising creator, Shane Molloy, sought to drive home.

Typical was an ad. with the banner headline 'Ireland in debt is Ireland unfree'. It showed a sombre-faced FitzGerald looking directly out at you, and bore this pointed message:

> Make no mistake, this election is about freedom. The freedom to manage our own affairs. That freedom cannot be ours until we reduce the massive £5,000 million debt incurred by Fianna Fáil between 1977 and 1981.
>
> To pay the interest on this massive debt, hundreds of millions drain away each year — money we should be using to create jobs, reduce taxation, look after the poor and meet the needs of our young population.

This was largely misleading. Fine Gael and the FitzGerald government was *not* cutting exorbitant public spending. It was simply seeking to feed the voracious monster with money raised from domestic taxes rather than money borrowed abroad.

The true situation was graphically spelled out by economist Brendan Walsh in an article in the *Irish Independent* on 28 January. The swingeing budget was only 'a modest first step on the road towards restoring order to the nation's finances.' To put the problem in perspective, he pointed out that the huge increases in VAT, excise duties, capital tax and post office charges in the abortive budget 'would not quite offset the cost of the increase in the public sector wage bill in 1982'. The entire amount of revenue expected from the higher VAT rates would just cover the rise during 1982 in the cost of paying the interest on the government's foreign debts. Bruton had only made minimal attempts actually to curb foreign borrowing. The 25 per cent social welfare rise would put pensioners well ahead of inflation, and the old age pension would have more than doubled in value between 1979 and 1982, a period in which industrial earnings would have only risen by 50 per cent.

But Fine Gael had struck broadly the right note with the electorate. From the outset, Haughey did not. It soon became clear that the public had been shocked by the unparalleled budget collapse. Since the government had introduced such stern fiscal medicine, and was now prepared to stick with it, then things must be really bad. That summed up people's feelings. The nation was finally ready to accept that they really did face a financial crisis.

Haughey misread the mood. At his inaugural press conference the day after the budget failure, he insisted there was an easier way forward. The country's capacity to borrow was still intact. He chided commentators for being 'hypnotised' by the deficit. He was in a buoyant mood, sharing the general expectation of the moment that the government were going to be trounced. And it wasn't just the budget handicap: Labour were also breaking up. How could the coalition offer themselves as a credible government?

On Thursday afternoon, Labour's Administrative Council

met. It was strongly anti-coalition, and had been inherited by O'Leary on his sudden accession to the leadership in June 1981. It was a bitter, faction-ridden meeting which only ended at 3 a.m. the following morning. O'Leary and other senior parliamentary figures battled desperately to keep the party behind the budget and a common government stance with Fine Gael. 'It would be absurd to run an independent election campaign, and at the same time remain in government with Fine Gael until the new Dáil meets on 9 March', he argued.

The outcome was inconclusive. A statement said that Labour would contest the election on the basis of its own social and economic policies, and the party leader undertook, with the support of the majority of his parliamentary colleagues, to negotiate with FitzGerald to have some of the worst features of the budget amended.

A cabinet meeting on Friday sought to tackle this dilemma. Some Fine Gael ministers were opposed to any changes, while others backed Labour's case for modifications. The upshot was a decision to exclude children's footwear and clothing from the proposed 18 per cent tax. A government statement stressed that this was the only alteration. Otherwise, the coalition would 'if re-elected maintain in full the provisions of Wednesday's budget'. The cost of the concession was £17 million. But fiscal rectitude now being the virility test of all true politicians, the statement said this would be made up by a further 2p tax on beer, spirits and cigarettes, and the foreign holiday charter tax was doubled to £20 per seat.

It should have been a bodyblow to government credibility. What Bruton and the Department of Finance found impossible because of 'major difficulties' and 'anomalies' forty-eight hours earlier was suddenly feasible.

On Saturday, FitzGerald and O'Leary held a joint press conference to underline coalition unity and to justify the change. The Fine Gael boss was asked about the broken promises on tax reform. He hid behind the exchequer crisis. 'The situation we found was much worse than we anticipated. It was so far beyond our worst imaginings that we have to put the economic solvency of the state before everything else.' Good patriotic stuff. But the plight of the exchequer was known to FitzGerald before he assumed office, although to be fair to him, even he did not realise the total extent of the difficulty. Alternatively, since the situation was indeed parlous, where were the spending cuts for 1982 to really tackle the problem? The abortive budget showed that public spending was actually set to rise by a further 16 per cent that year. Why was the 18 per cent tax no longer necessary on children's footwear and clothing? The answer was ingenious. 'So that the argument about getting the budget deficit down would not be trivialised by an argument about children's clothes'.

Predictably, Fianna Fáil attacked the VAT amendment as a budget climbdown. But it could not sustain its attack on the government's credibility, because it was behaving even more incredibly. Haughey's blazé approach did not impress the public. Not only were they shaken by the government's collapse, they also realised that the crunch was not how much the country could borrow, but the cost it was exacting in repayments. The penny had already dropped with some Fianna Fáil politicians. Under pressure from Martin O'Donoghue, George Colley and Des O'Malley, Haughey was forced to do a U-turn. By the weekend, he was publicly stating that a Fianna Fáil government would maintain the same budget deficit as the coalition had proposed. Now, even Haughey was on the bandwagon of fiscal rectitude. Soon the campaign was to become an extraordinary spectacle, Fianna Fáil and Fine Gael vieing with one another on how much harsh medicine needed to be administered. The days of manifesto giveaways were buried. But it all left Fianna Fáil at a psychological disadvantage because it was fighting on ground chosen by the coalition, and particularly by Fine Gael.

The immediate organisational need was to run off the selection conventions. Fine Gael's campaign was swiftly set in motion through the simple expedient of reviving the apparatus that had worked so well in the run-up to the June election. In most constituencies, the line-up chosen was similar also. Aside from Jim White and Richie Ryan, who had retired, and Dick Burke, who had announced that he too was opting out, all the outgoing deputies were re-selected.

The Dublin West convention was on Sunday evening. Burke was still insisting that he was retiring. He proposed that Jim Dooge should stand in his place, and he had actually suggested this to the Foreign Minister. After being used, insulted and cast aside in 1981, Burke was going to return to the bar and his three company chairmanships and other directorships. Nevertheless, on the Sunday morning FitzGerald rang and asked Burke if he could call to see him. He was on his way to RTE for a radio interview. But Burke gave him a flat no. FitzGerald asked if he could talk to Mary Burke. She was in the kitchen, but refused to come out. Through her husband she relayed the message that if he called back later, she would have time to talk to him. FitzGerald duly returned on his way back from RTE.

Once more he pleaded with the Burkes that Dick go forward again in Dublin West. He had a proposition to put. The government had nominated Richie Ryan for a vice-presidency of the European Investment Bank, which would require him to resign his seat in the European Parliament. FitzGerald hinted broadly that Dick could fill the vacancy.

But Mary Burke was very bitter over her husband's past treatment. 'And what about the Commissionership?', she asked sarcastically. That Irish post was vacant, because Michael O'Kennedy had returned from Brussels to fight for a Dáil seat. FitzGerald gave a cautious, loaded answer. 'Dublin West is a constituency Fine Gael could win.'

Mary Burke then accused him of trying to bribe them. The exchanges grew more heated, and FitzGerald became visibly distraught. He took his leave, still without a clear impression of what Burke would do. He insisted that Fine Gael had no hope of staying in power without winning their three seats in Dublin West — and without Burke, they would not do that.

But the wooing of Burke continued. Later in the afternoon, he received a call from his Dublin West colleague, Brian Fleming. The June contest had seen much in-fighting between the Fleming and Burke camps: Fleming felt his chance of a seat was being threatened by the arrival of the former EEC

Commissioner. Now Fleming was promising his full co-operation.

Finally, as the evening drew in and convention time approached the Burkes decided that Dick should go forward again. Why they so decided at the eleventh hour is not at all clear. He advanced no convincing, positive reason to balance the succession of plausible arguments he had been making for standing down. But at least he had had the satisfaction of seeing Fine Gael's new establishment almost on their knees before him. At any rate, he travelled to the convention and was duly selected. Fine Gael again had the dream ticket of its three outgoing deputies in this five-seater.

But things did not work out so well in all other constituencies. Louth again posed problems, as it had in June. The national executive ordained that just two candidates be selected. They were the outgoing deputy, Bernard Markey from Ardee and Councillor Brendan McGahon from Dundalk. The intention now was to add Paddy Donegan's son, Tommy, to strengthen the vote in the south of the country, including Drogheda. But Markey threatened to pull out if this was done. That would necessitate a fresh convention. Headquarters was stymied. The Louth line-up remained Markey and McGahon.

This incident later prompted an appropriate amendment to the constitution of the party. 'Where a candidate dies or withdraws, the national executive shall have the power to replace such candidate, irrespective of whether any addition or substitution has already been made.' Mount Street would run the show.

There was also a slight hitch in Sligo-Leitrim. Ted Nealon and Joe McCartin held a seat in each county in June. With Fianna Fáil breathing down their necks — they were only 1 per cent behind Fine Gael — what was needed was a judiciously placed south Sligo candidate to maximise the total Fine Gael vote. Joe Cawley, of Tubbercurry, was chosen by the local convention. However, some of the Mount Street strategists would have preferred a candidate from nearby Ballymote, which traditionally had its own Fine Gael TD, as a more effective form of insurance. It was a small thing, but it irritated the Mount Street boys not to be pulling all the strings.

Dublin South-West also threw up problems. The party harboured real hopes of advancing on its single seat in this four-seater. But outgoing TD Larry McMahon succeeded in blocking the most serious challenger for the task, Dr Con Brennan of Tallaght, who had survived to the final count in June on his first outing. But this time, he failed even to get a nomination. It was a good case of residual quota-squatting.

But it was North Kerry which provided the greatest example of Fine Gael's unpreparedness. This was the only constituency where they returned no TD in June. No real progress had yet been made, a situation epitomised by the selection of just one candidate, Tralee solicitor, Robert Pierse, unknown outside the town.

In Dublin, the Strategy Committee operated much as it had done in June. They convened at about 7.30 a.m. in the Berkeley Court, assessed the previous day's events and the media coverage, and moved on to the day's priorities. They wrapped up at about 9 a.m.

Derry Hussey was again in the chair. Marren, Bill O'Herlihy, Pat Heneghan, Seán Murray, Dan Egan and Shane Molloy were now joined by Frank Flannery. Occasional contributors were FitzGerald, who once more undertook an exhausting nationwide tour, and Jim Dooge. Government press secretary, Liam Hourican, provided direct liaison with government. There was a new factor in this campaign. The party was now in government, and its ministers continued to have a full round of functions. They also had their departmental back-up services. Co-ordination sometimes became a problem. Fitzpatrick provided daily reports from the constituencies, and Seán O'Leary as director of elections also helped sort out problems as they arose.

The other key issue was finance. Again Murray's dozen or so activists on the Capital Branch were the key fund-raisers. At this stage Murray had pared down the list of possible subscribers. He and his colleagues concentrated their attentions on the firms and individuals who had subscribed in June. An initial campaign target of £250,000 was set. But the business community still had confidence that Fine Gael, or more precisely FitzGerald, would deliver them a country fit to do business in. Less than a year after their first investment, they again got out the cheque books. The Strategy Committee was able to spend £400,000, thanks primarily to this private generosity.

The committee was also greatly heartened to soon find that their decision to stand by the budget was proving successful. On the first weekend, Jim Mitchell had a small opinion poll conducted in his constituency. To his great relief, it showed the party's support still solid. He immediately rang FitzGerald, who was elated. The first national opinion polls confirmed these surprise findings. Published by the *Irish Times* on 5 February, the IMS poll showed Fianna Fáil just 2 per cent ahead of the coalition: 44 per cent to Fine Gael's 34 per cent and Labour's 8 per cent. But more significantly, FitzGerald had a massive 20 per cent lead over Haughey as preferred choice for Taoiseach: 51 per cent to 31 per cent.

As in June, FitzGerald was Fine Gael's greatest electoral asset. And the converse of this proposition, so far as Fianna Fáil was concerned, was equally evident. The opposition was shocked. Despite Fine Gael's political incompetence, and FitzGerald's terrible gaffes and broken election promises, very many people accepted their central contention, that the country was in a serious economic crisis, and tough budgetary medicine was needed.

Fine Gael now piled on the fiscal arguments. They challenged Fianna Fáil to prepare its alternative budget. The credibility clincher was an offer to open up the Department of Finance books, and provide the department's expertise to the opposition for the task. Fine Gael's strategists thought they had Fianna Fáil trapped. Once more, Fine Gael was setting the agenda for the election debate and making Fianna Fáil fight on their ground. The central question now became: how did Fianna Fáil propose to raise the £119 million pounds which the coalition had calculated to save by introducing food subsidy cuts and by taxing footwear and clothing.

Fianna Fáil had no alternative but to take up the offer. But Martin O'Donoghue pulled a master-stroke. On Friday, 12 February — six days before polling — Fianna Fáil published their alternative budget. It did not include these unpopular impositions. Yet ended up with the same revenue and budget deficit as the coalition. O'Donoghue's less painful, ingenius alternative was to bring forward the payment date of various existing taxes, like those on banks and insurance companies. But most significantly, VAT on imports would be collected at the point of entry.

FitzGerald was campaigning in Cork. He made no response until the following day, following frantic consultation with Dublin. He then attacked the Fianna Fáil plan as spurious, and accused the opposition of creating funny money. But privately FitzGerald realised he had been trumped. Fianna Fáil had reached the same bottom-line figures by a much less painful route.

Earlier, Fine Gael had leaked a Department of Finance document to *Magill* magazine editor, Vincent Browne. It aimed to discredit Haughey. Published in an election issue of the magazine, it graphically outlined the gross under-estimations by Haughey's government in 1981. This was one of the documents drawn up for the incoming FitzGerald government.

It revealed, for instance, that in that year Fianna Fáil had only provided £80 million for special pay awards and pensions in the estimates, an *underestimate* of £89 million, or a full 53 per cent! Only £93.9 million was allocated for unemployment payments, a reduction of £33 million on 1980: yet unemployment was going up! And in the course of the 1981 election campaign, Haughey had increased food subsidies by £10 million and housing grants by £16.5 million, although no provision had been made for this money.

Fianna Fáil accused the government of leaking the document. Bruton denied this, and promised an inquiry. But the purpose had been served. Gone now was the fatalism and beleaguerment of Fine Gael on budget night. With each succeeding day, confidence grew. The Strategy Committee came to believe that they could hold their own. Flannery believed they would achieve another hung Dáil in their favour. FitzGerald too had been greatly buoyed by his reception around the country. On Sunday, 14 February, on RTE radio, he confidently predicted that the government would achieve a clear majority. He actually refused to rule out Fine Gael emerging as the largest party. Indeed, the biggest handicap Fine Gael had was the Labour Party, which was running a kind of pantomime campaign. The issue was whether or not they were fighting as a partner in government. Oh yes we are, was O'Leary's persistent line. Oh no we're not, was the equally emphatic response from party chairman Michael D. Higgins.

Fianna Fáil were proving less than effective opponents for two reasons: their lack of credibility on the economic issue — O'Donoghue's *coup de théâtre* notwithstanding — and the clear fact that Haughey was an electoral liability. Candidates were being told all around the country that people would vote for them, but not with Haughey in charge. By the middle of the campaign, Fianna Fáil headquarters had got the message loud and clear, and Haughey's picture was used less often in media ads. Fine Gael, meanwhile, were selling FitzGerald as an Irish Moses who would deliver his people from economic bondage. By the final week of campaigning FitzGerald's lead over Haughey in the personality stakes had grown to 23 per cent.

Yet for all his popularity, FitzGerald lacked the true common touch. It wasn't just the small feet blunder, or the 'trivial' matter of VAT on children's clothing and shoes. There were other connections which Garret failed to make.

On Saturday evening, 13 February, the 'Garret Bus' hit Cork North-West, probably the best organised Fine Gael constituency in the country. FitzGerald was welcomed by old-timers to 'Collins Country' like an Irish chief. Bonfires blazed; pipe bands and burning torches led him into Macroom, Millstreet and Charleville. It was an evening of passion and emotion, colour and drama.

FitzGerald stood on the steps of the bus in Millstreet, thanking the people for their great welcome. Urging them to get every last vote out on the day. Somebody in the crowd tossed him a large red-and-white teddy bear. A great cheer went up. He held up the teddy, and thanked the people. But something was puzzling him.

Microphone in the other hand, he asked the crowd: 'But is there any significance in the colours?'

'Dere de Cork colours, boy', someone groaned.

'Ah, yes. Yes, indeed.'

For all his faults, it's not a question Charles J. Haughey would have had to ask.

Early in the campaign, FitzGerald had taken the unusual step, for an outgoing Taoiseach, of challenging Haughey to a television debate. This time, unlike June, it would simply have to be a walkover, the *coup de grâce* to a beaten, discredited opponent. Indeed television had taken on unique importance in this campaign. Given the time of year, outdoor rallies and campaigning was at a minimum. The real battle for the votes of the people was fought out nightly on 'Today, Tonight'. Consistently, government ministers outperformed their Fianna Fáil opponents. Now, thirty-six hours before polling day, FitzGerald, the people's champion, would deliver the knock-out blow. Yet, the impossible again happened. Haughey was the clear winner. As in June, FitzGerald's addiction to statistics got in the way. The Fianna Fáil man was the smoother performer, the better communicator. How the Fine Gael backroom boys cursed, and groaned . . . and blamed themselves: they should have prepared their man better. He had been campaigning too much; he was too tired. If there was a next time, they vowed piously, things would be different.

It was the low point in another excellent campaign. With the government fighting a surprise election on the worst possible platform, the Strategy Committee, the party, and especially the members of the government had refused to be panicked. They stood their ground, and bravely defended their policies. Now, all they could do was wait and see what the electorate's verdict on them would be.

10

A Tail Wagging Two Dogs

It was remarkable, yet tantalising. Fine Gael had pushed up its vote to a new record level, but it also dropped two seats. That was the net outcome of the February 1982 election. In view of the panic that had gripped the party on budget night, the immediate reaction was one of immense relief. They had not been drubbed. And although Fianna Fáil had gained three seats, they were still three short of an overall majority. The second general election inside nine months had again thrown up a hung Dáil. But this time, it was clearly hung in Fianna Fáil's favour.

Eight of Fine Gael's outgoing deputies lost their seats, five to members of other parties, and three to party colleagues. The loss of five seats to non-Fine Gael contenders was partly compensated by three gains. In Dublin North-East, Maurice Manning took Seán Loftus's seat; in Wicklow, Gemma Hussey displaced Fianna Fáil's Paudge Brennan, and – in a remarkable outcome – Richard Bruton, a younger brother of the outgoing Minister for Finance, took the vacancy left by the retirement of Noel Browne, in Dublin North-Central. The net result, therefore, was a drop of two seats by the party, from 65 in the outgoing Dáil, to 63.

Labour had come back unchanged, with 15 seats, and Fianna Fáil now had 81. The WP had a good result, with three deputies being returned – Prionsias de Rossa, Paddy Gallagher and Joe Sherlock. That left four others: the outgoing Ceann Comhairle, John O'Connell, returned automatically; Neal Blaney, Jim Kemmy and Tony Gregory, who had taken Alice Glenn's seat in Dublin Central.

Fine Gael's organisational lapses, exacerbated by the untimely election and the absence of a general secretary, were punished. Again they took just one seat in Louth; they lost their second seat in Sligo-Leitrim; Larry McMahon was again the sole winner in Dublin South-West, and North Kerry remained the one constituency in the country where the party returned no deputy.

But there were also some remarkable performances, in particular from the Bruton brothers. In Meath, the hapless Minister for Finance topped the poll, with a quota and a half. The party organisation showed messianic fervour in defending their man for doing the brave, right thing by the country. Dan Egan, Fine Gael's press officer, was probably right when he said the people of Meath were ready to walk on water for him.

The most outstanding Fine Gael performance of all featured Bruton's younger brother, Richard. He stood in Dublin Central, alongside George Birmingham who had first won a seat eight months previously. On that occasion, Fine Gael had only one and a quarter quotas, whereas Fianna Fáil had two and a half quotas, thanks to the personal popularity of Haughey, whose constituency it was.

Fianna Fáil were better placed to exploit the retirement of Noel Browne in this four-seater. But Birmingham had a daring plan, and convinced headquarters that through judicious management, they might take the vacancy. Bruton (28), an economist, was chosen, although he did not even live in the constituency. His base, like that of his brother, was a farm in Co. Meath. The teeming estates of Coolock and Artane were another world.

An intensive campaign was conducted. But the key to success was a risky gamble by Birmingham, urging people in certain areas to give their first preferences to Bruton. This was done through leaflet instructions issued on election morning. To take a seat automatically in a four-seater requires 20 per cent. In the event, Fianna Fáil ended up with 51 per cent of the vote, just over two and a half quotas. Fine Gael had 32 per cent, just over one and a half. But Haughey's massive two-quota vote distorted his party's chances of taking Browne's seat. On the other hand, Birmingham and Bruton both emerged below the quota on the first count, but in second and third places, ideally placed to pick up transfers from all other candidates. In the end they won comfortably from Fianna Fáil. Birmingham was hailed as a hero in the party, and tactical vote splitting had arrived as a major weapon in the Fine Gael electoral armoury.

Fine Gael's national first preference vote was up just under 1 per cent, at 37.3 per cent. Running on a hairshirt budget manifesto, it had to rank as the party's finest performance to date. They had forced Fianna Fáil to fight on the financial issue, and at last the nation had accepted the reality of the economic crisis gripping the country. Fine Gael could take much credit for educating the electorate to the grim facts before them. But an extraordinary thing was now going to happen. Fine Gael was going to betray its commitment to fiscal rectitude in a pathetic scramble to hold onto power in the new Dáil. Power at any price would briefly intoxicate the party.

The new Dáil was to meet on 9 March. From the moment the full results were clear, the odds were obviously on Fianna Fáil securing the necessary minority support. Whether they or the outgoing coalition formed the government, both wanted John O'Connell to remain Ceann Comhairle. That would actually reduce an overall majority to 83. With Fianna Fáil's 81 votes, and the virtual certain support of Neal Blaney, Haughey needed only one more to become Taoiseach.

On the other hand, assuming Fine Gael could reach agreement with Labour (by no means a racing certainty) they would only have 78 votes. To hold onto power, FitzGerald would also require the support of the three WP deputies, as well as Kemmy and Gregory. Given the harsh economic policies Fine Gael were committed to pursuing, the prospect of winning the backing of all five socialist deputies looked well-nigh impossible.

Given the experience of the previous eight months, FitzGerald surely knew the impossibility of governing with such an arrangement. More than ever, it appeared the advice of people like Derry Hussey was now appropriate: opt out and let Fianna Fáil form a government. Arguably, it would not last that long anyway. But from the outset, the outgoing Taoiseach took up a totally different approach. On the Monday after the election, 22 February, he made clear his determination to remain in office.

'In a situation where there is no clear majority in the Dáil, I am naturally hopeful of being re-elected Taoiseach.' He had not met any of the socialist deputies yet, and he fended off questions about possible amendments to the budget.

Haughey, meanwhile, had internal party problems. Many of his deputies were appalled they had not won a majority. They believed that Fianna Fáil should have annihilated Fine Gael. But Haughey's lack of credibility was their Achilles heel. From the night of the count, veiled attacks on Haughey commenced. But he was quick to read the signs, and decided to bring forward the date of the first parliamentary party meeting. That meeting would consider a motion of his own re-selection as party leader. Immediately, the battle lines were drawn up by his supporters and opponents. Des O'Malley was the agreed choice of his critics to challenge the leader, but on the day his support evaporated and Haughey emerged triumphant.

When the coalition cabinet had their first post-election meeting, they assessed the options. FitzGerald maintained that they had a strong obligation to keep Haughey out if at all possible. He said that many people, including some Fianna Fáil supporters and civil servants, had been in touch with him to warn that a Fianna Fáil government, supported by the Workers Party, could pose a danger to the state. 'The security of the state is involved', he maintained. Other ministers, like John Boland, warned that their courageous attempts to arrest excessive public spending would be set at naught by Haughey's return.

But there were also baser motives in their attitude. Some feared that if Fianna Fáil got in, Haughey would revise the constituencies at the first opportunity to bias them in favour of his party. And for all the nightmares of being in government, some of the ministers were enjoying its trappings, prestige and publicity. They determined to try and hang on.

The next day, the Fine Gael parliamentary party met. Many of the arguments from the cabinet meeting were repeated. Haughey must be kept out. That was the bottom line, inspired by a mixture of principled concern and power-lust. FitzGerald was given approval to have exploratory talks with the five left-wing TDs. It was also accepted that some modifications of the budget would have to be entertained. Fine Gael was starting to lose its footing on the high ground of fiscal rectitude.

FitzGerald told reporters that after meeting the socialist deputies, he would be putting proposals to his party 'for their approval on the basis of which the leader of Fine Gael will be nominated as Taoiseach'. But the budget deficit figure would not be breached. Would there be any other changes though? The outgoing Taoiseach was coy: 'You can make your own inferences about that.'

That same day, Michael O'Leary, under severe pressure from his left wing, took the imminent-looking budget climbdown a step further. He maintained that the budget had been rejected by the electorate, and therefore could be modified. But it took plain-speaking Peter Barry to state bluntly what was afoot. On Sunday, 28 February, interviewed on the RTE radio programme, 'This Week', he said: 'As a pragmatic politician, if I can put a deal together that has something in it for me, and doesn't bend my principles, then of course I want to get into government.'

It was frank. But it also sat very oddly alongside all the talk of a financial crisis, and the government sacrificing itself to do the right thing for the nation. Meanwhile, John Bruton had ordered his officials to examine any revenue-raising measures that might make an alternative budget more palatable to the socialist deputies. It contrasted greatly with the failure to anticipate the problems of Kemmy and Loftus prior to the 27 January budget.

A week before the new Dáil met, on 2 March, the Labour parliamentary party came together. The chairman, Michael D. Higgins, was opposed to any renewal of coalition, but the great majority disagreed with him. They did, however, agree on modifications they wanted in the budget: the food subsidies must be retained in full; the 18 per cent VAT on footwear and clothing would have to be modified or eliminated; a £65 million capital taxation yield must be set for 1983; and a 45 per cent tax on speculative land introduced. Afterwards O'Leary declared: 'There is a link between our vote on Tuesday for Taoiseach, and how we will vote on the following week on the budget.'

That day FitzGerald had a ninety minute meeting with Kemmy, and later had a two and a half hour meeting with Tony Gregory at Gregory's office in Summerhill Parade. He was not the first caller Gregory had had: Charles J. Haughey had been there a week earlier.

On Wednesday, the Administrative Council of the Labour Party met. They endorsed the budgetary concessions demanded by their parliamentary party, but predictably they wanted more: more money for the National Development Corporation; implementation of the Kenny Report on land speculation; and a major urban renewal programme. They took no decision on which government option to back. They would meet again the following Monday, the eve of the new Dáil, to decide. Clearly there was no certainty that they would support Fine Gael. In fact, the AC mandated O'Leary, Barry Desmond and Higgins to have talks with all sides on their demands, and on the possible formation of a government.

Now the discussions were really hotting up. On Friday, FitzGerald met the three WP deputies and members of its árd comhairle in Government Buildings. The Taoiseach disclosed the government's willingness to retain the food subsidies, and to drop the planned 18 per cent tax on footwear and clothing. That would create a gap of £90.5 million in exchequer revenue for the year. Not only was such a move discrediting the entire government strategy, it was destroying Fine Gael's claims about 'putting the country first'. This climbdown was not immediately disclosed, but WP general secretary, Seán Garland, one of those present, said afterwards that the budget would be redrafted. One of their three deputies, Paddy Gallagher, said that if their objections regarding VAT and food subsidies were satisfied, they would have no problem supporting FitzGerald as Taoiseach.

But this was not the first tangible government betrayal of

fiscal rectitude. In a totally political move, the cabinet agreed to a state takeover of the Whitegate oil refinery in Cork, at a cost likely to be £20 million a year. Spurious strategic oil supply reasons were put forward. This move was now all the more incredible because FitzGerald had flatly refused to give such a commitment during the election campaign. But they were anxious to secure the backing of the WP trio, one of whom – Joe Sherlock – represented the Whitegate constituency of Cork East. There were 150 jobs at stake; the government takeover amounted to a subsidy per job of £133,000 annually. The public could have been forgiven for thinking that the grave national financial crisis of the general election campaign had suddenly vanished.

On the same day, the Fine Gael parliamentary party met again and FitzGerald gave an account of his talks with Gregory and WP. He told them that Gregory's demands were mainly constituency related. Kieran Crotty suggested that they offer the WP a place in the government to secure their support.

On Saturday, three days before the new Dáil met, FitzGerald was back at Summerhill Parade, accompanied by Jim Mitchell, seeking to do business with Gregory. On the Sunday, Haughey followed him. On Monday, the *Irish Times* carried two pictures beside each other of the two would-be Taoisigh suing for the lone deputy's vote. John Kelly summed the whole thing up by referring to it as a unique Irish phenomenon: a tail wagging two dogs.

Alone of the party leaders, Michael O'Leary refused to meet Gregory in the latter's office, and he had also advised FitzGerald not to go there: it was demeaning to have the Taoiseach going cap-in-hand to win the approval of a single deputy. For his meeting with Gregory, O'Leary chose Wynn's Hotel in Abbey Street. Subsequently he was criticised for choosing the hotel venue: it was supposed to reflect his feckless, bohemian tastes! O'Leary rightly scoffed at the notion. If he wanted a jazzy rendezvous, he would not have chosen solid, bourgeois Wynn's, with its complement of clergy and country folk. Anything less bohemian would be hard to find in Dublin.

On the morning of Monday, 8 March, the cabinet met

again. They knew from O'Leary the potential difficulties with Labour. Nor had Gregory been very forthcoming about possible support, although there was a newspaper report that he had made up his mind, but was not saying publicly. Nevertheless the upshot was a devastating budget revision that made nonsense of Fine Gael's entire general election campaign. The food subsidies were to be retained in full, and the 18 per cent VAT on footwear and clothing tax was scrapped. The revision of the school entry age to four years and two months was reiterated. The proposed taxing of short-term social welfare benefits would be reviewed. And the elements of a package to entice Gregory was also agreed: there would be an inner city programme, costing £500,000, and £350,000 of that would go to a Dublin inner city task force. A Dublin Corporation works scheme, due to finish in April with a loss of 150 jobs, would be continued. It would get £2 million and the workforce would double to 300. An additional £15 million would be provided for local authority housing in the capital. These changes would cause a gap of £93 million in the current budget for the year, and £15 million on the capital side.

One of the subsequent justifications put forward by FitzGerald for this stupendous *volte face* on Fine Gael policy was that exchequer revenue from Bord Gáis had been underestimated by £28 million. But that was still a long way from £93 million. The cabinet decided that the gap would be made up by further indirect taxation. Even higher taxes would go on drink and tobacco than already planned in the abortive budget. The standard VAT rate, already set to go to 30 per cent, would go even higher. It was economic lunacy and a total betrayal of party policy. Yet only two cabinet members voted against it, after a meeting which lasted two hours.

In the afternoon, FitzGerald met again with Gregory to convey his concessions. The WP árd comhairle met that evening and came down on the side of Fianna Fáil as offering the most stable option, but they did not make their intentions public.

The really crucial meeting was that of the Labour AC. Despite the massive concessions on the budget, the anti-coalitionists were *still* not satisfied. Finally, after six hours of bitter debate, they decided to pull out of coalition government with Fine Gael. The shock decision was taken at 2 a.m., thirteen hours before the Dáil met. It was decided on the casting vote of party chairman, Michael D. Higgins. O'Leary, despite the support of the overwhelming majority of his parliamentary party, had lost the battle to stay in coalition.

The AC decided to back FitzGerald on the vote for Taoiseach. But should he be successful, they would not join a government with Fine Gael. The notion of principled support from the opposition benches for a minority Fine Gael government was a farce. O'Leary and his parliamentary party colleagues who fought valiantly against the decision had been humiliated.

O'Leary now sought to contain the damage caused by the AC. He wanted them to keep their position secret until after the Dáil vote on the nominations for Taoiseach. If it was known that Labour was pulling out of government, there would be no chance whatsoever that the five socialist deputies would back FitzGerald. But the AC again snubbed him and so, on the morning of 9 March the papers carried the shock news that Labour were pulling out of coalition.

The die was cast. Fine Gael were on their way out of government after just over eight months. They had performed unparalleled organisational feats to get there. They had provided brave and committed government with their budgets of July 1981 and January 1982 especially. True, they had reneged on their election promises and taken the softer option on tackling the public finances. But at least they were confronting the crisis. Moreover, they had bravely defended a hairshirt budget in the February election. They converted the nation, including the Fianna Fáil opposition, to the reality of the national economic crisis. And they had actually pushed up their popular vote to a new record level.

But the last fortnight had witnessed a squalid flight from principle and policy. Nor had it any real chance of political success, as was now being painfully demonstrated. The parliamentary party met on Tuesday morning. Everyone knew the game was up. George Birmingham, interviewed by John Bowman on RTE radio, likened their plight to being 'three-nil behind with five minutes to go'. But realising the soccer metaphor held out no hope, he changed games in mid-sentence, and said two penalties, rugby-style, could still save them.

Strictly speaking, the issue did remain in doubt until after the Dáil convened at 3 p.m. As on 30 June, 1981, there was a tremendous air of drama and excitement. Fianna Fáil were odds-on to be the next government. But could one ever be sure in politics? All sides were happy to have O'Connell resume the chair. He was proposed by Neal Blaney, and FitzGerald seconded him. Then, the House swiftly moved on to nominations for Taoiseach. Brian Lenihan and Ray MacSharry proposed Haughey. Michael O'Leary and Peter Barry proposed FitzGerald, who had not yet publicly conceded defeat.

Now, as in June, it was the turn of the Independents and small party deputies to declare their intentions. The fortnight's grubbing would be out in the open. Joe Sherlock was the first on his feet to announce that the WP were backing Haughey. However, the afternoon's events really had as their primary focus a remarkable maiden speech by Tony Gregory. In explaining his voting intentions, he disclosed a £100 million plus development programme for Dublin, which he had agreed with Haughey.

An astonished House listened as the new deputy read into the record the terms of the 'Gregory Deal'. A twenty-seven acre Port and Docks Board site near the city centre was to be nationalised. Motorway plans for Dublin would be scrapped. Clondalkin Paper Mills would also be nationalised, saving 500 jobs. An Inner City Authority for Dublin would be set up. The deal was greeted with incredulity on all sides, not least on the Fianna Fáil backbenches. There were heckles and interruptions from Fine Gael deputies. Gregory said FitzGerald's promises 'did not approximate remotely' with the Fianna Fáil offer. While this was true, when their own mini-package for Gregory was added to the other changes in the budget, Fine Gael TDs had little moral right to their shock/horror response or to their ridiculing of Haughey.

So Gregory and the three WP deputies supported Haughey in the vote, and the Fianna Fáil leader cantered home by a margin of 86 votes to 79. Kemmy joined Fine Gael and Labour in voting against.

Fine Gael were back in opposition but things could have

been much worse for them. Although the media had duly reported their U-turn on the budget and on their economic policy that morning, the dramatic Gregory deal and Haughey's controversial cabinet line-up stole the subsequent headlines. The omission of George Colley from the new government was the big headline grabber, along with the Gregory Deal. Fine Gael was able to slink away from its abortive indulgence in auction politics, grateful that the spotlight was focused elsewhere.

Later FitzGerald would maintain it had been a case of 'state before party at the expense of our credibility'. But clearly the motivation of wanting power was just as great, if not greater, as any altruistic motive to keep Haughey out in the national interest. He accepted that the party should not have attempted to retain power, given all the adverse voting factors. 'It was a mistake and one of the things I regret in politics.'

———————

After the change of government on 9 March, FitzGerald spoke with political correspondents. He said he expected the Haughey government to last only about a year. The ex-Taoiseach said he had no fears for his continued leadership of Fine Gael. Besides, he would now be automatically going before the party for endorsement or rejection under their constitution.

That evening there were enormous recriminations in the Parliamentary Labour Party. Many deputies, including O'Leary, were enraged at their enforced subservience to the Administrative Council, some of whose members would scarcely get a hundred votes in a general election. Yet, under the party's crazy constitution, they were able to call the shots for the elected representatives. Liam Kavanagh, for instance, who had been a minister, was not on the AC. Yet that body could take decisions on fundamental party policy which were binding on him, but which he had no say in formulating. Such was the criticism of Michael D. Higgins that he left the meeting. Some Labour deputies even began to consider some form of more permanent coalition with

Fine Gael, and to hell with the Labour Party. This eventually led to a number of exploratory discussions later in the summer: O'Leary met FitzGerald to discuss the possibility of forming a new social democratic party, embracing Fine Gael and up to nine Labour TDs. However, the talks never advanced beyond the exploratory stage and FitzGerald did not take them too seriously, although he was well aware of the disenchantment of many Labour deputies with their party constitutional plight.

Meanwhile, Fianna Fáil's government got down to business. The new Minister for Finance was Ray MacSharry. He derided the 'doom and gloom' of his predecessors, and promised 'boom and bloom' in its stead. On 12 March, the new government introduced the higher excise duties in advance of their budget. The Dáil then adjourned while they prepared their alternative budget, which was unveiled on 25 March. It formally interred the controversial features of the Bruton budget, already ditched by the coalition. Food subsidies were retained. The 18 per cent VAT on footwear and clothing was dropped, as was the proposed taxing of short-term social welfare benefits. The application of VAT at point-of-entry for imports was introduced, and Corporations Profits Tax payments were brought forward.

However, the Haughey government did not proceed with tax credits in place of tax allowances. Nor did they see any merit in the famous £9.60 for wives in the home. MacSharry said that 'the response to this scheme had illustrated clearly that the general public saw no merit in a cumbersome and complex scheme, which merely transferred money from one spouse, via the Revenue Commissioners, to the other'. The response by applicants had been disappointing. But given the impact the measure made in the June '81 election campaign, it gave Fianna Fáil particular pleasure to dump it. The massive increases in PRSI and the raising of the payment ceilings did go ahead, however. They would soon cause immense difficulties and foment a taxpayers' revolt.

This budget seemed to signal Fianna Fáil's new-found commitment to sorting out the country's finances, a policy they had been forced to adopt in the election campaign. In fact, MacSharry proposed to outdo Fine Gael in fiscal rectitude. Whereas Bruton's budget had set a current budget deficit target of £714 million for the year. MacSharry lowered this to £679 million. That would be 5.6 per cent of projected GNP, whereas the 1981 deficit outturn had been 8.1 per cent. Time would tell, though, whether McSharry's figure was either realistic or attainable.

With the budget out of the way, Haughey set his sights on eliminating his dependence on Gregory's vote which, however costly, was not guaranteed for any specific period. As soon as the election results had emerged, he toyed with a daring scheme. The Irish EEC Commissionership was vacant since Michael O'Kennedy had come home and won a Dáil seat. If a Fine Gael deputy could be persuaded to take this lucrative £60,000 a year post in a constituency where Fianna Fáil stood a real chance of a by-election victory, Haughey's problems could be solved at a stroke, in every sense of the word.

No time was lost. On Tuesday, 23 February, MacSharry approached his fellow-Sligoman, the outgoing Junior Agriculture Minister, Ted Nealon, and offered him the Commissionership. But Nealon dismissed the overture. The same day in Dublin, Fianna Fáil was pursuing a more likely feeler. Albert Reynolds sounded out Dick Burke. He had been Commissioner from 1977 to 1981, and it was public knowledge he was greatly disappointed at being omitted from the first FitzGerald government. Burke gave no indication of his reaction. But he did not say 'no'.

The first the public were to know of this extraordinary possibility was a story in the *Evening Herald*. The paper was tipped off about the overture to Burke, and on Wednesday, 24 February, its main front page story declared: 'FF offer top Euro job to Burke'. But this was followed by a categoric denial from Fianna Fáil later that evening. 'No representations of any kind have been made to Mr Burke on behalf of Fianna Fáil'. Burke himself was quoted as saying that he would be voting for FitzGerald on 9 March. But he did not deny the overture. However, the whole story seemed so far-fetched, so outrageous, that the Fianna Fáil denial was readily accepted. Most people assumed the newspaper had got it wrong.

But once Haughey became Taoiseach on 9 March he renewed his efforts to win a by-election seat. Ted Nealon was again approached by one of his Junior Ministers, but again turned down the job. Fresh feelers were put out to Burke, and informal negotiations were conducted through Pádraig Ó hAnracháin, one of Haughey's closest confidants, who had been in the Department of Education when Burke was Minister there from 1973 to 1976.

Burke was keenly interested. He had enjoyed his first stint as Commissioner. His abiding interest had been European affairs. As far back as 1969, when he first entered the Dáil, he filled out a biographical questionnaire for RTE. Asked his ambitions, he stated: 'to further the ideal of European union'. On 21 March, Burke met the new Taoiseach. Haughey formally offered him the EEC job, and Burke agreed to consider it.

Burke had already approached possible staff members. They included Michael Lillis, a career civil servant, who was FitzGerald's diplomatic adviser in the office of the Taoiseach. Another was Liam Hourican who, with the departure of the coalition government, lost his job as head of the GIS. Both had worked in Burke's cabinet during his first stint in Brussels. Within twenty-four hours, the Dublin West deputy was prepared to accept the offer, and so informed Haughey. He saw no reason to consult FitzGerald or his parliamentary party. But he would not resign from the Dáil until after the budget vote on the following Wednesday.

On Monday Burke offered cabinet posts to Hourican and Lillis. The trio met again on Tuesday, and one outcome was that Lillis went and told FitzGerald what was afoot. FitzGerald was shocked by the news, but decided to be as helpful as possible to his estranged colleague. He was not hostile towards Burke; in fact, FitzGerald accepted that he had been hard done by. Lillis told him that the plans were that Haughey would formally nominate Burke to fill the EEC Commissioner's post in the Dáil on the following afternoon at 3.30 p.m.

FitzGerald said he would endorse the decision. But he made it plain to Lillis that he did not want it known that he had foreknowledge of the event. He wanted it to seem that he was being taken wholly by surprise.

But the next morning, Wednesday 24 March, things began to go badly wrong. Haughey had already informed the

President of the EEC Commission, Gaston Thorn, of Burke's forthcoming appointment. On that morning, Thorn informed the other members of the Commission. The story quickly leaked, and reached RTE's man in Brussels, Eamonn Lawlor. He rang Dublin. In the RTE newsroom, the Head of News, Mike Burns, immediately decided to ring his friend, Maurice Manning, in the Dáil. It was close to 10.30 a.m., time for the Order of Business in the House. Manning was amazed, and on his way to the chamber, met Jim Mitchell and told him what he had heard. Mitchell went to FitzGerald, and the party leader duly reacted to the news as if hearing it for the first time.

A meeting of the Fine Gael parliamentary party was due to start at 11 a.m. in the College of Art annexe. It was the meeting at which the secret ballot on FitzGerald's leadership was to be held in accordance with the party's constitution. This was the first business, and a ballot box and papers had been duly prepared.

In all, 86 people were entitled to give their verdict on FitzGerald's leadership. The 63 TDs, 20 outgoing senators, and the three MEPs. This trio, Clinton, Ryan and Joe McCartin, were not there. All were on European Parliament business.

The ballot was quickly completed, without any speeches on the subject. The outcome was sixty-two votes to five in favour of FitzGerald. Later there would be much speculation on who the five were. But many of the probable no-confidence voters were either not there or were to deny that they had voted against FitzGerald. Oliver J. Flanagan, a frequent critic of FitzGerald, actually showed his vote to Enda Kenny, the secretary of the parliamentary party. It was for the leader. Neither John Donnellan nor Tom O'Donnell, two of the men let down in June, were at the meeting. Michael Joe Cosgrave, another who was critical of FitzGerald, subsequently denied that he was one of the five. Only one was definitely revealed. That was Austin Deasy, who would soon show his hand in dramatic terms.

When the ballot was over, someone stated there had been a report on the RTE news at 11 o'clock that Burke was taking the EEC post. Burke was sitting at the back of the room. It was the first time the bulk of the attendance had heard of it.

FitzGerald was asked if he knew anything. He said that he had just heard it. This was untrue; he knew from the previous day. There was consternation in the room. After the budget debacle, the tough election campaign, and their eventual dismissal from government, most deputies were in no mood to countenance one of their colleagues improving Haughey's tenuous hold on power.

It could copperfasten him in office for a full term. If Burke had done this, it would be betrayal and treachery; betrayal of Fine Gael and treachery to his colleagues. The moment FitzGerald confirmed the rumour, the meeting rounded on Burke. Many TDs attacked him openly, none more vehemently than Jim Mitchell, the man who had invited him into Dublin West. Mitchell assumed that Haughey would win the by-election, given that he had a ready-made candidate in former deputy Eileen Lemass. 'She would get my vote', he said. 'What do you mean?', someone asked angrily, assuming that Mitchell meant that *he* would vote for Lemass. He explained that he meant that his working-class Ballyfermot support would go to her.

Eddie Collins and others also attacked Burke. There were calls on him to withdraw. Peter Barry was unhappy with the bitterness and division. He suggested that they discuss the matter with him. Barry and FitzGerald left the meeting with Burke and went into an adjoining room.

Burke was shattered by the venom of his colleagues. He did not know what to do. Just then Mary Burke arrived. She too had heard the story had broken on RTE, and she was anxious to support her husband. She found FitzGerald, Barry and Liam Hourican, who had also joined them, all urging him to change his mind. She told him of messages of support arriving at their home, and urged him to take the job. Burke did not know what to do. He agreed to go for a walk with FitzGerald around the car-park on the Kildare Street side of Leinster House. FitzGerald sought to mend fences, telling Burke he must now come on the front bench. Yet again, Burke was being invited back.

When they returned to the party room, Burke announced that he had re-considered. He would not take the Commissionership. They gave him a standing ovation. But he was now in a woeful dilemma, because he had broken his word to the Taoiseach. Confused and shattered by the venomous onslaught of his colleagues, he agreed to issue a statement saying that he had turned down Haughey's offer. At 2 o'clock, Haughey received a message stating that 'while grateful for the honour conferred on him, he was declining the offer'. Ninety minutes later Haughey had been due to announce his coup to the Dáil.

FitzGerald too had been taken aback by the viciousness of the party's reaction. He regarded the information from Lillis the day before as confidential. Unwittingly, this led to Burke being portrayed in an even worse light for allegedly not telling his leader. The following days' newspapers referred to FitzGerald being 'kept in the dark until the final moment', and of him being 'amazed' when Jim Mitchell broke the news to him on the Order of Business. Now it was Haughey's turn to take the flak. He denied that there was any political advantage in offering the EEC job to Burke, and pointed out that Fianna Fáil had only 42 per cent of the vote in Dublin West. He had chosen Burke for his experience. But why had he not re-appointed Michael O'Kennedy? That would have presented political difficulties, he said.

Burke was in a daze. Maurice Manning met him and urged him to come for a drink in the Members' Bar. 'That is the first kind thing anyone has said to me all day', he said. Afterwards, Burke went home, utterly shattered by his topsy-turvy day. But Fine Gael were jubilant. Haughey would not get his overall majority. They had nobbled his stroke.

But that was not the end of the affair. Burke had had his heart set on that return to Brussels. He was racked by third and fourth thoughts, and by the following day the temptation was too great: he started to renew his interest through some Fianna Fáil acquaintances.

That weekend, Brussels celebrated the silver jubilee of the Treaty of Rome. As a former Commissioner, Burke was invited, and he flew out on the Friday and booked into the Hyatt Regency Hotel. On the Sunday, Haughey and Pádraig Ó hAnracháin arrived and also booked in to the Hyatt Regency. Burke later denied that he had any discussions with Haughey beyond an exchange of salutations, but he had detailed conversations with Ó hAnracháin who naturally urged him to take the Commissionership. In a sense, he was pushing an open door. Burke was revelling in the atmosphere of Brussels, meeting other Commissioners, past and present, and renewing old acquaintances. On the previous day, he had met Gaston Thorn and had taken the precaution of sounding out the President of the Commission about his possible return. No problem: Thorn made clear his willingness to have him back.

On Monday, 29 March, Burke flew to Dublin. It was his fiftieth birthday. He picked up a copy of the *Irish Times* on the plane. Inevitably, the story had persisted and all weekend the speculation had been growing. There it was on the front page: maybe Burke will change his mind again. The paper also reported on the previous day's radio interviews with Jim Mitchell and the party chairman, Kieran Crotty. If Burke accepted the post, Mitchell said, 'it would not be in the national or party interest, or in the best interests of Mr Burke himself.' To do so would 'cement Mr Haughey in power, and would be remembered by his colleagues.' Mitchell had no doubt what the priority of any true Fine Gael TD was. 'Our duty to the country is to ensure that the Haughey government lasts the shortest possible time. If Dick Burke accepted, and Haughey won the by-election — which is the only reason for the offer — he would have an overall majority, including Neil Blaney, which would cement him in power for the next four and a half years.'

Crotty was asked would Burke be expelled from Fine Gael if he accepted, and have the whip withdrawn. 'Yes, all these things are on. Somebody did raise the possibility of the whip being withdrawn from him at the last meeting of the parliamentary party should he accept the position. But I didn't get a proposal to that effect.'

Burke was outraged by these threats. His mind was made up to take the Commissionership. The following morning, he wrote a brief letter to FitzGerald. He declared it his 'duty' to accept the job, and then went on to beat the parliamentary party to the draw. 'It is clear that opinion in the party is divided on the question of my nomination. I believe that in the interests of party unity, and with a view to limiting the

165

further public expression of this division, it is right for me to tender my resignation [from Fine Gael]'.

In a longer public statement, he said he had been mistaken in changing his mind the previous week. Nor did he feel that the views of the parliamentary party represented the consensus in Fine Gael. It was his 'urgent duty to ensure that there is an experienced Irish voice at the Commission table in these difficult times for our country and the Community'. There were some who regarded this declaration as an example of that pomposity and arrogance with which Burke was charged from time to time.

He did not think his resignation 'will confer any decisive advantage on the government. Had it done so, I would not have felt free to consider the government's offer.'

Burke did not hang around this time to be dissuaded by his colleagues, or to face another 'fascist onslaught', as he termed his treatment by the party the week before. He and his wife packed their bags, and headed for Dublin Airport and a flight to London. FitzGerald did move to head him off again. He called to his Ailesbury Road home, but the Burkes were already on their way to the airport. There they received a message to ring FitzGerald. This Burke did. But there was very little to say. 'Well Garret, it isn't today or yesterday that differences grew up between us.'

That evening, the Fine Gael leader issued a brief statement accepting the *fait accompli*. He had drawn up an earlier, hard-hitting one, but decided to consign it to the dustbin. Haughey also issued a statement confirming Burke's acceptance. He had achieved his masterstroke.

Haughey's primary motivation in the whole business was to win a by-election through dispensing the Commissionership. On the previous Tuesday morning, when Burke finally announced his acceptance, he first rang Ó hAnracháin, who was still at the Hyatt Regency Hotel in Brussels. He told him that he would be taking the job.

Ó hAnracháin was ecstatic. He asked Burke to hang on a moment, and dashed down the corridor to Haughey's room with the good news. Haughey came up to hear for himself. He spoke to Burke and heard the confirmation again. 'Let me be the first to congratulate you, Commissioner', the Taoiseach said in grave tones.

When he put down the phone, he was beaming. 'We've got it', he told Ó hAnracháin. And with that Haughey danced a little jig on the floor.

11

The Famous Twenty-Mile Pain Barrier

'You're a lousy politician', Austin Deasy declared. He was looking directly at FitzGerald. 'We blew the election and threw away power, and the reason was political ineptitude.' The inquest on the February election was now in full spate, raw and bitter. It was Wednesday, 31 March, just twenty-four hours after Dick Burke had finally decamped for Brussels. With Haughey now odds-on favourite to win the by-election, four and a half years in opposition again loomed.

Deasy had just declared that he was one of the five who had voted against the leader the previous week. He said he did not want a different leader; that he was a member of no caucus. 'But I had to register my displeasure at how the party was run since last June.' Deasy spoke with passion and conviction. Some of his colleagues thought he was close to tears. His pent-up anger and humiliation at being overlooked in the June government burst out. It had been top-heavy with academics and Dubliners. There was a lack of communication through the party, a lack of contact with the grassroots members of Fine Gael.

Deasy (45) knew all about the grassroots. He had carved out a second seat in the Waterford constituency as an outsider since 1977 by dint of hard slogging. A hungry, professional politician, this ex-teacher had been on the front bench from 1977 until June 1981. Then when the allocation of ministries came, he got nothing. He said nothing to FitzGerald at the time. Bottling up his anger, he redoubled his work rate. He put down an extraordinary number of Dáil questions. More like an opposition than government backbencher.

Now he was letting fly. He told the meeting, and FitzGerald in particular, that he trained a football team at home in

Stradbally. If he was going to drop a player, he would go to him and explain the reasons. He would not leave him to find out from others. 'I was on your first team, and you dropped me. And you didn't have the guts to tell me, or explain why you dropped me.' FitzGerald listened without interruption to this frank, passionate outpouring.

It was not the only onslaught on the leader and his former cabinet colleagues. But it was the most telling. The youngest member of the party, Wexford's Ivan Yates (22) had some stinging comments also. He attacked the lack of political nous in the budget, revealed by the government's capacity to drop the children's footwear and clothing tax *after* they fell. 'You would have been better advised by Chrissie in the restaurant'. Chrissie was one of the waitresses in the Dáil restaurant.

Maurice Manning, just elected in February for Dublin North-East, had been appalled by the budgetary climbdown in the bid to hold onto power after the election. 'It undermined our credibility, and we were doing what we accused and attacked Fianna Fáil for doing.' His theme was re-echoed by David Molony and by former Minister, John Kelly. Mary Flaherty attacked the 'selfish' constituencies like Louth and Sligo-Leitrim, where they had thrown away seats. The inquest was so intense that it had to be prolonged for a second day, into Thursday.

John Boland, who had been Minister for Education hit back for the ex-government. They never really had a chance, facing crisis after crisis; the backbenchers did not understand how parlous the financial situation was; moreover, they had rebelled on various issues, like the school entry age and the proposed abolition of the death penalty. 'What are ye made of, are ye mice or men?'

FitzGerald, too, responded. He was shaken by the onslaught, but did not seek to counter-attack. His was a conciliatory tone. He conceded that the children's footwear and clothing tax had been a mistake. He told them he would be reshuffling his team after Easter. He pledged his willingness to repeat the 1977-81 reorganisational work so that the next time Fine Gael could govern on their own.

After the meeting a press statement referred only to Burke's desertion, and regretted that he had 'repudiated his assurance' to the party of the previous week. Of course, the two day inquest heard further criticism of the new Commissioner. Nor was it confined to him. The former government Press Secretary, Hourican, and another FitzGerald civil service aide, Lillis, who had joined Burke, were dismissed as 'gallóglaigh' (mercenaries).

All this internal Fine Gael unhappiness was further exacerbated when the *Sunday Tribune* political correspondent, Geraldine Kennedy, carried a detailed account of their verbal blood-letting the following Sunday. Upheavals were no longer an exclusive Fianna Fáil preserve.

In fact, in a radio interview, Deasy went on to repeat openly much of his criticism of FitzGerald. He said that 'like practically everyone else in the country', he admired FitzGerald as an economist and statesman, but added that 'there is a question mark about his judgment in tight political situations'. In his view, the government had not had the proper blend; it was 'overloaded with academics and intellectuals. None the less, he was both generous and frankly realistic in his overall assessment of FitzGerald: 'he is the best thing we have going for us.'

When the promised re-shuffle came a few weeks later, perhaps the most surprising feature of it was that, despite all that he had said, Deasy was back on the front bench, as spokesman for Foreign Affairs. It was a testimony to the generous, open side of FitzGerald; he was no bearer of grudges. The front bench now comprised a staggering twenty-four people, and among the new faces were Gemma Hussey, Paul Connaughton, George Birmingham, Michael Noonan and Nuala Fennell. Moreover, there were a further eighteen 'spokespersons' on various matters, so that no fewer than forty-two out of the sixty-three Fine Gael TDs had got some kind of job or other. FitzGerald was all for getting his troops involved. As Maurice Manning observed: 'for every three called, two were chosen!'

The early spring of 1982 was a miserable time for FitzGerald. Having attained the glittering prize of government, he had let it slip away again through political ineptitude. He then rallied his troops in a brilliant campaign, but afterwards led a discreditable scramble to hold onto power. If the attempt had even succeeded, it might have justified the effort but in fact it failed. Now Haughey was back and was set fair to consolidate his position by taking a further seat from Fine Gael. The party was disgruntled and morale was at a very low ebb.

The tide was turned by two of the more able young deputies, Gemma Hussey and George Birmingham. In a couple of important speeches, they struck the right note – a positive, but critical, assessment of Fine Gael's progress over the past five years. These speeches helped to dispel the glum introspection of the party and refocused its mind on the task ahead.

Gemma Hussey drew an analogy with marathon running. 'Fine Gael began a political marathon in 1977 . . . the 1982 general election represents the famous twenty-mile pain barrier before we finish hard by becoming the biggest party in the country.'

George Birmingham advised against merely 'studying our political navel'. The champion of the Dublin North-Central two seats coup was well placed to criticise organisational weaknesses elsewhere. They would assert that 'never again will our prospects of office be allowed to be jeopardised by selfishness which allows seats to drift to Fianna Fáil by default.' Birmingham pointed out they now had two Fine Gael seats in Dublin North Central, whereas there was not even a coalition seat there in 1977. 'As a constituency I think we are entitled to feel outraged that seats which on paper were far more winnable were easily thrown away.'

He was not the only one concerned about this lapse. The new general secretary, Finbarr Fitzpatrick, had seen the problems closely during the recent election. One of the driving forces behind a splendid reorganisation of his own Cork North-West constituency, he now had remedial plans for the others. On his initiative, FitzGerald and the national executive set up a special Constituency Review Committee to examine all problem and marginal constituencies. It was a small, compact group. The chairman was Seán O'Leary. Enda Marren was also on board, as was Peter Kelleher from Fitzpatrick's own constituency: he had been the Munster regional director of the Strategy Committee in the June and February elections. The fourth member was Frank Flannery. The thirty-eight-year old chief executive of the Rehabilitation Institute had demonstrated uncanny electoral knowledge on the night of the February count on an RTE radio programme. With the other pundits and the resident computer all predicting that Fianna Fáil would get up to 86 seats, only Flannery struck a discordant note. Long before many counts were complete, he said that Fianna Fáil would not get more than 81. He was spot on.

These four backroom boys were complemented by four TDs: George Birmingham, Michael Noonan, Paul Connaughton and Jim Mitchell. Their brief was to visit twenty constituencies, to meet local and national public representatives and local officers; assess the party's problems in each, and make proposals on the best location and spread of candidates for the next election.

The target constituencies were Louth, Kildare, Sligo-Leitrim, Clare, Dun Laoghaire, Laois-Offaly, Wexford, Cavan-Monaghan, Kerry North, Meath, Roscommon, Mayo East and West, Galway East and West, South Tipperary and, in Dublin, South-Central, South-West, North-West and Central. The exhaustive, time-consuming task would proceed for the next five months.

After Easter, however, the more immediate electoral consideration was the unwanted Dublin West by-election. From the time of Burke's final departure on 30 March, Fine Gael had been looking desperately for a winning candidate. Speculation focused on Jim Dooge and Fergus O'Brien, one of the shock losers in February. Both came under severe pressure to stand. By mid-April, party branches in Ballyfermot, Lucan and Inchicore had nominated Dooge. But on advice from his doctor, he decided not to run. Moreover, he wanted to devote more time to his academic career. His refusal to stand in both the February election and now in this crucial by-election angered many TDs, who had seen him accept a ministry but now saw that he was unwilling to put in the hard slog on the ground. Fergus O'Brien toyed with running, but in the end decided that his best chance lay in building up his support in Dublin South-Central.

Jim Mitchell was the powerbroker in Dublin West, and he had a poll carried out to ascertain what the people wanted.

It suggested that Fine Gael should opt for a local candidate. All the better if he could appeal to both the working-class (Ballyfermot and Inchicore) and middle-class (Castleknock, Lucan and Blanchardstown) ends of the vast constituency. Naturally, there were a number of local aspirants. Deputy Brian Fleming was championing Seán Lyons from Clonsilla. Dr Tony Collis, from Castleknock, with a large Ballyfermot practice, was a strong contender. And there were others. But Jim Mitchell was not satisfied. His choice was a kind of identikit of himself, another working-class Inchicore boy made good.

Liam Skelly (40) was five years older than Mitchell. But they knew each other since their primary school days in St Michael's NS in Inchicore. Furthermore, Skelly had gone to secondary school in Ballyfermot; he lived in Chapelizod, and was a minister of the eucharist in a church in Castleknock.

A qualified barrister and a successful businessman running his own company, he personified the dual appeal candidate Dublin West needed. However, there was a little snag. Skelly was not a member of Fine Gael. True, he had worked with Mitchell in the last two election campaigns. In February he was actually Dick Burke's campaign manager. But he had not yet formally joined the party.

By now it was the week of the selection convention. Skelly became a member of the Blanchardstown branch, but under the constitution this was irregular: he had to be in his local branch. This necessitated an emergency meeting of the Castleknock branch, which promptly made him a member. Mitchell, in the meantime, arranged for the Navan Road branch — which had a meeting scheduled for early that week — to nominate Skelly as the by-election candidate. The convention eventually had to be put back by two days in order to accommodate these last-minute hitches.

Not surprisingly, the other candidates did not take kindly to Mitchell's steamrolling of the election process. The complaints flowed into Mount Street. Obviously, the convention would require delicate handling: Fitzpatrick called on Peter Barry to preside, and it was decided that FitzGerald would also go along. The atmosphere at Sarsfield House in Inchicore, where the convention was held, was electric. There was a lot

173

of anger, and complaints about a candidate being parachuted into the constituency. But Mitchell and headquarters had their way. Skelly came through.

Of course, the public response was 'Liam Who?' Compared to the Fianna Fáil candidate, Skelly looked a no-hoper. Eileen Lemass had a famous name; she was the widow of Séan Lemass's son, Noel. She had failed to win the seat in the by-election after he died in June 1976, but she was a member for Dublin Ballyfermot from 1977. In June 1981, she was elected for the current Dublin West constituency, but had lost her seat in February. She was a member of Dublin City Council since 1974. Altogether she was a very experienced, well-known politician. She also relied on her Dáil salary for an income, and this could be an emotive, vote-winning plea. And against her Fine Gael were pitting a total novice. Who is this 'S. Kelly'?, many people asked. After blowing their hold on government, it looked as if Fine Gael were going to throw away the by-election.

FitzGerald asked John Boland to be director of elections. He resolutely refused. He had never run an election campaign outside his own constituency before. Besides, he had arranged a two-week Easter holiday in Portugal with his family. But Mitchell, who had suggested him, did not give up easily. Peter Barry was produced to apply the persuasive touch. Finally Boland relented. But he was going to take his holiday first. Sitting by a pool in the Algarve that Easter, he pored over feet of telexed data from Dublin providing every possible detail on the constituency and the candidates.

Over the fortnight his attitude began to change. What started out as a damage control exercise began to take on a more optimistic appearance. Slowly, Boland came to the conclusion from all the data that Lemass could be beaten. She had been beaten in the by-election on the death of her husband in 1976 and she had lost again in February. He returned home in the last week of April in a very positive mood.

The by-election writ was moved, and voting day was fixed for 25 May. It was impossible to exaggerate its importance. It was almost a general election in miniature. Victory for Haughey would mean an end to dependence on unreliable left-wing deputies and the prospect of a full term with an effective majority.

The new tax year in April had seen the introduction of the swingeing increase in payroll taxes (notably PRSI) from 4.75 per cent to 7.5 per cent of gross income every week. After the first wage packets were opened, there was an immediate outcry by workers: it sparked off a fresh campaign for tax reform by the trade unions. At first, Haughey and MacSharry stood firm. But with Dublin West looming, they decided to soft pedal. On 22 April, the Minister for Finance announced a £45 million PRSI tax concession.

But this failed to assuage workers' anger. Major PRSI protests were threatened for May day. The three Workers Party deputies had put down a motion opposing the tax rises, and Gregory and Kemmy had indicated support. The government announced that the children's allowance increases planned for July would now be brought forward and paid from May.

Although Fianna Fáil had belatedly accepted the Exchequer's fiscal constraints in the February election and had introduced a responsible budget on 25 March, the obsession with winning the by-election dictated that the purse-strings be loosened afresh. The electors of Dublin West were in for some very special treatment, on top of the tax and children's allowance concessions to the whole country. Schools and sports centres were promised; so were extra gardaí, and a major US forklift plant for Blanchardstown.

Meanwhile a tanned and reinvigorated John Boland was finding it difficult to motivate many of his colleagues. They had enough elections in the last year. But some of the older deputies were the key. Many of them had come into the Dáil in 1969 with Dick Burke, and now felt strongly that he had let the party down. It was a strong Cosgraveite trait. Men like Pat Cooney and Peter Barry took the lead from the start of May. They worked morning, noon and night in Dublin West. From 7 a.m., Cooney was out on the platforms of the newly-opened Maynooth commuter line. Soon the newer crop of deputies were also responding to the challenge.

But the party faced a daunting task. Skelly would need an incredible marketing campaign. Boland prepared various budgets, and went to Mount Street to get the money. He wanted a staggering £60,000. Yet after the party trustees had him explain his plans, they approved them. Having run an early newspaper ad., the campaign team decided to drop this approach. It was too costly; besides, this was not a national contest. The money would be used in an intensive constituency canvass to get Skelly's name across. Saturation opinion polling and qualitative research was also done.

Everyone worked hard, but no-one worked harder than Mitchell. He had felt particularly betrayed by Burke. He had stuck his neck out for him, inviting him into Dublin West in 1981. He got him elected then, and again in February. There was a lot at stake for this hard-working professional politician. The constituency was saturated with leaflets. The tactic was to get Skelly identified with Mitchell, and get the latter's vote to transfer. Slogans like 'Jim's man', 'Mitchell's man' and 'Jim says' predominated.

Besides the PRSI revolt, the other major issues impinging on the campaign were the government's attitude to the escalating Falklands war, and to new devolution proposals in Northern Ireland. Increasingly Haughey's stance on the Falklands was seen as crudely anti-British, with consequent risks to Irish exports and jobs. He also flatly rejected Northern Secretary, Jim Prior's plans for a new, elected Assembly. Fine Gael played up the Taoiseach's extreme stance on both issues and elevated the suitability of Haughey as leader of the country to a major campaign issue. The message was clear: it would be dangerous to give him a clear mandate.

The uphill task, however, faced by Fine Gael was dramatically disclosed when, on 14 May, the *Evening Herald* published a constituency opinion poll. It gave Lemass 45 per cent; Skelly just 21 per cent, and Workers' Party leader, Tomas MacGiolla, 15 per cent. Although the poll had been taken a week earlier, it still made grim reading.

The PRSI revolt remained a major irritant for Haughey. To maximise their protest, the trade unions had planned a major demonstration for Dublin on Monday, 24 May – the day before polling.

The government piled more goodies on Dublin West. A convenient national anti-crime campaign was launched. One of Fianna Fáil's campaign ads reflected the emphasis. It showed Lemass with the Minister for Justice, Seán Doherty, and the banner 'Crackdown on Crime'. Beneath were the many promises: '2,000 new gardaí. New garda stations and extra gardaí for Dublin West. Action programme in crime prevention. New legal aid clinic for Ballyfermot. Drug squads to stamp out drug abuse.'

Another advertising theme was the need to 'strengthen the government's hand'. Haughey pressed the need for stable government after two 'hung' Dáils. It was a powerful, logical appeal, but only if the people were willing to repose that degree of trust in him and Fianna Fáil. Already, however, Fine Gael knew this tactic was backfiring. Qualitative research told Shane Molloy that the people did not want to give Haughey a clear mandate.

So, going into the last week of the campaign, Fine Gael felt that they were still in with a chance. Naturally, there were problems, but the party was thinking positively. One problem was rather unusual. Skelly was not a compliant Mitchell alter ego. He had very strong views of his own, and he was fiery and outspoken. A true idealist, he was also a strong social reformer. However, the Fine Gael strategy team wanted him simply to stick with the script and get the contest over. There was no time for a candidate with strong preferences of his own. The campaign actually had to detail two deputies, George Birmingham and Richard Bruton, to chaperone Skelly around the constituency, to keep him out of controversy and keep him moving: these were the priorities.

The frenetic commitment of both main parties to winning was underlined on the final Sunday before polling. Outside Ballyfermot Church, no fewer than twenty-four members of the Oireachtas were lined up to sweet-talk the voters. On Monday, the big PRSI protest went ahead, and about 20,000 people marched through the centre of Dublin.

The lengths to which Fianna Fáil were prepared to go to win were grotesque and unbelievable. That night, the eve of polling, the Minister for the Environment, Ray Burke, arranged to have a crop of trees planted in a new housing estate in Clonsilla. There had been many complaints on the canvass about the uncompleted estate. Two days later the trees were removed.

In a final statement on the issues of the campaign,

177

FitzGerald warned that Haughey should not be given a free hand. 'There is a deep suspicion of this government.' And a fine piece of political audacity saw him proclaim that there was 'intense dissatisfaction with the PRSI and tax system which has emerged from the Fianna Fáil government.' The payroll tax increases, which were causing all the trouble, had also been proposed in the abortive Fine Gael January budget.

Polling day arrived with grave concern for the turnout, despite the saturation campaign. This was the constituency's third election in eleven months. Poll fatigue and boredom were inevitable. The general expectation was that Lemass would win. Admittedly, the Fianna Fáil vote in February was only 41.7 per cent to Fine Gael's 42.5 per cent. But the Labour vote had already collapsed, and Labour's candidate was a political nonentity and a strong anti-coalitionist. The Workers' Party President, Tomás MacGiolla, was the other big vote-getter and was likely to pick up most of the old Labour vote. In February he had got 7.3 per cent. Now his party was supporting Fianna Fáil. Did that mean his vote would eventually transfer to the government?

As the great day approached, Haughey maintained that Lemass would win 'easily'. Peter Barry, however, was claiming that a party opinion poll showed Lemass and Skelly both with 33 per cent; MacGiolla, at 8 per cent, and 18 per cent undecided. After an intensive drive on 25 May to get the vote out, both camps anxiously waited for the following day's count. Early indications from Palmerstown national school, the count centre, showed the two main candidates running very closely. 'Liam Who?' and 'S. Kelly' was not going to be wiped out: that much was certain.

The counting went on amidst great tension and excitement. The first count result was terribly close. Lemass led, but only barely: 17,095 (39.7 per cent) to 16,777 (39 per cent), a difference of only 318 votes. MacGiolla had 6,357 (14.8 per cent), and the Labour candidate, Brendan O'Sullivan, just 703 votes. The quota was 21,531. It would all depend on transfers.

Next, the elimination of seven minor candidates together saw Skelly jump into a slight lead: 17,736 to 17,571. Now

MacGiolla was eliminated. To Fianna Fáil's consternation, his vote went more than two to one in favour of Skelly. The former Fine Gael unknown emerged the incredible winner, just short of the quota of 21,388, to 19,206 for Lemass.

It was a remarkable outcome. Fine Gael's finest hour, then or later. They had stopped Haughey's masterstroke at the final fence. Party mentors had long envied Fianna Fáil's election machine, in particular the skill of men like Neil Blaney and Kevin Boland in winning by-elections in the sixties. But now the Fine Gael machine had actually outperformed their legendary opponents.

It was the beginning of the end of the second Haughey government. He was still reliant on fickle left-wingers, and his failure to win Dublin West further damaged his electoral reputation. Worse still, he had gambled heavily with the sorely over-stretched Exchequer.

For Fine Gael, the Burke humiliation was buried. They had had the last laugh. Their campaign for the next general election started in Palmerstown national school on 26 May 1982.

It was obvious that the PRSI revolt had damaged the government. On this Fine Gael had been totally opportunistic in their criticism. The entire blueprint for the increases was mapped out in their abortive budget. But this policy inconsistency was brazenly pursued from the day the new Dáil met on 9 March. U-turns were enthusiastically embraced by FitzGerald and most of his colleagues in a persistent bid to topple Fianna Fáil. They justified this later by pleading necessity: that it was absolutely imperative because Haughey was endangering the security of the state. Within weeks of the change of power, Fine Gael were aware that allegations of serious political interference with the gardaí were being made against the new Minister for Justice, Seán Doherty.

But one man was not happy with this summary abandonment of Fine Gael policy. John Kelly had never been partial to the idea that the two major parties were natural opponents when they really had so much in common. Moreover he was no longer enamoured of coalition with Labour. Labour in government after June 1981 was a vastly different Labour Party to that in the Cosgrave government in 1973-77. They were looking over their shoulders at the Workers' Party and had pursued a much more independent, left-wing stance in government.

Kelly had been Minister for Trade, Commerce and Tourism in FitzGerald's government. He found Labour a terrible handicap. There were grindingly long meetings which yielded only miniscule cuts in public expenditure. Kelly also favoured a much sterner line on public sector pay. He favoured going down with all flags flying on the issue if necessary. He had also been appalled by his government's decision to provide further cash to build Knock Airport, against all relevant departmental advice. He felt that they should have stood by their commitment to cut the budget deficit and not reneged on their election programme.

After the February election, he watched his former cabinet colleagues throw many fundamental aspects of the coalition budget overboard in a bid to cling onto power. Now, when the new Dáil met, they were continuing to sacrifice their political principles. The final straw was a Private Member's motion put down by the party supporting the National Development Corporation. This was a Labour project which had been foisted on Fine Gael as part of the coalition deal. But now the party — which had never concealed its contempt for the NDC and had regarded it as a piece of daft socialist dogma — was embracing it solely to embarrass the Workers Party, and to try and detach them from Haughey. Kelly's name was on the motion, but he had never been consulted about it. He was sickened by the pure opportunism of it all.

Kelly decided he could no longer serve on the Fine Gael front bench. He could not endorse this shoddy compromising on party principles. After Easter, he wrote a letter to FitzGerald explaining his position. On 28 April he issued a statement confirming his unavailability. He said he told his leader that there were 'certain matters on which I wish to be free to speak with greater independence than I think is compatible with membership of the front bench.'

He did not elaborate further, but he made it clear that he

was not challenging FitzGerald. His confidence in the leader 'remains undiminished'. Did he not, however, have the same difficulties being in the parliamentary party that excluded him from the front bench? 'There are difficulties, but I want to remain a member of the Fine Gael party. Where else would I go?' On the backbenches, Kelly went on to argue repeatedly for a political reconciliation between Fianna Fáil and Fine Gael, Siamese twins as he called them.

Kelly's criticism went to the heart of a dilemma that stayed with Fine Gael for the nine months that Haughey was in power. Should they stick to their policies and principles, even if this meant supporting — or at least not attacking — the government on some issues and thus probably extending its life? Or should they simply use any weapon that came to hand in order to try to defeat a government they believed to be uniquely damaging to the national interest and apparently indifferent to the conventional usages of democratic government? Kelly wanted the party to keep its hand clean. The leadership took the more pragmatic line: Charlie out at all costs. Naturally, this line entailed the party standing on its head a fair bit.

Haughey's GUBU government is now part of the folklore of Irish life. Everything it touched seemed to turn to ashes. But Haughey — for all his undoubted faults — was also extraordinarily unlucky. His first piece of bad luck came, ironically enough, with the fall of the coalition on the budget issue. Had the coalition survived that, they would almost certainly have fallen in April or May as a result of the PRSI revolt. They would then have had to fight an election on the tax issue — something that no group of handlers could have won for them. Indeed, senior party figures reckoned later that Fine Gael could have lost as many as twenty seats in such a contest. One way or another, Haughey would have had a handsome majority. Maybe the coalition had reason to thank Jim Kemmy after all.

The Fianna Fáil defeat in Dublin West meant that the politics of promise had failed them once again. Moreover, they had flung money at the electorate at a time when the cash was running out at an alarming rate. The entire deficit for 1982, which MacSharry had set at £679 million in the

March budget, was going to be used up by the end of June.

The cabinet now had no choice. They simply had to adopt a tough budget strategy and announce that there would be no more concessions. In effect, Haughey's government had at last come round to Fine Gael's economic policy. Fine Gael's response to this was cynically to oppose the government's new measures, once again for reasons of expediency: what mattered was to defeat the government.

The pattern was repeated at the end of June, when Fine Gael supported a series of Workers' Party amendments to the Finance Bill. The government only survived on the casting vote of the Ceann Comhairle. In the course of the debate FitzGerald actually tried to make a virtue of the coalition's January budget débâcle.

> Politics, we were told, was the art of survival. Never mind the public interest and the public good. Never mind towards what national disaster your action may lead. Politics is about staying in power for its own sake, we were told. Those who sought in vain to persuade us of this debilitating doctrine had an apt pupil waiting in the wings . . . we need a government that will govern us as we governed for seven months, without flinching from the task, without trimming, without stroking.

This little oration was made in support of amendments with which FitzGerald disagreed, with which his party disagreed — which, indeed, could hardly have been farther removed in spirit from everything that Fine Gael stood for. If that was not trimming or stroking, what was? It was all of a piece with Fine Gael's undignified attempt to cling on to power after the February election. As the context for a sermon on the moral superiority of Fine Gael, it was less than appropriate!

This kind of *realpolitik* can, moreover, acquire a momentum of its own which quickly carries a political party beyond mere cynical calculation. And so it proved with Fine Gael. In March 1982, the Fieldcrest towel manufacturing plant in Kilkenny went into receivership with the loss of 600 jobs. It was a major crisis for the region and by the end of June no rescue plan had emerged. The Labour Party put down a Dáil motion calling for its re-opening, with the IDA involved as a majority partner if necessary.

Liam Cosgrave (*above*) and Garret FitzGerald did not always see eye to eye. Cosgrave, a keen horseman, had once referred to his rivals in the party as 'mongrel foxes'. Was Garret a mongrel fox?

Garret on the stump. He is not the most natural shaker of hands or kisser of babies. Still, he works hard at it. These photographs show him in Mayo East looking at a picture of someone familiar (*above*); across the road from a certain pub in Ballyporeen (*above, right*); and arriving at night in Kanturk, Co. Cork (*opposite*).

General secretaries past and present. Peter Prendergast (*above, left*), seen here with Michael Noonan, was the driving force behind the organisational reforms that revived the party in the late 1970s. His successor, Finbarr Fitzpatrick (*below, left*), seen talking to Jim Dooge, established his reputation as a formidable constituency organiser in Cork North West before taking over in head office.

John Bruton, his wife Finola, and their three children. Bruton has been less conscious of his public image and more conscious of the need for coherent and consistent policies than most of his contemporaries in Fine Gael.

Garret and friends. Charlie Haughey seems to be putting the evil eye on him (*above*). Are the smiles really as wooden as they seem (*above, right*) when Garret and Margaret Thatcher watch the birdie? At least the laughter seems genuine (*opposite*) as the Taoiseach shares a joke with the Archbishop of Dublin, Dr McNamara. But what can they possibly have to joke about? The photograph was taken only a few days before the coalition government introduced their amended family planning bill in February 1985.

Peter Barry, Minister for Foreign Affairs, taking the weight off his feet after a hard day's diplomacy.

Fine Gael, however, wished to go further. It would have been one thing to support the Labour motion, even though it would have meant endorsing a policy of throwing good public money after bad: the state had already invested millions in the venture. Not very logical for the party of fiscal rectitude and reduced public expenditure, but at least consistent with the strategy of attacking the government at every opportunity. It was quite another thing to do what they did: table an amendment to the Labour motion, in the names of their two Carlow-Kilkenny deputies, Kieran Crotty and Des Governey, calling on the government to re-open the plant, 'to provide the necessary finance, and to take whatever steps are necessary to effect this in 1982'. This was absolutely irresponsible and outrageous: it was the negation of everything Fine Gael said it stood for.

In fact, Fianna Fáil lost the vote — the first time since the sixties that a Fianna Fáil government had been defeated in Dáil Éireann — but it was hardly a resigning matter. The Dáil went into recess until October shortly afterwards, but the government's financial crisis was mounting daily. It resulted in what was effectively a mini-budget at the end of July. Every government department had its budget cut; a public sector pay round was deferred; food subsidies were reduced. The aim was to cut public spending by £120 million in 1982, and to try and curb the massive overrun on the current budget deficit. That was now heading for over £900 million, compared to MacSharry's original target of £679 million. After just a few months back in office, Fianna Fáil had again allowed public spending to get out of control.

The cuts were announced on the Friday of the August bank holiday weekend not by government ministers — most of whom had already cleared off for their weekend break — but by civil servants. Fine Gael's response was interesting. John Bruton endorsed the cuts initially and repeated this line in a radio interview on the Sunday. He said that there was a limit to what the state could afford to pay its employees. Bruton knew the score.

But Labour and the trade unions were up in arms and the rest of Fine Gael now jumped aside and let the revolt grow. By mid-August, the party's front bench had met and jumped on the opportunistic bandwagon as before. They decided to oppose the cuts in the Dáil when the House resumed in October. It was the same old story: anything to damage Haughey. Bruton had implied at the outset that Fine Gael might abstain: that was quickly forgotten. John Kelly had urged the party to back the cuts: that was ignored.

Kelly actually called for a parliamentary party meeting over this latest piece of opportunism, and he got it. But there was only minimal support for his stand. Moreover, the party's front bench renewed its offensive against the government in September, giving particular emphasis to its condemnation of Fianna Fáil's curb on public service pay. Yet here was the biggest single item of public expenditure, and the cutting of public expenditure was supposed to be the central pillar of Fine Gael economic policy.

It all boiled down to a clear case of party before country. Or did it? There is no question that Fine Gael behaved unscrupulously in opposition to Haughey's government in 1982. But it was also a time of rising hysteria in Irish public life, as one scandal after another enveloped the government. Moreover, FitzGerald claimed later that from the end of the summer he and some of his colleagues had information that the government was 'behaving improperly, and was a danger to security and democracy. There was a sense of urgency about the serious damage being done to the state. The first opportunity to get rid of them had to be taken.' It emerged later that Haughey's government had been interfering with the routine operations of the gardaí and had been tapping journalists' telephones. Telephone tapping was a particular Fine Gael neurosis ever since Peter Prendergast's suspicions of 1980. Senior party figures, particularly the former Minister for Justice, Jim Mitchell, were being tipped off and they passed their information on to FitzGerald. Derry Hussey was warned during the summer that his telephone was being tapped. Senior party members believed that Haughey was going to attempt a constituency gerrymander.

At a time when the political temperature was uniquely high, this kind of information was bound to influence Fine Gael's actions. It would, however, be naive simply to take them at their word: to believe that they did what they did simply because of the overriding necessity to unseat Haughey. The national interest was mixed with some very traditional party political calculation. They knew that Haughey was an electoral liability to Fianna Fáil: it only made sense to keep the heat on him, and if that meant compromising their principles — well, that's politics.

———————

Since Dublin West the party had sensibly begun to gear up for another general election. The Strategy Committee was again meeting regularly. Hussey was in the chair once more, and O'Leary, Flannery, Marren, Heneghan, O'Herlihy, Murray, and Shane Molloy were all there as well. So too were general secretary, Fitzpatrick, press officer, Dan Egan, and Michael Conry, who worked with the Agricultural Institute and had been adviser to Alan Dukes as Minister for Agriculture. In addition, the Constituency Review Committee — Mitchell, Connaughton, Noonan and Birmingham — was also continuing its special work, with delegations making sorties into the twenty target constituencies. Fitzpatrick was in regular touch with key constituency officers: he was especially concerned with maximising their potential seats under the PR system. He kept pointing out that they got sufficient votes to have gained more seats in four or five constituencies in both June and February, but the failure had been one of vote spread. The lessons of Dublin North-Central were being learned.

Fitzpatrick also paid special attention to the Western seaboard constituencies. In every one of those they had the minimum representation of one TD with the exception of Kerry North where they had none at all!

Shane Molloy set up two sub-committees dealing with advertising and PR. The party also turned once more to a tried and trusted technique from previous elections: qualitative research. Groups of people around the country were again assembled to establish what were their priorities. As ever, the results were fascinating. People felt that the country was in a deep financial crisis, exacerbated by the obvious political instability. There was also a strong perception that FitzGerald was the man best equipped to clean up the mess.

Here then was the key theme for any early election. People wanted certainty and stability and they wanted the government in good hands. They wanted somebody who would solve the persistent and worsening financial crisis. FitzGerald was the man: FG might not bring salvation, but there was a high expectation that GFG might do it. The party leader was set to play a more dominant role than ever in Fine Gael's electoral strategy.

No election preparation, of course, could overlook the need to fund the campaign adequately. Seán Murray and his Capital Branch colleagues were also back in business. Another round of meetings, addressed by FitzGerald and some former ministers, were arranged on professional and sectoral bases. The secret list of subscribers, running to about 400 was updated and fresh appeals were made. Only Murray and a secretary who did his typing, were familiar with the full contents: the names of all the subscribers, and how much they had donated in June and February. Confidentiality was everything. Murray was so secretive about the list that he gave an assurance that if anyone else pressed to see it, he would first destroy it. As usual, this rugged, hard-working accountant was thinking big. He began to map out a campaign that would cost half a million pounds.

By the end of the summer of 1982, Fine Gael were virtually ready for another election. For all the key personnel, this was their third time over the course. They had learned much, and at this stage were an extremely professional tough-minded outfit.

At the end of September, the Constituency Review Committee presented a comprehensive report to the national executive. Its recommendations were specific to the constituencies under review, but there were also some general points. The conduct of selection conventions, for example was seen as crucial: the committee suggested that well-briefed senior party members should always preside at such conventions. The most alarming revelation was 'a serious lack of potential candidates and efficient branches in almost all of the large towns of rural constituencies'. In many areas, party branches and district executives were not meeting regularly. In other words the fundamental problem in the weak constituencies was that the FitzGerald reforms of 1977-78 had not yet penetrated to them, especially in the case of the Western seaboard constituencies.

Turning to the specific problems of the constituencies under the microscope, the committee threw up invaluable conclusions on what needed to be done. In Louth, they found that the performance had been 'little short of disastrous', and the sitting deputy, Bernard Markey, to be 'unhelpful'. They now proposed that three candidates should be selected: one each in Dundalk, Drogheda and mid-Louth. The committee also noted that in February, only 40 per cent of the Labour vote transferred to Fine Gael; nearly 2,000 votes did not. They urged a specific canvass to seek No. 2s from Labour voters.

In Kildare, the party had pushed up their vote by 0.6 per cent to 32.1 per cent in the February election. Nevertheless, they lost one of their two seats in this five-seater. The problem was to split the vote better. The solution: run only two candidates. In June and February, there had been three: Alan Dukes, Bernard Durkan (who lost out in February) and Patsy Lawlor. The latter said she would not object to a two-candidate strategy and the committee commended her 'extremely helpful attitude'.

In neighbouring Laois-Offaly, Fine Gael had not won a third seat since 1973. In February, they were 5 per cent short of three quotas, whereas Fianna Fáil were just over the three quotas and duly took as many seats. There was long-standing factionalism between the three main candidates, Oliver Flanagan, Tom Enright and Charlie McDonald. 'Canvassing in general was done on a highly personalised basis for individual candidates, rather than for the party ticket, and the party organisation on polling day was very deficient.' But the committee had no obvious solution to offer in the case of this intractable constituency.

Another five-seater, Wexford, had returned two TDs in June and Febuary, Michael D'Arcy, from Gorey, in the north and Ivan Yates, from Enniscorthy, in mid-county. But they had no strong candidate for the key town of Wexford in the south, the base of the now retired Labour leader, Brendan Corish. That area had 18,000 voters. In February, Fine Gael only got 30 per cent of the town vote, and only one of its eighteen branches in the Wexford electoral area was actually in the town. The committee saw Wexford town as the key to a possible third seat. They wanted more town branches set up, and the next selection convention to choose one of three candidates from there.

Moving to the electorally weak Western constituencies, the primary conclusion was a pattern of declining Fine Gael support since 1977. In 1973, they had taken two of the three seats in Mayo West, Sligo-Leitrim and Roscommon-Leitrim. In 1977, they took only one seat in each, and the pattern was repeated in June 1981 and in February 1982.

One of the reasons for this was the slow evolution of Fine Gael into a more liberal party under FitzGerald. The committee neatly summed it up: 'Aspects of Fine Gael policy and image which have enabled us to make such great progress in other areas of the country are not working to our advantage . . . a result of the different social and cultural attitudes held by the electorate in the Western part of the country.' Two of the committee members were uniquely placed to measure this factor. Marren and Flannery, now living in Dublin for many years, were from Mayo and Galway respectively.

Their primary recommendation was that a separate Western policy should be developed by Fine Gael. The party's image there also needed to be improved. But they concluded that there was a large disaffected Fianna Fáil vote along the Western seaboard which could be tapped.

Turning to individual Western constituencies, they identified badly organised conventions in February as the root of the loss of two seats. In Sligo-Leitrim, the south Sligo candidate had been from the wrong electoral area. It should have been Ballymote, not Tubbercurry. The proposal was three candidates for next time: from north Sligo, Leitrim, and Ballymote.

East Mayo had twin problems. Fianna Fáil were resurgent on the strength of the Knock Airport project, and Fine Gael had internal divisions. The former deputy, Martin Finn, who won a seat in 1973 and was an unsuccessful candidate in 1977 and 1981, had fallen out with Mount Street. The proposal was that three candidates — in Ballina, Claremorris and Swinford — be selected.

In the Galway West five-seater, the party had only won a single seat in June and February. Fianna Fáil took three, and Labour's Michael D. Higgins the remaining one. But Fine Gael were as close to two quotas as Higgins was to one: in February, they had 28.4 per cent to Higgins' 11.8 per cent.

The problem was that there was too much leakage in Fine Gael transfers: up to 20 per cent to other parties. They promised more research, but concluded generally that Higgins's seat was winable. The fact that Higgins had been crucial to Labour's withdrawal from coalition in March made this prospect particularly attractive to Mount Street.

Clare, the heartland of Fianna Fáil, had never returned a second Fine Gael deputy, not even when it was a five-seater in the forties. But in the two recent elections they were close to this historic breakthrough. The committee found that they were weak in west Clare, and much of the county area had been badly canvassed in February. There should be three candidates next time: sitting deputy, Donal Carey from Clarecastle, near Ennis; former deputy, Madeline Taylor from Kilrush, in the west; and someone from the north-east of the county.

Kerry North was Fine Gael's ultimate black spot: the only constituency with no sitting Fine Gael deputy. In the February election, the vote had dropped to its lowest level since 1965. There were still lots of problems to be overcome, not least being the lack of a strong candidate in the key town of Tralee.

The review of some Dublin constituencies was also vital. The capital's forty-eight seats were becoming more and more crucial to the destiny of the government. It was also potentially the area of greatest appeal to FitzGerald's more liberal Fine Gael. But the committee identified some alarming problems.

With the exception of Dun Laoghaire, all other Dublin marginals had a serious manpower and good candidate shortage. It was recommended that potential candidates should be offered some secretarial assistance to help compete with the highly organised Workers' Party.

Dublin South-Central saw Fergus O'Brien lose in February. Fine Gael had enough votes to take two seats in February, as they had done in 1981. But there was intense rivalry and division between the O'Brien and Gay Mitchell camps. The committee's role here was to impress on the local organisation that a proper vote split would give them back their second seat.

Dublin South-West had major organisational problems. The sitting deputy, Larry McMahon, was clearly opposed to younger, able running mates. In February the 1981 vote was down 5 per cent and the second seat, which had been so close then, now looked quite elusive. The committee also reported that there was a serious lack of working-class support for the party there, with its burgeoning Tallaght suburbs. They proposed the convention select two candidates only, with headquarters to hold the discretion to add a third.

Dublin North-West had two Fine Gael deputies in 1981 — Hugh Byrne and the newcomer, Mary Flaherty. But the camp followers of the traditionalist and the Young Fine Gaeler had never got on together. In February Prionsias de Rossa of the Workers' Party took Byrne's seat. Fine Gael's problems were compounded by having run four candidates. The proposal now was that just two be selected at convention, with Mount Street reserving the right to add a third.

In Dublin Central, Tony Gregory had ousted Alice Glenn in February. After all the publicity attending the Gregory Deal, he was reckoned to be safe. The committee targeted Michael O'Leary who had only taken the fifth and final seat without reaching the quota, as the most likely victim if Fine Gael were to regain their second seat.

In Dun Laoghaire Fine Gael had enough votes, 48.2 per cent, to have taken three seats in February, but they had been badly managed. The opportunity here lay with Monica Barnes, who had been pipped for the final slot by Martin O'Donoghue. But she was greatly feared by the two sitting Fine Gael deputies, Liam T. Cosgrave and Seán Barrett. In June and February, they blocked her from getting a nomination, but each time headquarters added her.

In those two campaigns she had some party people actually canvassing against her. They told the voters she was too radical, that she was not really Fine Gael. But February had finally shown the local organisation that all three could take

190

seats. The electoral committee also drove this point home with the local party officers.

By September then, Fine Gael was well prepared for another election, better even than in the run-up to June 1981. But there was one very noticeable parallel with that election. There was very little policy development. One man, John Bruton, was single-handedly tackling this. All summer he worked on a comprehensive economic policy. But otherwise headquarters was not concerned with this key issue.

In fact, their previous coyness in dealing with controversial issues while in opposition had re-emerged since March. In May, the Labour Party had brought forward a bill to curb profiteering in building land. It proposed that local authorities acquire such land at existing use value. However, Fine Gael decided not to back it. Instead they settled for the painless and non-controversial device of suggesting an all-party committee to examine the issue.

Their remarkable attention to electoral detail was further borne out in mid-September. Fitzpatrick, who had not yet had a break since he was hurtled into the general secretaryship on budget night in January, got all his forty-one constituency organisers together. He gave them a briefing document outlining the procedure to be followed once an election was called. The national executive would meet and issue its convention directives to all constituencies. The conventions would then be held, and finally the panel of candidates would be ratified by the executive, with any additions it might make.

The document also emphasised the need to identify which Fianna Fáil candidates were pro- and anti-Haughey. By September, his government was succumbing to one crisis and scandal after another and Fianna Fáil was increasingly divided on the issue of Haughey's leadership. It would be an issue that Fine Gael would exploit on the ground for all it was worth.

12

The Ship Comes In

It was an historic day for Fine Gael. For the first time ever, they were level with Fianna Fáil in popular electoral support. Admittedly it was only an opinion poll sampling, but the *Irish Times*-MRBI survey of 27 October did mark a major breakthrough. The polls had been seen as remarkably accurate since 1977, especially by the party's hierarchy. Furthermore, the placing of the two major parties at 36 per cent confirmed the trend of another sample the previous week. On 22 October, an *Irish Independent*-IMS survey had Fianna Fáil at 38 per cent to Fine Gael's 36 per cent. FitzGerald and his colleagues were euphoric. The Dáil also resumed on 27 October. The consensus in the country was that yet another general election was probably only weeks away. What better tonic could they hope for?

The month had already seen some remarkable political developments. On 1 October, Fianna Fáil backbencher, Charlie McCreevy put down a motion of no confidence in Haughey for debate by the parliamentary party. The internal Fianna Fáil divisions culminated in a bitter and raw show-down on 6 October. Preceding it, Des O'Malley and Martin O'Donoghue resigned from the cabinet rather than pledge personal loyalty to Haughey. For twelve hours the party tore itself apart. It ended with Haughey's survival, but with the depth of divisions symbolised by the 58-22 vote on his leader-ship. The great Fianna Fáil national movement was riven from grassroots to national executive and parliamentary party.

Three weeks away from a crucial Dáil term, the government was in a sorry state. Their July mini-budget meant that Gregory and the Workers' Party were threatening to withdraw their support. The financial crisis was simply getting worse. The three-quarters exchequer returns at the start of October showed the deficit at £960 million, and Haughey admitted it would end up 'in excess of £900 million' for the year. His March budget had set a target of £697 million.

All this Fianna Fáil discomfiture was a tremendous boost to Fine Gael. The party's árd fheis on 16-17 October saw the leadership consciously project the image of Fine Gael as a credible alternative government. FitzGerald's presidential address was all about offering honesty and open government: courageous and fair policies for the country's ills. He made a virtue of having no immediate solution: 'No political party can solve the problem entirely. To promise that, as was done in 1977, we would have to be knaves or fools — and you would be fools to believe us.' Obviously there would be no repeat of the June 1981 manifesto.

It was a relatively low-key conference, with few references to the recent convulsions in Fianna Fáil. FitzGerald did not refer to them at all. A deliberate decision had been taken by Fine Gael's strategists, who believed that many anti-Haughey Fianna Fáil voters were ready to cross over and vote for them. Knocking Fianna Fáil might dissuade them.

Only one small thundercloud loomed on Fine Gael's horizon that weekend: the proposed constitutional amendment to outlaw abortion. In the run-up to the June and February elections, FitzGerald had given commitments to the promoters of the referendum. But as a deeply divisive national debate raged on the subject, amidst charges of sectarianism and moral blackmail, FitzGerald sought to U-turn on his commitment. His Justice spokesman, Jim Mitchell, spelled out at the Sunday session of the árd fheis their preference for a multi-amendment review of the constitution. FitzGerald was also very conscious that the proposed referendum sat very oddly with his much-vaunted 'constitutional crusade' of September 1981. In his presidential address he said that, back in government, this crusade would be revived. 'To bring together my father's people and my mother's people is my undying passion.'

On 14 October, in the run-up to the conference, the party had published its new policy document. 'Jobs for the '80s' was almost entirely John Bruton's work. It comprised a masterly analysis of the problems facing the economy and outlined a raft of reforms.

It is important not only because it was to be the effective election manifesto of the party. It also shaped much of the policies of the second FitzGerald government.

It presented a stark analysis of the economic crisis. 'The public finances are dangerously overstretched, inflation is running at twice European levels, unemployment has reached one in eight of the labour force, and the net debt of the state to foreign banks now exceeds £6,000 for every PAYE taxpayer in the country. The total cost of servicing the national debt now exceeds agricultural income.'

It warned of several tough deflationary years being necessary. Government was living beyond its means, and strict control of current and capital spending was needed. An economic and social plan for a number of years was urged. All spending programmes must have clearly-stated objectives, including how many jobs they would provide, and when.

'The myth that all government capital spending is necessarily productive must be exploded.' The capital programme needed re-classification. State companies should be given an honest mandate and 'should not be forced by the government to carry on unsubsidised loss-making duties'. Companies like CIE and Aer Lingus should be given specific budgets for the social and strategic duties imposed on them by government.

Incomes had to reflect prevailing economic realities. Public sector pay increases had to be reduced because they were leading to increased charges for electricity, communications and transport, and higher taxation on the productive sector. Bruton's document did not actually mention the public sector – a key electorate – but the vaguer 'sheltered sectors'.

Ironically 'Jobs for the 80s' did not set out specific job creation targets. Instead it cited the need for cost competitiveness to attract foreign industry. To promote the work incentive, it urged a reduction in tax and social insurance for the low-paid. Welfare increases should not increase faster than comparable wages.

The government had to give a lead in beating inflation by strict control of those prices and incomes within its ambit. Bruton urged acceptance of new technology and a strong open economy. Major reform of the public sector was also required. 'Two-thirds of all activity in this country takes place, directly or indirectly, under the aegis of government. If the public sector of the economy is inefficient, there is little hope for the rest.' The need for civil service and Dáil reform was also outlined.

Settling public sector pay claims on the basis of 'comparability' was irrelevant when the money had to be borrowed abroad. Arbitration schemes took no account of government ability to pay, the document said. 'It is obviously wrong that any outside discussions should be capable of completely overturning the validity of the government's budget estimates, as agreed democratically by the Dáil.' Bruton wanted all public sector pay to be settled on the basis of 'the availability of tax revenues to pay for it'. The relevance of this would become painfully clear three years later.

He also put forward radical proposals for employee shareholding in industry. A National Development Corporation which would set up strictly commercial enterprises, 'either on a wholly-owned or joint venture basis' was also advocated. One aspect of his NDC policy would embroil Bruton in major clashes with Labour later on. 'Jobs for the 80s' said the aim of the NDC 'should be to build up the projects to a stage of profitability so that they can be sold off to the private sector, and the proceeds re-invested in future projects'. Obviously, this idea was anathema to any party of the left, even one whose socialism was as uncertain as the Irish Labour Party's.

Agriculture was just coming out of its worst post-war recession. Incomes were down 40 per cent on their 1978 levels in real terms. Bruton argued the value of low inflation and interest rates for the industry, rather than throwing grants at it. To develop food processing, he wanted long-term supply contracts between farmers and processors.

Finally, the document detailed a number of work schemes for young unemployed, including a job sharing scheme, and a work experience programme. It also recited the long-standing Fine Gael dogma about eliminating the current budget deficit, and set down a four-year deadline for this goal.

Altogether, it was a formidable, imaginative plan. But there were two major defects. It failed totally to spell out what precise areas of state spending or jobs would be cut so that the deficit could be eliminated in four years. It also failed to tackle the burning problem of tax reform and evasion.

Exactly a week after the Fine Gael economic plan was published, on 21 October, Fianna Fáil published theirs. 'The Way Forward' essentially represented Haughey's way back to his famous January 1980 television broadcast. It too was a hairshirt blueprint. After many twists and turns of policy Haughey was finally back to fiscal rectitude.

The government's plan also proposed eliminating the budget deficit over four years, job cuts in the public service, and charges for various state services, including local government levies that would again raise the spectre of domestic rates. Was Haughey going to attempt to steal Fine Gael's clothes a second time?

Both documents were launched as veritable election manifestoes. It was an ironic twist. After the auction elections of 1977 and 1981, with their giveaway manifestoes from Fianna Fáil and Fine Gael in turn, both parties were now virtually vying with one another to clobber the electorate.

An election was very much in the air. The Workers' Party, Labour and Fine Gael were all waiting to challenge the Fianna Fáil mini-budget measures when the Dáil resumed. Haughey's position had been made even more tenuous by the death of Clare backbench deputy Dr Bill Loughnane on 18 October. The next day more disaster befell the party. Jim Gibbons, a long-time opponent of Haughey, had suffered a heart attack, and was seriously ill in hospital. Haughey was now totally reliant on the Workers' Party in the Dáil.

The following weekend, the Labour Party annual conference was held in Salthill. The conference divided hopelessly on the question of coalition. In the end former leader, Frank Cluskey, saved the day with a compromise proposal that a decision be put off until after an election, when the party would negotiate with all sides. That was agreed. But Michael O'Leary was desperately unhappy. He felt that this was a cop-out and was totally unfair to the electorate. Labour would be negotiating behind closed doors *after* the people had voted: far better a pre-election pact like the one that brought Liam Cosgrave and Brendan Corish to power in 1973.

It was a desperate time for the Labour leader. This was the second occasion inside eight months that he had been rebuffed by his party. He left Galway thinking hard about his political future.

On the following Wednesday, 27 October, the Dáil resumed. Election speculation was rampant. That day's MRBI poll not only showed the two main parties dead-heating, it high-lighted a dramatic slump in the government's standing. There was little doubt that Fianna Fáil's internal bloodletting had badly damaged its popularity.

All this came on top of the summer of the GUBU govern-ment, dominated by the MacArthur affair. The mini-budget had set the public sector unions on the warpath, and since September newspaper stories had surfaced regularly about political interference with the gardaí. These culminated at the end of that month in the extraordinary Dowra Affair. A gárda who was the brother-in-law of the Minister of Justice, Seán Doherty, faced charges of assault against a Fermanagh man. But on the day of the hearing at Dowra, Co. Cavan, the complainant was arrested in the early morning by the RUC, and held until after the court hearing in Dowra was over. The charges were dropped. Media reports on this im-mediately focused on the relationship between the defendant and Doherty. People began to draw their own conclusions about this novel form of cross-border security co-operation.

When the Dáil resumed, Fine Gael was more determined than ever to bring down the government. Their front bench was now meeting almost daily to assess the situation. At the meeting of the parliamentary party that week, John Donnellan urged the leadership to put down a motion of no confidence. He had travelled up from Galway on the train, and was speak-ing to a number of Fianna Fáil deputies, and they all expected an election. But FitzGerald told the meeting that the question of putting down such a motion was a matter of fine judgment. This had to do with doubts about the Workers' Party. True, they were indicating opposition to the national plan. But they had backed the government on the Finance Bill in July, and again on the opening day of the new Dáil session. If they lost their no-confidence motion, Fine Gael could not table another one for six months. That was why they had to be certain.

There were some in Fine Gael who favoured waiting until after the budget: the government would be even more unpopular then. Finbarr Fitzpatrick would also have liked more time. He told a national executive meeting that if there was no election until March, everything would be shipshape. Kerry North had still to be sorted out, as had Louth and Dublin South West. And in Roscommon, the party was faced with a High Court injunction over candidate differences! Constituencies' funds were another problem. Many had not yet recovered from the two previous elections, and Fitzpatrick was now finalising plans for a major fund-raising lottery.

But the counter-argument was that they should do as they had been doing for months: attack Fianna Fáil non-stop, especially now when they could take advantage of the government's depleted ranks. There was always the danger that if Haughey hung on, he would attempt a constituency gerrymander. (Fine Gael's fears were well founded. Haughey had actually raised the possibility shortly after assuming office in March. However, some Fianna Fáil backbenchers had been worried about the implications for their own seats. But Haughey was now returning to the idea in late October.) There was also genuine concern about the whiff of scandal surrounding Seán Doherty's administration of the gardaí. Fine Gael called publicly for a judicial inquiry into political interference with the Force. Michael Noonan rang in from Clare, where he was director of elections in the by-election caused by Bill Loughnane's death. He was hearing stories 'of guards being blackguarded in every constituency'. FitzGerald, Mitchell and others were receiving even more reliable information about the tapping of journalists' telephones. By this stage, FitzGerald had no doubt that the security of the state was being threatened by some 'very improper behaviour by the government'.

It took only one more dramatic occurence to swing it. On the evening of 28 October, FitzGerald was in Ennis at the selection convention for the Clare by-election when the news reached him from Dublin that Michael O'Leary had announced his resignation as leader of the Labour Party. Moreover, he was quitting the party entirely. He said he could no longer abide his party's negative electoral policy, and he indicated that he would work to secure a change of government. It was as good as an application to join Fine Gael.

The following day, Friday, FitzGerald issued a statement praising O'Leary's 'honourable and courageous' decision. He also announced his intention of meeting him to discuss 'how our common purpose to provide our country with an alternative government at this critical time can best be achieved'. Sure enough, the two men met the following Tuesday, and O'Leary emerged from the meeting as a member of Fine Gael. But other politicians also were anxious to exploit O'Leary's move, and the consequent Labour Party dissarray. The Workers' Party saw their chance to raid the Labour vote. Tony Gregory saw his chance of capitalising on O'Leary's defection in Dublin Central.

This was the position when the Fine Gael front bench finally agreed to table that no confidence motion in the Dáil. Ironically, FitzGerald was not at the meeting which took the decision. He was in RTE recording an interview for French television. With the pace of events really hotting up, his colleagues were growing more anxious and nervous that the moment might pass. The rumours were flying that the Workers' Party was about to ditch Fianna Fáil. Jim O'Keeffe, from Cork South West, referred the front bench to what Joe Sherlock was quoted as saying in the *Cork Examiner*: that it was difficult to see how the government could now survive a no-confidence vote.

It was clearly time to move. Catherine Meenan, FitzGerald's private secretary, who was also secretary to the front bench, left the meeting to phone him. He agreed with his colleagues. They would table the no-confidence motion. Later that day, when the news broke, the Workers' Party declared that they would be supporting it. Fine Gael had calculated correctly.

As the crucial debate got under way on Wednesday, 3 November, Haughey tried a desperate stratagem to stay in power. He sought talks with the Labour Party. Labour's new leader, Dick Spring, was a surprise choice to succeed O'Leary. He was just thirty-two years old, and less than a year and a half in the Dáil. Haughey obviously hoped to exploit Spring's inexperience, but he never got the chance. The new Labour leader rejected any question of talks out of hand. It was a particularly brave decision. Labour needed time as much as Fianna Fáil; yet they shunned a deal.

The debate set the scene for a bitter election campaign. Fianna Fáil speakers accused Fine Gael of a campaign of vilification against Haughey. It was a term that would rival 'fiscal rectitude' as the predominant catchcries of those two crowded political years, 1981 and 1982. Fine Gael was trying to clamber to power, they cried, over the grave of Bill Loughnane and the sick-bed of Jim Gibbons.

FitzGerald and Peter Barry alleged second-class behaviour by Fianna Fáil and low standards in high places. But from Fine Gael's point of view the most significant speech of the two-day debate was Dick Spring's. Although Labour was officially neutral on its electoral options, he made it very clear where he stood.

> Labour stands alone in this election, but not apart. I left the last government headed by Dr FitzGerald [he had been a junior minister] with no sense of shame. No one in that administration could say that Dr FitzGerald did not strive to give the country decent and honest government.

He felt sure Labour voters around the country would register their opinions on the respective merits of Haughey and FitzGerald. A nod was as good as a wink. In the Labour party the pro-coalition leader was dead: long live the new pro-coalition leader.

The end was inevitable. By a vote of 82 to 80, Haughey's second government was toppled. In a repeat of May 1981,

Fine Gael's election machine was purring, ready for the 'off'. It was to be their best campaign. This time the errors of June and February would be put right. They had high hopes. George Birmingham, a member of the Constituency Review Committee, felt they could take up to 73 seats and actually top Fianna Fáil.

Polling was set for 24 November. It would be a short, sharp campaign. Just as well. People and politicians alike were suffering from election fatigue. It was winter time, and party coffers all round were none too healthy. All the major parties were now agreed on the serious economic crisis facing the country. This time there were no goodies and giveaways, just two hairshirt economic plans vying with one another in harshness. The focus of the November 1982 contest lay elsewhere.

Ever since FitzGerald's stinging attack on Haughey in December 1979, the two men were remarkable for their total domination of their respective parties. The bitter antipathy between them was increasingly the factor on which Irish politics turned. The scene was now set for the ultimate presidential-style general election between them. Trust and credibility would be the touchstones.

FitzGerald and Fine Gael attacked Haughey's credibility on the economy, his U-turns, his strokes and deals. The electorate were being asked: would you trust another government to this man? To this party?

Ironically, Haughey also focused on this issue. 'I don't trust him', he said of FitzGerald. But *he* was referring to the constitutional amendment to outlaw abortion. The government had issued the proposed wording on 2 November, and Haughey was well aware of FitzGerald's attempts to back off the commitments he had given to legislate for such a measure in the two preceding election campaigns. Fine Gael were fully aware of their vulnerability on this issue. As a result, within twenty-four hours of the wording being published, FitzGerald gave it a fulsome welcome and promised to support it in government. The party's election manifesto, published on Friday, 5 November, duly gave a commitment to put the amendment to the people before 31 March 1983.

Haughey also made it clear that he did not trust FitzGerald

to maintain an independent nationalist position on the North. That would later develop as a major issue in the campaign. But now it looked like a desperate ploy.

It was an immensely confident FitzGerald who kicked off his party's programme. Fine Gael's opinion poll rating had jumped to a record 42 per cent, which he reckoned would give them 72 seats and could make them the biggest party in the Dáil. He said they would win extra seats in Louth, Kildare, Sligo-Leitrim, Clare, Dun Laoghaire, Laois-Offaly and Wexford. A slightly bigger swing would bring them further extra seats in Cavan-Monaghan, Kerry North, Dublin South-Central, Meath, Roscommon and Galway West.

The manifesto primarily comprised the 'Jobs for the 80s' document. It identified two main election issues: credibility and key economic policy differences between themselves and Fianna Fáil. It lauded their own 'consistent' tackling of the country's economic woes in contrast to five U-turns it recorded against Haughey. Moreover, Fine Gael had refused to be 'diverted from this course by promises of soft options'. Nothing about its own soft-option U-turn the previous March.

On taxation, the manifesto had none of the grandiose, expensive promises of June 1981. It did renew the promise of tax credits, a family income supplement for the low paid, and lower PRSI for those on incomes below £6,000. On overall tax reform, there was merely a commitment to examine the blueprint of the Commission on Taxation set up by Fianna Fáil in 1980. It was a case of older and wiser.

In government, they would also regulate building land prices; upgrade the status of women in the home, and appoint a Minister of State for Women's Affairs. There would be a judicial inquiry into allegations of political interference with the gardaí over the previous two years; reform of the criminal law; a garda authority, and an independent garda complaints body. On Northern Ireland, they would restore a working relationship with the British government.

FitzGerald was asked about the feasibility of eliminating the budget deficit over four years. He remained firm on principle, but devoid of detail. 'If the budget deficit runs on for more than four years, the seriousness with which the government is tackling the economic difficulties could be doubted.'

But he did not spell out any of the cuts that Fine Gael would make, just the same wooliness on this fundamental issue as existed in the run-up to the June 1981 election. In fact, many economists and commentators doubted the efficacy of such a policy because of the severe deflationary effect it would have. In the *Irish Times*, Paul Tansey wrote that getting rid of the deficit over four years would send the economy 'through the floorboards'.

The first weekend of the campaign was taken up with selection conventions. The party had a couple of problems. In Limerick, Tom O'Donnell intimated that he was not going forward. Since February, he and Neil Blaney were the only dual mandate representatives in the European Parliament, and it was a very arduous routine. It was impossible to get a pairing. However, the local Fine Gael councillors prevailed on him to stand again, and a few days later he received a letter from FitzGerald thanking him for his decision.

The Strategy Committee, with Seán O'Leary again director of elections, decided to run the other O'Leary, the former Labour leader, in Dublin South-West. He was willing to stand in any constituency, except for his old Dublin Central base. There was a strong feeling that he should be well treated. Otherwise, any other possible defectors to Fine Gael might think twice about doing so. The sitting deputy, Larry McMahon, was not informed in advance. Fitzpatrick was sure that McMahon would object, and therefore presented him with an effective *fait accompli*. He knew the Dublin South-West set-up intimately. Declan Fitzpatrick, the former constituency organiser there, was his brother. McMahon was livid, but O'Leary duly got through the convention, along with McMahon and Dr Con Brennan. Mount Street was adamant that the strategy was to win two seats. McMahon was not so sure. He reckoned that he was a marked man, that head office had written him off as an obstructive quota squatter, and that they were only too pleased to catapult O'Leary in on top of him.

Roscommon was a particularly thorny problem due to a court injunction which prevented a convention vote being taken. There were deep divisions between the camps of Liam Naughton, the outgoing deputy, and John Connor, the man he had displaced in February. The only way around the legal constraint was to have the candidates unanimously selected. Fitzpatrick travelled down for the vital meeting, and engaged the experienced Pat Cooney to chair the proceedings.

It was a tense, angry meeting. There was much wheeling, dealing and bartering. But finally Fitzpatrick got his plan through. He persuaded Naughton and Connor to propose and second Boyle solicitor, Tom Callan, who thus joined them on the ticket which was then agreed without a vote. In this way, the injunction was not breached.

In most other constituencies, conventions went smoothly. The findings of the Constituency Review Committee were carefully followed. West Galway was probably the finest example of the blueprint in action. The committee had identified too much leakage in the party's vote. The National Executive's directive now was to nominate two candidates, one of them from Connemara. With John Donnellan from Dunmore in the east of the county certain to be selected, Mount Street was effectively reserving to itself the choice of a Galway city candidate. Pól Ó Foighil and Donnellan were duly selected at the convention.

The national executive now had a choice between Padraic MacCormack or Fintan Coogan jnr from the city. MacCormack, a native of Athenry, had been unsuccessful in June 1981 and February 1982. In the latter contest, he and Coogan virtually cancelled each other out, with 3,900 and 3,700 votes respectively.

The verdict was that MacCormack was taking some votes from Donnellan, was depressing Coogan's vote, and was unlikely to make it on his own. Coogan was the one added. The target was a seat to be gained at the expense of Labour's Michael D. Higgins.

In Cork North-Central there was a surprise development at the convention. February's party poll-topper, Bernard Allen, failed to get a nomination due to the machinations of his outgoing colleague, Liam Burke, who felt threatened by the younger man. However, Mount Street duly added Allen to the ticket.

Otherwise the campaign was away to a fine start. A week

into it, the first *Irish Independent*-IMS opinion poll provided very heartening news. Fianna Fáil were at 44 per cent, Fine Gael, 40 per cent and Labour 10 per cent. A clear 6 per cent lead for a possible coalition and a bridgeable gap for Fine Gael. At the beginning of the campaign, Haughey had firmly ruled out the possibility of coalition. Fine Gael was urging transfers for Labour, but the former junior coalition partner remained its old divisive self on the matter.

There was more good news for Fine Gael. The poll confirmed the record low standing of the outgoing administration which the late October polls had marked. Dissatisfaction with the government was running at 71 per cent; with Haughey, a new record 64 per cent. In contrast, FitzGerald was smelling of roses, with a 56 per cent satisfaction rating. He was the preferred choice as Taoiseach of 57 per cent; Haughey was preferred by only 32 per cent. The deep internal divisions in Fianna Fáil were underlined by 46 per cent of party supporters declaring themselves dissatisfied with their performance in government.

If Fine Gael did not win handsomely this time, they never would. Haughey and his party were in desperate trouble. His initial attempts to elevate the proposed anti-abortion amendment into a major issue was unsuccessful. FitzGerald's unqualified endorsement of the measure had stymied it. Nor was the North taking off as an issue.

In desperation, Haughey decided to hype the national question, and to accuse FitzGerald of colluding with the British. Demands that Britain stay out of the election were made by the outgoing Taoiseach a week into the campaign. Since the Falklands War earlier in the year, formal Anglo-Irish relations were at a very low ebb. That followed Fianna Fáil's failure to endorse EEC sanctions against Argentina. Now Haughey's allegations against FitzGerald centred on the latter's alleged support for Jim Prior's Assembly initiative in the North.

But people simply did not believe the Fianna Fáil boss. And the proof of this was a further poll on 15 November — nine days before polling. Also in the *Irish Independent*, it revealed that 73 per cent of people felt that 'you can believe little or nothing' of what Fianna Fáil politicians say.

For Fine Gael, things could not have been better. Their

planning and strategy were going a dream. They were now virtually on auto-pilot. One shrewd change saw them move from the Berkeley Court Hotel. Given the grim state of the economy, they decided that operating from this luxurious hotel might spark off stories about Fine Gael living in splendour while 170,000 people were on the dole. Their early morning campaign review meetings were now held in party headquarters.

Seán Murray was again dusting off his secret list of business subscribers. He and his Capital Branch colleagues repeated their marathon begging phone-arounds. About £160,000 was also levied on the constituencies. Once more, there was a remarkable response by business. Murray had been nervous at a third appeal in eighteen months. But they ended up being able to spend half a million pounds on the campaign.

Not surprisingly GFG rather than FG was the primary focus of their campaign. His picture dominated the election posters and the newspaper advertisement. In the post-budget election in February, the slogan across the top of his poster was simply: 'He's Right'. Now it was 'Put the Right Man Back'. All over the country, candidates and canvassers alike sold FitzGerald as the economic messiah come to deliver Ireland from the trough of despair and insolvency.

However, the great man himself was proving remarkably coy when it came to explaining his message. On 15 November, for instance, when asked if he would have to bring in another savage budget, he waffled. He did not want to depress the economy 'more than we have to, because we are in a very deep recession, and that aspect will have to be considered in our budget strategy in our first year.'

That suited the strategy team — soon to be dubbed the National Handlers by political columnist, John Healy — who were into more bland, superficial concepts. Now they wanted their hero to impress the youth electorate also. What better way to do this than to stage a photocall of FitzGerald with the Irish rock prodigies, U2, who were acquiring an international reputation. This was duly arranged for the Windmill Lane studios in Dublin on Friday, 19 November, where the group were recording an album. While there could be nothing more incongruous than FitzGerald as rock music groupie, there was actually a genuine basis to this stroke.

Some months earlier, U2's lead singer, Bono, had seen FitzGerald at London Airport, and talked to him. Subsequently, he had corresponded with the Fine Gael leader, he told journalists. Bono was also fulsome in his estimation of FitzGerald: 'He is what he is. He does not hide behind a face. I'm a Garret supporter. It's a very personal thing.' The next day, the papers carried pictures of FitzGerald, his wife Joan and Bono, wearing headphones and looking very pleased with themselves. The strategy boys were overjoyed.

Not everyone was impressed. Certainly not the outgoing Minister of State for Education, Niall Andrews. 'I suppose he will now be known as Garret the Groover. Perhaps he will be bringing in his version of "Blue Suede Shoes", except that in his case it will be "Don't Step on my one red, and one blue suede shoe".' This was a reference to the celebrated incident where FitzGerald turned up at a function wearing odd shoes.

There was only one mishap in an otherwise impeccable Fine Gael campaign. It centred on Haughey's persistent accusations that Britain was interfering in the election on the side of Fine Gael. Then the Northern Secretary, Jim Prior, who was in the United States, said that he understood Dr FitzGerald would be making a campaign speech supporting an all-Ireland court and police force.

The next day Haughey seized on this very odd foreknowledge of Prior's. 'The fact that the Secretary of State for Northern Ireland knew in advance what Dr FitzGerald would say in his speech on Northern Ireland reveals now the degree of collusion that exists between the leader of the Fine Gael party and the British government.' A feature of the election campaign, he claimed, was the support by British government circles, radio and television networks, and leading newspapers for FitzGerald. The situation now revealed 'represents one of the most serious threats to our political independence since the last war. Once again, I demand that Britain stay out of our general election.'

Later in the day FitzGerald pointed out that he had made the all-Ireland police and court proposals in his televised Dimbleby Lecture the previous May, when Prior was in the audience. 'Mr Prior has rightly guessed that I am standing by this suggestion as part of the long-term process of bringing peace to Northern Ireland.'

The next night, he duly made the only speech of the campaign on Northern Ireland. He urged the establishment of 'a joint court and police force, under North-South control'. Haughey saw his chance. The Green Card was going to be elevated to a Green Scare.

Immediately Fianna Fáil interpreted the all-Ireland police force idea as bringing RUC men onto the streets of the Republic. The further away from the border, the more lurid the picture was painted. Down in Kerry South, the party's director of elections, Jackie Healy-Rea, resurrected the RIC from their graves of sixty years and had them stalking the land. Kitchener-style posters appeared, showing FitzGerald as a British recruiting sergeant. Even in parts of Dublin there were posters declaring 'no' to 'armed RUC patrols'.

The Strategy Committee was horrified. Haughey had seized the initiative, and his party's wild, alarmist claims were having the desired effect, especially in the more republican constituencies. Irate calls began to come to Mount Street from Kerry, and border counties like Sligo, Leitrim, Cavan and Monaghan. The strategy people quickly decided that the thing to do was to defuse the issue, not to counter-attack.

Jim Mitchell believed this was wrong: that they should have stood their ground, that it was a good proposal and well worth defending. He felt that an Irish-style FBI, which crossed state boundaries, was the way to overcome no-go areas like South Armagh. They could also have exploited the fact that the great united Irelanders of Fianna Fáil were now the ones opposed to all-Ireland institutions.

But the word from Mount Street was to back off the issue. FitzGerald, for his part, showed his personal pluck. On the Friday night, he went ahead with plans to present the annual Ewart-Biggs Award of the British-Irish Association in Dublin.

On Thursday, 18 November, in the midst of the Green Scare, Haughey also tried to counter-attack on the economic issue. As ever, he was a touch unorthodox. He published the estimates for 1983, which normally would not appear until January. It was a brave gamble, because it spelled out some very harsh medicine. CIE fares were to go up 25 per cent;

short-term social welfare benefits were to be cut; the secondary school free transport was to go, and there would be charges for local services. There would also be a further £160 million in tax increases. The annual deficit was set at £750 million. It was truly, as Haughey declared, 'a unique electoral platform'. He also had a plaintive plea for the public. 'We know they are not popular, but it is the honest thing to do ... we don't get credit for much, but I hope we get credit for that.'

They didn't. Fine Gael's response was evasive: they would have to wait until they were in government to see if these measures were necessary. Sectoral groups affected by the proposed cuts reacted angrily. Fine Gael played it cute and waffled, while the brickbats were hurled at the government.

Overall, it had been a rather lacklustre campaign. Given the time of year, and the poll weariness of the nation, it was very much a campaign waged in the media, and particularly on television. FitzGerald did not make a sustained nationwide tour: just occasional sorties to key constituencies.

To sustain interest, the Strategy Committee had devised some clever television party political broadcasts. They were primarily the inspiration of Bill O'Herlihy, a veteran television performer. A first cousin of Seán O'Leary, this other shrewd Corkman set out to exploit the divisions and lack of credibility in Fianna Fáil.

One film interposed clips of pro-Haughey and anti-Haughey deputies. The accompanying tune was: 'You can't have one without the other.' Another showed a man walking along a road. First he is seen reading the 1977 Fianna Fáil giveaway manifesto: next Martin O'Donoghue's plans; then Haughey's programmes, and finally 'The Way Forward'. At that point he disappears down a manhole.

On the final weekend of the campaign, Fianna Fáil kept up the Green Scare. It had Fine Gael rattled, and it deflected some attention from their own harsh estimates. The Attorney-General, John Murray, issued a detailed statement claiming that FitzGerald's security proposals could undermine our sovereignty. On the Saturday, Haughey accused FitzGerald of colluding with 'a trained British spy', a reference to the elderly Duke of Norfolk — the former head of British intelligence — who in a recent speech had referred to having lunched with FitzGerald.

The Fine Gael leader replied to the collusion allegation, and other charges by the outgoing Taoiseach, in a detailed statement. The very fact that he issued a rebuttal showed that he and his advisers knew the Fianna Fáil campaign was doing them damage. He accused Haughey of having three times during the campaign 'vilified my motives or actions'. Firstly, there was the abortion referendum. Then there was the collusion charge: 'This is a lie and Mr Haughey knows it is a lie.' Finally, there was Haughey's 'big lie' about RUC involvement in an all-Ireland police force. FitzGerald ended his statement: 'I have no alternative but to defend myself against the unprincipled and vicious attacks of a man desperate at the prospect of losing office.'

On the final Sunday, Dick Spring made it abundantly clear that he would not do business after the election with Haughey, whatever about his party obligation to treat with all parties. 'I can say point blank that I won't be negotiating with Mr Haughey as leader of Fianna Fáil.'

Now, in the final days, all attention turned to the ritual television confrontation of the party leaders. As we have already seen, FitzGerald had greatly disappointed in the two previous showdowns. Haughey had won both. But this time it would be different. The strategy people vowed to have their man properly prepared this time. They turned FitzGerald out like a world boxing championship contender.

In the preceding week, a number of televised trials were conducted. O'Herlihy wanted to get back to a repeat of 1973 when FitzGerald had 'whipped' George Colley. On Monday, their champ had his hair cut and styled; his clothes were carefully chosen. In the afternoon, he rested. He also had a two-hour political briefing with O'Herlihy, O'Leary, Sutherland and Peter Prendergast.

The handlers wanted a decisive, straight-talking performance: no scattered allusions, no speech-slurring, no racing ahead. 'Keep it simple, avoid technical budgetary terms like GNPs and deficits'. That was the message.

But their attention to detail really showed on the night. They arrived at RTE just after the 9 o'clock news. In February, FitzGerald and Haughey had joked nervously as they posed for photographs, exchanging a prolonged handshake. This time there would be no handshake with the opponent. Nothing must be done to break concentration, to trivialise the event. Afterwards, in an ironic comment, FitzGerald said he did not shake hands because he did not want it to look like a prize fight. In every other respect, the preparations resembled nothing else. The duellists, along with the lesser contender, Dick Spring, then got together with RTE anchorman, Brian Farrell, for the opening 'shots' of the programme. It was to proceed with a twenty-minute interview of the Labour man. The real contestants would wait off camera until this was over. Then the real contest would start.

But the handlers had other ideas. They took their man out of the studio, leaving Haughey sitting there on his own. They retired for a last minute pep-talk. They also taped FitzGerald's glasses behind his ears. He had a tendency to take them off and put them on again when reading something. But that was too like what a university professer would do. It would have to stop.

FitzGerald returned to the studio just before the Spring interview finished, and took his seat. Soon the great bout was under way.

Haughey again showed what an adroit performer he was. But he had an impossible task. There were so many inconsistencies. FitzGerald made hay with all the changes in economic policy, and the embarrassment of Fianna Fáil's 'Club of 22'. He also delivered a neat winning punch when they moved on to the North. He handed Haughey a copy of his controversial speech of the previous Thursday, and challenged him to find anywhere in it a reference to a 'British-Irish' force. That was what Haughey had dubbed his all-Ireland police force idea. Haughey took it up, but then he put it down, refusing to pursue the issue.

All through, FitzGerald avoided GNPs and other technical data. He did everything asked of him. When it ended, there was no doubt about the winner. FitzGerald had finally outpointed Haughey, his first victory in three contests. O'Herlihy was both jubilant and modest: 'He created the right impression on the key issues of leadership and credibility. All we did was to improve the talent that was already there.'

Except for being put on the defensive on Northern policy, the whole campaign had been a superb Fine Gael performance. This time they had positive images to sell. Unlike June 1981, many of the Fine Gael front bench were now well known after their first stint in government. 'Garret's Team' was highlighted. But once again, it was FitzGerald who was plugged remorselessly. The message was: 'you can't have Garret FitzGerald if you don't vote Fine Gael.'

On voting day, the final newspaper advertisements summed it up. A big picture of FitzGerald, and below the legend: 'More than ever the country needs a leader it can trust. Garret FitzGerald leads the united team that will give Ireland a government that *works*. An economy that *works*. A community that *works*.'

Another ad. attacked Haughey more explicitly. 'A vote for Fianna Fáil is a vote of confidence in the Haughey government. Is that what you really want? Fine Gael — Change for the Better.'

However, the final opinion polls showed a slight recovery for Fianna Fáil. Clearly the Green Card had been important. The day before voting, an *Irish Times*-MRBI poll gave Fianna Fáil 44 per cent, Fine Gael 41, and Labour 9. The breakthrough had not occurred. FitzGerald led Haughey comfortably as preferred choice for Taoiseach. As the people trundled to the polling booths for the third time in less than eighteen months, the odds were clearly on a Fine Gael-Labour coalition, and an end at last to hung Dáils.

Fine Gael resorted to vote management on a large scale, bearing in mind the evidence of the Constituency Review Committee. The aim was to emulate the Birmingham-Bruton Dublin North-Central result in other key marginals and to rectify the vote mismanagement of February that had lost seats in Sligo-Leitrim, Dublin South-Central, Dun Laoghaire, Kildare and Galway West. There was no point in having poll toppers who failed to elect running mates.

To reinforce the case there were special 'Good Morning' leaflet drops in many constituencies. These carried personalised messages from FitzGerald, with pictures of the leader. They explained that the best chance for the party's candidates was for the people of that area to vote for a specified named candidate, and give their subsequent preferences to the others. Thus in Leixlip, Celbridge and Naas, the leaflets urged first preferences for Bernard Durkan, who had lost out in February. A similar exercise urged preference for Fergus O'Brien in parts of Dublin South-Central. There the ploy was to check the highly personalised campaign of Gay Mitchell. Similar exercises were undertaken in other parts of the country.

Then it was an agonising wait for the ballot boxes to open on 25 November. In Fine Gael headquarters the mid-morning tallies were looking good. Hopes were soon rising that they would indeed realise their ambition, now a fairly realistic expectation, of equalling Fianna Fáil. When FitzGerald became leader in July 1977, his central ambition had been to make Fine Gael the largest party in the country. Was this incredible notion now going to be realised less than five and a half years later?

The long count eventually stretched into the next day, due to recounts in Clare and Kerry North. The final outcome was a further remarkable breakthrough for Fine Gael. For the third time in eighteen months, the party's vote was up again to new record levels. This time it was 39.2 per cent, bettering even the 39 per cent vote of Cumann na nGaedheal's first Free State government in 1923.

And naturally the extra votes had brought extra seats this time. They made a net gain of seven on February, taking them to 70. But the marvellous performance had its tantalising factor. Despite all the adversities facing Fianna Fáil, they had not been eclipsed, as the first campaign polls had suggested was possible. They got seventy-five seats. Labour confounded the political prophets under their new leader; far from sliding to oblivion, they actually got an extra seat, taking their total to 16. The Workers' Party had two deputies elected, including party president, Tomas MacGiolla, and there were three others: Gregory, Blaney and John O'Connell, who was returned automatically.

In historical terms, Fine Gael's narrowing of the forty-one-seat lead which Fianna Fáil had over them in 1977 to a mere

213

five was a magnificent achievement. FitzGerald, above any-one else, had to be credited with this enormous resurgence. Yet he was also probably the author of the party's failure at least to draw level with Fianna Fáil. His all-Ireland court and police proposal had been the lifeline that saved Fianna Fáil from a greater collapse.

In most constituencies, however, the party had secured the optimal result. Lost seats were recovered by Fergus O'Brien, Bernard Durkan, Alice Glenn and Joe McCartin. In all cases, the remedial strategy of the Constituency Review Committee had been invaluable. In some cases it worked nearly too well. In Kildare, for instance, Durkan ended up heading the poll, 1,500 votes ahead of Dukes, and was elected on the first count.

In Galway West, the plan was also a winner. Fintan Coogan's city vote was up over 80 per cent, and he took the third seat, with John Donnellan taking the second. Exactly according to strategy, Michael D. Higgins was the casualty: there was much glee in Fine Gael at *that* outcome. In Sligo-Leitrim, a Ballymote candidate, Tom Lavin, had been selected, as head-quarters had instructed. He got 4,300 votes and duly helped elect Joe McCartin.

There were two remarkable gains in two five-seaters, Dun Laoghaire and Wexford. For the first time, Monica Barnes made it safely through the convention. She now had the last laugh, storming home on the first count and topping the poll. In the process she ousted the chief architect of Fianna Fáil's 1977 manifesto, Martin O'Donoghue. In that constituency, Fine Gael took a remarkable 52 per cent of the vote.

In Wexford the prescription of adding a Wexford town candidate was obeyed. Avril Doyle, a member of the Dublin Belton family, was the successful candidate, and again the party took 52 per cent of the vote.

However, the winning of a second seat in Clare was the most important advance psychologically. Fine Gael was now taking on Fianna Fáil in their very heartland and beating them. It was a long, unbearably tense count and in the end Donal Carey edged out Sile de Valera, no less, for the final seat. It was one thing to win a second seat in Clare, but to win it in a head-to-head battle with The Chief's own grand-daughter was sensational.

There were also the failures. In Dublin South-West, Michael O'Leary duly won a seat, but it was the one held by the party's outgoing deputy, Larry McMahon. He was very bitter at the outcome, alleging that O'Leary supporters had stormed through his part of the constituency in the final days. While it was disappointing not to win a second seat, we can assume that there were many dry eyes in Mount Street at the departure of McMahon.

In FitzGerald's own Dublin South-East constituency, an elaborate attempt to defeat Labour's Ruairi Quinn came unstuck. In February, FitzGerald had urged transfers to Quinn by name on the party's literature. But there was a strong feeling that he had not reciprocated: he had been very critical of coalition after that election. But the Fine Gael vote spread went wrong. The sitting deputy, Alexis FitzGerald, simply lost out to colleague, Joe Doyle, the Donnybrook Church sacristan. A fourth candidate, John McKenna, from Quinn's Sandymount base, polled a poor 1,700 votes. The leader's own vote was whittled down by 4,000 on February, but it was not sufficient to achieve a seat gain.

Nor did Louth come right. Fianna Fáil did lose one of their three seats. But Labour's Michael Bell was the beneficiary. Brendan McGahon replaced Bernard Markey as the party's sole deputy there. And Kerry North remained the only constituency in the country not to have a TD under FitzGerald after an election. To regain the seat there Fine Gael last held in 1973, headquarters turned to one of the myriad football heroes in the Kingdom, recent all-Ireland winning captain, Jim Deenihan. And in true sporting style, he put up a magnificent fight, only being edged out by 144 votes for the final seat. Laois-Offaly was also an abject failure again. Here they had not held three seats since 1973, and pleas for vote management fell on very unreceptive ears. Oliver J. Flanagan was long used to doing his own thing, and was not going to change at this, his fourteenth successful election on the trot.

One interesting pattern to the three elections under FitzGerald was that Fine Gael had actually done better under Cosgrave in Louth, Cavan-Monaghan, Roscommon, East and West Mayo and Laois-Offaly. This was the price the party paid for its less conservative, social democratic orientation under the new leadership.

The new deputies returned for the party were Michael O'Leary, Monica Barnes, Fintan Coogan, Avril Doyle, Dick Dowling (replacing Des Governey who retired), Joe Doyle (displacing Alexis FitzGerald), Brendan McGahon (displacing Bernard Markey), while former deputies elected were Hugh Coveney (replacing Jim Corr, who retired), Bernard Durkan, Alice Glenn, Joe McCartin and Madeline Taylor. Four outgoing deputies had been defeated: Alexis FitzGerald, Larry McMahon, Brian Fleming and Bernard Markey. Fine Gael had lost one of its outgoing seats — in Dublin West to the Workers' Party — and gained eight new ones: Clare, Dun Laoghaire, Dublin Central and South-Central, Galway West, Kildare, Sligo-Leitrim and Wexford.

The Labour Party held the balance of power in the new Dáil. But despite that, there was little doubt that a coalition would be formed which would end the era of political instability. On the eve of the election, Spring had again made clear his antipathy to doing business with Fianna Fáil. 'Mr Haughey doesn't have the confidence of his own party, while the vast majority of the people of this country feel he shouldn't be Taoiseach. And we in the Labour Party feel he shouldn't be Taoiseach.'

That weekend a large banner draped the front of Fine Gael's headquarters in Mount Street. It carried FitzGerald's picture and his signature, and the simple message: 'Thank You.' It was an appropriate message, too, for the Strategy Committee. From the spring of 1981 they had moulded an anonymous, policy-less party, with only a single discernible asset — Garret FitzGerald — into a political party that in less than two years was outperforming the legendary Fianna Fáil machine in election campaigns. Along the way FitzGerald had also infused it with a more democratic, vibrant constituency organisation. Along with Prendergast he had broadened its appeal to women and young voters. But it was the Strategy Committee that welded these factors into a winning force at election time.

Now at the end of November 1982, they were set fair to resume government, and for a full term. But it would have to be remembered that Fine Gael had not won the election. Ultimately they were at the mercy of the Labour Party. On 25 November, as the final outcome of the election began to emerge definitively, FitzGerald said it all: 'It is now up to Labour.' By even entertaining coalition, Fine Gael were, by definition, committed to compromising on their policies.

13

Labour Calls the Shots

The coalition deal was worked out in a most unlikely venue. FitzGerald and Spring spent the best part of a fortnight in and out of the Good Shepherd Convent on Eglinton Road, Donnybrook. The suggestion came from Spring. One of his close friends and advisers, John Rogers, knew members of the community and through him they agreed to place their drawing room at the disposal of the two leaders.

It was a soothing place. Before a nice big fire, and under the gaze of a statue of the Child of Prague, FitzGerald and Spring argued out their compromise. The nuns ferried in tea and coffee on a regular basis.

The negotiators were something of an odd couple. Although Spring had been a junior minister in the first FitzGerald coalition, the two men hardly knew one another, which created obvious difficulties. FitzGerald, at fifty-six, was the most popular politician in Ireland. Spring, at thirty-two, was almost totally unknown. As journalist Vincent Browne observed caustically: prior to these talks the biggest thing Spring had ever negotiated was his mortgage. FitzGerald's party had captured nearly four times the support of Spring's party at the election, and they had diametrically opposed policies in some areas, yet Fine Gael and Labour were thrown together in this way as the only feasible government potentially on offer to the country. They were going to put together a compromise agreement, but the question was: could it stick?

In time, this private compromise proved unworkable in many key areas, and led to stagnation and indecision, rather than to positive action. This was the very situation which Michael O'Leary regarded as unfair to the electorate: far better to have a joint coalition programme put plainly before the people in an election.

218

Nearly 85 per cent of the electorate had in fact voted for the hairshirt policies of financial retrenchment of Fianna Fáil and Fine Gael. That was John Kelly's fundamental argument against coalition with Labour; he went on urging the logic of an alternative coalition with Fianna Fáil. But for both parties, a grand coalition was unthinkable. In practice, it was Fine Gael-Labour or nothing at all.

There were fundamental differences in Fine Gael and Labour priorities. To combat the jobs crisis, Labour wanted an aggressive National Development Corporation to spearhead state investment in natural resources, with £500 million working capital. Fine Gael had proposed an NDC also, but operating in a more restrictive way. Labour wanted major increases in capital taxation, a wealth tax and a property tax. They sought a referendum on divorce and they were unhappy about the Fine Gael commitment to eliminate the budget deficit over four years. They also wanted social welfare payments indexed to the cost of living. In short, they favoured state-led involvement in job creation, taxation of property and wealth in addition to wages and salaries, and high state investment.

On the other hand, Fine Gael wanted to get the books balanced in four years; they did not want to be explicitly committed to indexing welfare payments, they were strongly opposed to additional capital taxation, and deeply divided on the question of divorce. Despite all these difficulties, however, the vast majority of Labour TDs favoured joining another coalition government with Fine Gael. Only Mervyn Taylor struck a discordant note, favouring support for a minority FitzGerald government. For their part, Fine Gael saw Labour as a nuisance . . . but an indispensable one, if they were to achieve power.

The two party leaders had their first meeting on Wednesday, 1 December. It was exactly a fortnight to the meeting of the new Dáil. Spring made clear from the outset his preference to participate in government: 'I am far more interested in sharing power and having Labour Party policies implemented' rather than 'propping up some other party'. His was a unique mandate from the October party conference: he was empowered to negotiate alone, without encumbrance by any

219

other party officer. That meeting, and a second on the Friday, were essentially getting-to-know-you sessions and occasions for exchanging basic position papers on all aspects of policy.

Both men conducted almost all the direct negotiations alone. Unlike June 1981, advisers were only consulted, not directly involved. FitzGerald referred back primarily to his mentor and friend, James Dooge, and also to Gemma Hussey and Alan Dukes. Spring's aides were John Rogers, Pat Magner from Cork, and friend and fellow Tralee man, Joe Revington. Each morning the Labour team met in Roger's flat in Ballsbridge over breakfast and planned their strategy for the day's talks ahead.

It became clear from the outset that the talks would be tough. Spring had behind him a party deeply divided on the very issue of coalition. He was determined to put an impressive package to the special delegate conference in Limerick on Sunday, 12 December where the fate of a possible government arrangement with Fine Gael would be decided. The talks were sufficiently prolonged and difficult for FitzGerald to cancel a planned visit to Paris on Monday, 6 December. The word was also out that Labour were pressing for an extra £200 million in capital taxation.

FitzGerald wanted a largely aspirational programme for government. Labour, on the other hand, were insisting on specific commitments. Capital taxation, the role and financing of an NDC, the budget deficit, and possible referenda on divorce and abortion were to remain stubbornly resistant to compromise. It was easier to agree the broad parameters of the problems the government would have to tackle. These were set down as halting and reversing unemployment, then standing at 170,000, and a 'fundamental reform of the taxation and social welfare systems'.

On many issues it was a case of FitzGerald having no personal difficulties with Labour's demands, but he argued that he could not get them accepted by his party. For instance, he accepted Spring's demand for a residential property tax. Much of the detailed work on this proposal was done for Labour by their Dublin Co. Councillor economist, Eithne FitzGerald, who was FitzGerald's daughter-in-law, being married to his economist son, John. The Fine Gael leader saw nothing wrong with high income earners in expensive houses paying a special tax towards the cost of local authority services.

The compromise on the NDC was that it would have £200 million equity capital, 'to be taken up over a period of years' instead of the £500 million sought by Labour. The NDC would get involved primarily in developing the natural resources area, like food processing, forestry and fisheries.

Tackling the budget deficit was another stickler. Likely to run to a billion pounds in 1982, Labour were extremely concerned at the deflationary impact of pulling that much money out of the state services sector in four years. The finally agreed target was elimination over five years. But they failed totally to spell out where the necessary cuts would be even attempted to ensure this. Indeed other sections of their government document seriously begged whether they were serious at all with that target. There was a commitment to 'minimising the impact of the less well off' of the public spending cuts already announced in the 1983 book of estimates published by Haughey's government during the election campaign. That had pointed towards school transport cuts, local authority charges, 25 per cent CIE fare rises, and £160 million more in unspecified cuts. Another pullback was signalled in the FitzGerald-Spring agreement to review the 900 items withdrawn from medical card holders under Fianna Fáil's July mini-budget.

FitzGerald and Fine Gael were obviously deeply compromised on their most fundamental items of economic policy long before getting into government.

On capital taxation, Labour were promised half what they wanted. New taxes and anti-avoidance measures which would yield £100 million by 1984 were agreed. There was also to be a crackdown on tax evasion and welfare abuses, along with a 'minimisation' of indirect tax rises so as to reduce inflation.

Fine Gael influence in the document was evidenced by the identification of competitiveness as the key to job creation, through increased productivity and incomes restraint. They would have liked an incomes policy, but that would be unlikely to get the benediction of the comrades in Limerick. A Ministerial Task Force, a national planning board and sectoral committees would all be committed to the task of bringing forward an economic plan. Emergency employment measures were to get up to £200 million in 1983.

All these compromises were not easily achieved. By mid-week, both leaders had briefly introduced their deputy leaders, Peter Barry and Barry Desmond, to help smooth out some of the difficulties. On another occasion, Labour brought along Frank Cluskey, former leader and anti-coalitionist, 'to frighten the shit out of Fine Gael', as one of the Labour advisers explained. Cluskey pushed the property and capital tax proposals through.

Surprisingly, one of the people *not* consulted by FitzGerald was John Bruton. This was all the stranger given that he was the author of much of their policy. It was only when he read in the newspapers during the negotiations that FitzGerald was consulting with Alan Dukes that he realised something was amiss. He was extremely angry. Ironically much of the final coalition programme — on competitiveness, backing for the Telesis industrial strategy, venture capital and developing small firms — was lifted directly from his 'Jobs for the 80s' document. Commitments to Oireachtas and public service reform, and the appointment of an ombudsman were also his.

Labour secured indexation of social welfare payments. They did not get a divorce referendum, but a promise of an Oireachtas committee to examine the problem of marriage breakdown. Fine Gael insisted on their commitment to have the anti-abortion amendment put to the people before 31 March 1983. But Spring reserved the right of a free vote for his party, a very wise caveat.

He also won a dilution of Fine Gael's commitment to taxation of short-term social welfare payments. A 'may be' proviso was now inserted. The two leaders also agreed to legislation to curb land speculation, and a 10 per cent annual tax on derelict sites. The repeal of Haughey's Family Planning Act of 1979 was promised; it was to be replaced by 'full family planning and advice'. Local authority housing output would be raised to 30,000 units annually. There would be a judicial inquiry into alleged political interference with the gardaí, and a garda authority and an independent garda complaints board would be set up.

On Northern Ireland there was ready agreement. Both parties favoured devolved power-sharing, and full recognition of the Irish identity in the North alongside the 'existing recognition of the British/Irish identity' of the unionists; both accepted that Irish unity could only come about by consent.

The intensive negotiations went into the second week of December, and final agreement was in doubt right up to forty-eight hours before the Labour delegate conference.

Along the way, the media had sought in vain to track down the secret negotiators. The *Irish Times* half cracked the mystery one morning when they tailed FitzGerald from his Palmerston Road home in Rathmines to a house in Belgrave Square, just a few hundred yards away. But that was merely a side-conference at the home of his friend Martin McCullogh. Later in the day the real talking resumed under the kindly aegis of the Good Shepherd sisters.

Another item Spring had to attend to was a meeting with Haughey. This was part of the Labour Party conference mandate: negotiate with all sides. Both party leaders merely went through the motions. One of their conversation items was Haughey's herd of deer on Inisvickallaune.

When the party delegate conferences came around on Sunday, 12 December, most interest was naturally focused on Labour's meeting in Limerick. About 1,500 were expected to attend: the anti-coalitionists would swarm in from Dublin while the rural deputies would strain might and main to get all their delegates along to offset them. Despite his youth and inexperience, Spring was in a formidable position. He had taken a leaderless, demoralised party into a general election fearing annihilation, and yet emerged with an extra seat. At the end of the day, he came out of the Savoy Theatre with a good victory margin of 324 votes: 846 for the coalition package, 522 against.

Meantime the Fine Gael parliamentary party was meeting in the Burlington Hotel, Dublin. Deputies had no advance knowledge of what was in the pact with Labour. Copies were distributed, but it was impossible to digest the contents so quickly. Moreover, FitzGerald showed himself quite impatient and reluctant to entertain detailed queries. David Molony wanted to know if there would be no other new taxes in the life of the government. FitzGerald agreed that was the case.

Despite misgivings by many over the capital taxation measures, they were reluctant to voice their criticism. Over the next two days, the leader would be forming his government. There was not a single man or woman in the room who did not harbour some hope of getting a junior ministry at least. It was no time to antagonise him.

But John Kelly was not following the herd. He was opposed to coalition with Labour on principle. 'In today's conditions, my feeling is that the Labour element is likely to make the government's task more difficult . . . There are certain measures which might be desirable dealing with the general finances of the state, and the relationship between private enterprise and the state, which Labour cannot accept. In tough times, there is no room for the ideology of the left.' He also made clear his strong opposition to the proposed residential property tax. Moreover, he voted against the agreement. He was the only one to do so. Nor did he confine his objections to the party meeting. Afterwards he made public his misgivings about the property tax. It proposed that people with incomes over £20,000 and with homes worth over £65,000 would pay a 1.5 per cent annual tax on the value in excess of £65,000. Kelly saw it as a crude and arbitrary measure, 'neither rational nor capable of being fairly implemented'. As he saw it, it had been banged into the programme by some Labour ideologue. He pointed out some of its absurdities. Substantial wealth could be owned by people in homes valued at under £65,000, and people living in rented apartments, with huge fortunes, would also be exempt. There was little doubt that he spoke for many members of his party. For instance, a key Strategy Committee member, Frank Flannery, saw this proposal as simply screwing Fine Gael supporters. It was also seen as a blunt concession to socialism. Furthermore, immediate differences between the proposed coalition partners were emerging that Sunday night on the issue. At a press conference in Dublin, FitzGerald said that it would be the income of the main breadwinner of a household which would be reckonable for the new tax. In Limerick, Spring said it would be the aggregated household income.

The immediate focus after the proposed coalition was ratified in Limerick and Dublin, was forming a cabinet. There was ready agreement between FitzGerald and Spring on Labour getting the same number of ministries as in June 1981. For his part, the Tánaiste-elect had no experience of any economic department, and decided he would take a post he could readily grasp. Hence his choice of Environment. This was greeted with disappointment by some Fine Gael TDs who saw it as a powerful brokerage department, with its tentacles reaching into local government all over the country.

Labour had come to regard tenure of Health and Social Welfare as virtually axiomatic for a left-wing party, committed to looking after the less well-off. Deputy leader Barry Desmond took these huge spending portfolios. Labour was another department which the party was keen on holding, and Liam Kavanagh was the automatic choice. He held the same post in the first FitzGerald coalition. Frank Cluskey got Trade, Commerce and Tourism; here he looked after another Labour priority, price control.

In choosing his ministers, FitzGerald again turned to Jim Dooge and Peter Barry for advice. He asked Dooge to serve again as Foreign Minister, notwithstanding the outrage his previous appointment had provoked in the party. But FitzGerald's attitude was that Dooge had done a very good job. However, Dooge's health was not good, and he declined to serve. Given that he had refused to stand in the February general election, and in the Dublin West by-election, and had not offered himself as a candidate in November, there is no doubt that a further massive outcry would have greeted his re-appointment. Still, the story demonstrates the party leader's guts, and his capacity for being his own man.

Given the importance of EEC affairs and Northern Ireland, which came within the ambit of Foreign Affairs, he wanted somebody utterly reliable. Peter Barry was willing to take the job, and was to prove an inspired choice.

But who would get the key Finance portfolio? The writing was already on the wall for John Bruton when he was not involved in the coalition negotiations. In FitzGerald's view a number of considerations dictated a change. Given the tough decisions he knew were ahead, he feared that Bruton was too combative and fiery to work with the Labour Party. Moreover, he feared that Bruton's association with the abortive January budget would tarnish his image if he was back again in Merrion Street. Four more years of tough budgeting could ruin his political career, and blight him in the way Richie Ryan had been blighted by his period in that office.

However, Bruton was very angry, and felt he was being made a scapegoat for the January budget failure. It took some time for FitzGerald to convince him that by-passing him was not a repudiation of his term at Finance. In fact, FitzGerald regarded Bruton as one of the deputies in the party who would be in the contest to succeed him as leader when he eventually stepped down.

He now turned to another former student, Alan Dukes. A brilliant technocrat and absolutely unflappable, he would provoke less animosity from Labour. Dukes was totally surprised at his elevation. He did not regard being consulted on the negotiations with Labour as indicating that he was destined for greater things. He actually expected to be returning to Agriculture House.

Two of the biggest surprise appointments were those of Michael Noonan to Justice and Gemma Hussey to Education. Hussey was a close personal friend of FitzGerald, and a very able politician. She had been a particularly effective leader of the Seanad in his first government, but was only a TD since the previous February. Noonan was first elected in June 1981, but was a very effective deputy. He was marked down for greater things when FitzGerald included him in his front bench reshuffle in April 1982. The leader was also anxious to have somebody utterly reliable who would investigate the various security irregularities which had come to his notice.

But the biggest surprise of all among a trio of people with no previous ministerial experience whatsoever was Austin Deasy's appointment to Agriculture. Nobody was more surprised than the Waterford deputy, who frankly admitted after his selection that he knew little or nothing about agriculture, and did not know why he had been appointed. There was a lot of speculation at the time that FitzGerald was actually getting his own back on Deasy for the latter's bitter attack on his leadership the previous March. But the leader said he had chosen him for Agriculture because he was stubborn and tenacious: vital qualities for the tough negotiations at EEC level on farming.

There was consternation in many ranks of Fine Gael at the appointment. After all, Fine Gael was traditionally the farmer's party, and here was Garret appointing an ex-school teacher. At least Dukes, although a Dubliner, had been the IFA's economist, and was an expert on the EEC, where Irish farmers now looked for aid. When he got over the shock of his appointment, Deasy came to accept that FitzGerald was actually being magnanimous. Nor did he accept that his leader wanted him to fall on his face. If that was the case, then it would reflect as much on FitzGerald as on himself.

Early on, Deasy betrayed his lamentable knowledge of farming — and in the wrong place. At a function he was sitting beside Paddy O'Keeffe, editor of the *Farmers' Journal* and one of the most powerful figures in Irish agriculture. 'Tell me', said Deasy to him, 'what is the difference between the Agricultural Institute and an Foras Talúntais?' It was bad enough not knowing they were one and the same body, but confessing as much to the likes of Paddy O'Keeffe was a real gaffe. Deasy was to have a stormy relationship with the IFA and its outspoken president, Joe Rea. He once ridiculed Deasy's alleged ignorance of the industry by stating that 'if someone told the minister that cows could fly, he would ask "how high?"'

But the rugged Waterford man was tough and wiry. In time, he got to grips with his portfolio and was a fearless critic of the IFA's double standards. They were constantly complaining about any tax impositions on farming and at the same time looking for ever more hand-outs for the industry. He was also one of the few cabinet ministers to defend the need for drastic public spending cuts.

Apart from this trio of newcomers, the other cabinet members chosen by FitzGerald were all former Ministers. Pat Cooney was appointed to Defence, Paddy O'Toole returned to his old portfolio of the Gaeltacht, and this time Fisheries and Forestry were also included. Along with Liam Kavanagh, he was the only man to resume his former ministry. Jim Mitchell had been in Justice in 1981, and was one of the hardest-working members of the party. But he had also come under fierce attack from Fianna Fáil, and Seán Doherty made damaging allegations against him in the no-confidence debate in November. He revealed that a blood sample showing that a brother of Mitchell was over the permitted alcohol limit while driving had been lost in the post while the Fine Gael man was minister. 'Was the case prosecuted? I am told, and the dogs in the street are barking it, that it was not.' Doherty made other allegations of Mitchell calling in individual gardaí without the knowledge of the Commissioner. There is little doubt that the charges damaged Mitchell. Afterwards he was dubbed 'the Fixer' Mitchell by Fianna Fáil. FitzGerald switched him to Posts and Telegraphs, and Transport. Another of the surprise appointments was John Boland to the Public Service. He was not too happy with his portfolio and did not know what it would entail. But it underlined FitzGerald's commitment to reforming the civil service. Boland would be a tough opponent who would take on the entrenched rules and traditions.

As in June 1981, FitzGerald appointed his ministers at separate audiences, and this time did not repeat his inquiry about any of them being members of a secret organisation. But in subsequent letters confirming their terms of appointment, FitzGerald set down this as one of a number of requirements. Others included the obligation to inform him of any planned overseas trips. He also wanted to be informed in advance of proposed appointments to boards under the aegis of their departments.

The vocational composition of the new government was interesting. It had a distinct academic bias. FitzGerald and Dukes were economists. O'Toole, Noonan and Deasy were school teachers, and Hussey was involved with the same discipline: she had been co-founder of the English Language Institute. Cooney was a solicitor. Boland was a former auctioneer, but he had been a full-time politician since his first election to the Dáil in 1977. But a party whose core support was farming and business barely represented these interests. The only farmer was Bruton, but he was more a farm-owner than a farmer. He had been a member of the Dáil since 1969, when he was just twenty-two years old.

Peter Barry was the only businessman proper on the cabinet, being head of the famous family tea firm in Cork. Mitchell had been a computer operator with Guinness in Dublin, until his election to the Dáil in 1977.

On the Labour side, Spring was a barrister, Cluskey a butcher by trade, but later a trade union official. Kavanagh was a rate collector, and Barry Desmond a trade union official.

When the new Dáil met at 3 p.m. on 14 December, there was none of the drama and tension of the two previous hung Dáils. This time the destiny of government was not in doubt. This was underlined by the coalition's decision to oust John O'Connell from the chair. FitzGerald proposed Tom Fitzpatrick, one of the party's veterans, and Peter Barry, seconded him. O'Connell was also proposed. Fitzpatrick's nomination was carried by 86 votes to 80, a margin that was positively overwhelming when compared to the knife-edge votes of the previous eighteen months.

It was a similar formality when it came to nominations for Taoiseach. Party chairman Kieran Crotty proposed FitzGerald, and he was seconded by one of the party's nine women deputies, Nora Owen. The first vote was on the nomination of the outgoing Taoiseach, and Haughey lost that vote by 88 votes to 77. The Workers' Party and Gregory voted with the Coalition, and O'Connell and Blaney backed Fianna Fáil. The vote on FitzGerald was carried by 85 to 79. The missing TD was O'Connell, who did not vote.

The Fine Gael leader was then driven to Árus an Úachtaráin to receive his seal of office, and the Dáil resumed at 6.15 p.m. When he led his cabinet into the chamber, most comment focused on Dukes replacing Bruton and the inclusion of the three newcomers to office. FitzGerald also announced the appointment of Seán Barrett as Chief Whip, and Peter Sutherland's reappointment as Attorney-General. He would announce his Ministers of State later. Clearly he had learned the lesson of rushing all the appointments. The remaining posts he announced that evening were Peter Prendergast as Government Press Secretary, and another Strategy Committee member, Joe Jennings, as head of the Government Information Services. The old partnership of FitzGerald and Prendergast was back in business.

There were a number of disappointed deputies on the Fine Gael benches. Michael Keating and Paddy Harte had been hoping to be elevated from their junior posts of the first Coalition. Tom O'Donnell was hoping that this time he would not be overlooked. FitzGerald had written to him thanking him for standing again in Limerick East. He had polled very well again, finishing second to Des O'Malley. This time he was making sure FitzGerald had no excuses. He went to him after the election and informed the leader that if he wished to appoint him, he (O'Donnell) would be willing to serve and to give up his Euro-seat. But he received no summons. He was disappointed, but not as upset as he had been in June 1981.

The most disappointed of all was former Tánaiste and Labour leader, Michael O'Leary. He had had three separate meetings with FitzGerald in the weekend before the Dáil met. He argued strongly for his inclusion. He was the greatest coalitionist of all. He had given up his leadership of the Labour Party because he rejected their anti-coalition stance. But for his defection to Fine Gael, Haughey might be still in office. He could be a real bridge now between the two coalition parties.

Unfortunately that was not how FitzGerald, or the Labour Party, saw it. His former party colleagues were especially infuriated with O'Leary. Spring had been one of his supporters in Galway at their conference, and he and others had gone out of their way to back his stance then. But when O'Leary quit, he informed none of them. Spring learned of it the following day from a journalist who rang him up for a comment. So when he was discussing the government line-up with FitzGerald, he made it absolutely clear to him that O'Leary would not be acceptable to Labour. The Fine Gael boss was also made aware by his own party colleagues that O'Leary would also be disapproved of. He was only in the party a month, and his preferment over veteran deputies would cause problems. There would have been some chance if O'Leary had won an extra seat. But he had simply displaced another Fine Gael deputy. FitzGerald was in a dilemma. He and O'Leary had been friends for many years. But now he came to realise that 'his appointment would have been unacceptable to either party. It became clear from both sides that he could not be a member of the government. It would have been a destabilising factor.'

The next day, the Dáil elected Labour's John Ryan as Leas Ceann Comhairle, and FitzGerald completed his selection of junior ministers. Most deputies were still hopeful of inclusion on this second row. On Thursday, Seán Barrett rounded up the lucky ones and informed them that the leader wanted to see them. This time they were informed individually of their appointments. Unlike June 1981, it was the junior appointments, rather than the cabinet line-up, that was to cause consternation and alienate some party deputies for years to come.

FitzGerald decided to drop five of the junior ministers who served in his first government: Michael Keating, Michael Begley, Paddy Harte, Gerry L'Estrange and Mary Flaherty. But at least he sought to rectify his previous mistake of not speaking to those who were disappointed.

He asked Peter Barry to contact this group and tell them to come and see him. Barry would later describe it as 'one of the most difficult days of my life'. Effectively it was he who had the task of telling men like L'Estrange, Harte and Begley, all of whom were in the Dáil since his own arrival there in 1969, that they were being dropped. He informed each of them that FitzGerald wanted to see them, while making it plain that it was not for what they might assume. They were immediately aware that they were not being appointed.

With the exception of Mary Flaherty, the others were stunned and shattered. When Keating went to see FitzGerald there was a very stormy session. Keating pressed him for an explanation, but was given none. It was a totally inconclusive encounter, and Keating left the room very unhappy. Harte was equally appalled at his treatment. Like Keating, he had been very disappointed at not getting into cabinet in June 1981. Yet he had really buckled down to his junior job at Posts and Telegraphs, and was looking forward to returning there, at least. He was terribly upset. He accused FitzGerald of destroying the structures of seniority in the party. The Taoiseach told him he had to give some younger men a chance: that did not impress the Donegal man. What about fellows his own age or older, like Fergus O'Brien, Ted Nealon and Donal Creed who were being appointed? Harte felt he was done a major injustice, and for years afterwards his confidence in himself was destroyed. He faded from the Dáil chamber, and saw little point in maintaining a good performance there.

L'Estrange did not feel well enough to take a junior post even if it had been offered. But he would have liked FitzGerald to ask him. FitzGerald was upset when the Westmeath man told him this.

Only Mary Flaherty readily accepted her demotion. She had come to realise that her earlier appointment was random and out of turn. She also accepted that many more senior, and rural deputies, had felt genuinely aggrieved at her spectacular elevation on her first day in the Dáil. The period in office that followed was a hectic one. She suffered an incredible baptism of fire answering questions in the House because her senior minister, Eileen Desmond, was often out through illness. Naturally, she was disappointed at what was perceived as a demotion. But she had no row with FitzGerald over it. In fact, she felt that she needed a period on the backbenches to establish herself within her constituency. She put it behind her very quickly.

The junior appointments announced in the Dáil on that Thursday evening by FitzGerald represented a better geographical spread than had been the case in 1981. Half of them — Eddie Collins, Fergus O'Brien, Donal Creed, Michael D'Arcy, Ted Nealon and Jim O'Keeffe — had also been juniors in that government. The other six included Nuala Fennell, who was made Minister for State for Women's Affairs. That was a specific commitment in the party's programme. Two more, John Donnellan and Paddy Hegarty, had made their anger at their exclusion in 1981 very plain to FitzGerald at that time.

The other three were all younger deputies who had been first elected in 1981. Two of them, George Birmingham and Paul Connaughton, had been members of the key Constituency Review Committee. Birmingham, now just 28, had been a very able Dáil performer and won promotion to FitzGerald's front bench in April 1982. Connaughton, a Ballinasloe farmer, who had topped the poll in East Galway, was a very good choice for a junior agriculture post. That left the Chief Whip, Seán Barrett, a junior at the Taoiseach's office. He was one of the party's three deputies in the Dun Laoghaire five-seater.

It was a difficult business for FitzGerald. He was on a hiding to nothing in making his selection. He felt it was very important to establish the principle of change in the junior line-up and to give some more novice deputies the opportunity to serve in a government post. When he announced his list, the leader also informed the Dáil that the government planned to discontinue the availability of state cars for juniors. At the time, the state car fleet was costing £2.5 million annually.

A notable omission was John Kelly, who had been Minister for Trade, Commerce and Tourism in the 1981 government. Given his resignation from the front bench, his persistent argument against coalescing with Labour and his preference for a coalition with Fianna Fáil, he did not expect a call. He was right. FitzGerald did not offer him anything or inquire if he would be willing to serve. Notwithstanding his views about Labour, Kelly had enjoyed his ministerial stint and would have been tempted to say yes had he been offered a post in December 1982.

———————

As the new government got down to business, they inherited Fianna Fáil's tough budgetary plans for 1983. The difficult decisions Fine Gael had fudged and dodged during the November election campaign could no longer be avoided. In that period FitzGerald had run away from stating whether he would implement all the cuts in school transport and health, along with the imposition of local authority charges. The lame excuse was that they would have to see the books for themselves. Now it was decision time. First into the breach was Gemma Hussey, who during the Christmas holidays announced the introduction of charges for the school transport scheme.

All hell broke loose. She was attacked from all quarters. The school transport system touched every village in the remotest corner of the country, and was long recognised as political dynamite. Indeed Fianna Fáil could be excused a

233

secret pleasure at the torrent of outrage now heaped on the new government. In April 1980 their minister, John Wilson, had proposed precisely such a system of charges. He was finally forced to withdraw them. Fine Gael had denounced Wilson's plans as 'ill-conceived, anti-social and discriminatory'. Now it was simply a case of reversing roles. Hussey pleaded that she was only implementing policy already agreed by the outgoing government. Nobody wore that. Were Fine Gael now not masters of government? By the end of January, the government had rowed back severely on its plan, excluding children of social welfare recipients from the new charges.

Fiscal rectitude was going to be no easier to achieve now than in 1981. The publication of the Exchequer returns for 1982 at the start of 1983 underlined the size of the task facing FitzGerald's administration. The deficit had ended up at £988 million, £309 million greater than targeted by Fianna Fáil, in other words out of line by over 45 per cent! The main reasons for this were the shortfall in tax and the un-anticipated high level of unemployment payments. This underlined the depth of the recession. Income tax for the year was £131 million below target; VAT, £138 million short, and payments to the jobless £35 million more than targeted. The end of year out-of-work total had soared to 180,000, with the record total of 10,000 added in December.

The inherent conflict between Fine Gael and Labour policies was quickly evident. Cutting public spending was FitzGerald's priority; it was not Spring's. They had not faced up to the implications of eliminating the deficit over five years in the Good Shepherd negotiations, just as Fine Gael had not worked out for themselves how this central policy would be achieved. Again, as in July 1981, the easier option of increasing taxation, rather than cutting spending, was adopted. In an ominous pre-emotive strike, the government announced a veritable mini-budget on 7 January. Excise duties were sent soaring on the old reliables, and petrol went up by 21p per gallon. The measures would add about 1.5 per cent of the cost of living, but by moving then, rather than waiting for the real budget in February, a badly needed £10 million was recouped in January. In a full year, the measures would bring in £119 million.

The following Sunday the new Minister for Finance, Alan Dukes, disclosed that the real budget would have to raise a further £380 million. That meant total tax increases of just under £500 million in 1983: the abortive January 1982 budget had sought to raise £278 million. What was happening was very clear. It was a total replica of July 1981 and January 1982: to the extent that the books would be balanced, it would be through raising taxes rather than cutting spending.

Dukes did, however, signal his intentions to cut the deficit. Despite indications that it would be over £900 million for the year, he made clear that he wanted it cut to £750 million. The next day, Jim Mitchell warned that CIE workers might have to take a 10 per cent wage cut that year. Were Fine Gael serious at last about cutting public spending?

Perhaps. But they had reckoned without their Coalition partners. Dick Spring was in Dublin's Dr Steeven's Hospital for minor surgery and from there he issued a statement disowning the sentiments of his cabinet colleagues. There had been no agreement on the size of the deficit. He also made his anger known to the Taoiseach when the latter visited him that day. On the Wednesday, a formal government statement after a cabinet meeting pointed out that there had been no agreement on a £750 million deficit. Moreover, it added, they were concerned to avoid deflating the economy excessively, since it was already in severe recession. 'There has been concern on the part of the Taoiseach, the Tánaiste and a number of Ministers of both parties, that the figure of £750 million, which the Minister of Finance has mentioned as a target to aim at, should be taken as reflecting a government decision on a matter that is still under review.' The statement was an open rebuke to Dukes. Fine Gael's pursuit of financial orthodoxy had lasted just three days. Moreover, fundamental divisions were evidenced in a government not yet a month in office. It was an ominous development.

But it would be wrong to suggest that but for Labour, Fine Gael would definitely have pursued major spending cuts in 1983. Many of its own backbenchers would have screamed as loudly as any socialist at the prospect. For instance, on 13 January, Liam T. Cosgrave issued a statement warning that the economy should not be depressed further:

the living standards of the weak and defenceless had to be protected.

Welcome relief for the government from these inter-party rows, and the adverse media attention they attracted, came with a dramatic disclosure by Minister for Justice, Michael Noonan, on 20 January. After various teasers were tossed to the media, the eventual announcement lived up to its billing. Noonan told a press conference that the previous Haughey government had improperly tapped the phones of two journalists, Bruce Arnold and Geraldine Kennedy. Ray MacSharry had bugged a conversation back on 21 October with Dr Martin O'Donoghue. And the Garda Commissioner and his assistant, Joe Ainsworth, would be retiring on 1 February.

These dramatic findings were the results of an intensive investigation commenced by Noonan on his first day in office, 15 December. The previous evening, when the cabinet received their seals of office at Árus an Úachtaráin, they had their first meeting there immediately afterwards. FitzGerald informed Noonan that he wanted him to inquire immediately into rumours that Arnold's and Kennedy's phones were tapped. He had also heard that unsuccessful attempts had been made in the Department of Justice to destroy some documents. This would be the first opportunity to check the veracity of all the reports reaching the Fine Gael leader over the previous three months. That information was 'from several sources, and in a very complete way, of improper telephone tappings and interference with the proper role of civil servants'.

Some reports of the government inquiry appeared in the *Irish Times* before Christmas, but the country was stunned by the extent of the revelations on 20 January. It triggered off a fresh crisis within Fianna Fáil. For the third time inside a year, Haughey's leadership came under seige. His GUBU government stood disgraced. It was, by contrast, a major fillip for the new administration and for Noonan who performed admirably on the media.

From then until 7 February, the entire focus of public attention was on the bitter opposition divisions. Fianna Fáil was tearing itself asunder. For a time Haughey's demise as leader appeared inevitable. Yet when the votes were finally counted he again emerged triumphant, by 40 votes to 33. But the divisions in the party were now deeper and more bitter than ever.

The government meanwhile were finalising their budget for Wednesday, 9 February. The total disarray in Fianna Fáil, and the public's shock and gratitude to the new government, were a glorious opportunity to make really dramatic cuts in public spending. That is what some ministers wanted. Noonan had no doubt, for instance, that in that budget they could have done anything. They should have cut, cut and cut. Many other ministers in later years would look back on their 1983 budget as a glorious opportunity missed. Even Alan Dukes would later accept that they should have achieved more.

In the event, it was a complete replica of July 1981 and January 1982. In fact, it was one of the harshest budgets in decades, according to economic commentators. But the emphasis again was on massive increases in taxation, rather than on expenditure cuts. Tax bands were unchanged, meaning that inflation would attract £280 million in income tax. The top tax rate was pushed up 5 per cent to an incredible 65 per cent. That would now apply to single people at their marginal rate on an income of just £10,000. The *coup de grâce* delivered to the PAYE sector was a 'temporary' 1 per cent income levy on gross income to raise £47 million in 1983. Payroll taxes (PRSI) were upped to 7.5 per cent and were to apply to incomes up to £13,000 (the old limit had been £9,500).

The 'low' VAT rate had gone from 10 per cent in July 1981 to 15 per cent, then to 18 per cent in January 1982. Now it would go to 23 per cent. And the standard rate was also raised, from 30 per cent to 35 per cent. The Residential Property Tax got the go-ahead. Colour TVs, road tax and telephones would all be dearer. And petrol got a further wallop of 12p a gallon. From 1 March, a gallon of petrol would be £2.80, and retailers in border counties especially would be poleaxed.

The current budget deficit was set for the year at £897 million, meaning that Labour had won on this crucial issue. The overall effect of the budget was estimated to add 3 per cent to the cost of living. Social welfare payments were raised 10 per cent, but Labour's much vaunted NDC was only getting £7 million. By the end of the month, the jobless total had

237

risen to 188,000, and dole payments were costing the state £1.3 million per day.

––––––––––––

Tension between the coalition partners persisted throughout 1983 in one damaging public disagreement after another. In March, Labour had a dose of the jitters over a Social Welfare Bill to effectively cut weekly pay-related benefit. But in the face of some determined statements from FitzGerald, the government held its nerve and its majority. But Labour had two casualties. Michael Bell resigned from the parliamentary party and voted against, and after agonising all over the media for weeks, Frank Prendergast finally voted with his party.

Against a threat of fresh tax protests, FitzGerald did a state-of-the-nation television broadcast on 18 March to underline the extent of the economic crisis. He correctly identified the core problem: 'to try to start living within our means after years of national overspending'. Fine Gael's persistent failure since 1980 to map out the structural reform of the public service and state services was now glaringly obvious. It had been easy to cry 'eliminate the deficit, balance the books': it made perfect sense. But not even their painful experience in government in 1981-82 induced Fine Gael to confront the implications of this. There was no blueprint to shake out wasteful semi-states; to make the tax system more efficient and broadbased; to make the public sector more accountable and to measure the cost-benefit of state services. Instead there was the daft and inoperable residential property tax while the absence of realistic proposals for reform was underlined by the introduction of a £10 application fee for civil service jobs on 7 March.

For the second time inside two years, Fine Gael's introduction to government was proving immensely traumatic. In March and April the party was tearing itself apart over its commitment to honour the anti-abortion amendment to the constitution. That culminated in a humiliating defeat for its alternative wording for the amendment. Eight party backbenchers refused to back it. It was a very damaging time for FitzGerald in particular. His constitutional crusade was in

238

tatters. Until September, when the amendment was finally put to the people, the government presided, incoherent and divided, over a piece of legislation it really opposed. The nation rent itself in a 'moral' civil war. It was another symptom of Fine Gael's wooliness in opposition being visited with a vengeance upon it in government.

Divisions on the central economic issue went on apace. On 13 April, while tax protesters were marching in the streets of Dublin, Alan Dukes was addressing a business gathering. He said that tax relief would have to wait until the finances were balanced and warned that a whole range of subsidies, covering housing, food, agriculture and CIE, would have to be reviewed. The public would have to pay for health and education services which formerly were free. These were all part of a standard of living which, he said, could not be afforded.

Labour's response was predictable. It was time for another pow-wow between Spring and FitzGerald, and the young Labour boss laid it on the line: 'The timing and tone of the Minister's remarks are totally unacceptable to me as leader of the Labour party.' In a public speech afterwards, he rubbed it into Fine Gael: 'The Labour Party stands for high public expenditure, efficiently allocated in the interests of equality and employment recovery . . . the question of the overall tax base is of critical importance, especially in the area of capital taxation.' John Kelly must have had apoplexy when he read that. The essential, irreconcilable difference within the government could not have been more starkly stated even by the most stern critic of coalition. Fine Gael stood first and foremost for cutting public spending. Labour stood for high public expenditure. Labour wanted more capital taxation. Fine Gael, with the damage of the wealth tax in 1977 very vividly implanted in its folk memory, did not.

Again Dukes had to take it on the chin. He said his speech had been 'an analysis of issues which have to be examined in the context of re-establishing the public finances'. But no government decisions had been taken. And he added a comment not in his controversial speech: they were committed to greater equity in the tax system. Another round to the Labour Party.

To his credit, Dukes persisted in reminding the public of the fundamental problem. On 21 June he made clear his unhappiness with many semi-state companies. Profit-making must be their criterion. 'It is clear we are going to need a different approach to the operation of these companies. And it may mean restructuring operations, or closing off part of their operation.'

Another dogged trier, Jim Mitchell, presented more tangible evidence of doing something. On 30 June, he informed CIE that no overrun on their £86 million subvention for the year would be tolerated. And he ordered the board of the company to cut spending by 12 per cent in real terms over the following five years.

The half-yearly exchequer figures in early July reflected an all-too-familiar picture. Three-quarters of the year's projected deficit was already eaten up. On 3 July, Dukes made .clear that he would need about £75 million to bridge the emerging gap. He did not regard further taxation as feasible, so spending would have to be cut by that amount. By now, it would not take a great political analyst to predict the next move. Oh, no you can't, came the Labour reply.

'There are other ways of dealing with the shortfall situation', insisted Frank Cluskey. What about capital taxation? Barry Desmond, battling to keep his huge Health and Social Welfare budgets, wanted to know if farmer taxation was sufficient. To resolve the problem, the cabinet took off for Barretstown Castle in Co. Kildare for two days in mid July, where there was a great deal of haggling about spending cuts or new taxes.

The fruits of that were a hotch-potch of measures. The deficit was revised upwards by £53 million to £950 million. Another 5p was added to the packet of cigarettes and £3 million was to be collected in farmers' health contributions. A planned family income supplement for the low-paid would be delayed. The government's barrenness of ideas was revealed in Dukes' comment: 'We have searched every area, looked in every corner, scraped the bottom of the barrel.' The package of measures was to yield £67 million.

And what about spending cuts? The fifteen junior ministers were to lose their state cars from October, as FitzGerald had promised earlier. Instead they would receive a mileage allowance. And the government state cars would be reduced in size.

This was piddling stuff beside the really big items of public spending, like public sector pay. Here the government was making no real progress. On 1 September, a new pay deal, the 23rd round, commenced. It was to run for nine months, after a brief pay pause. Totalling 8 per cent, it helped push the public sector pay bill to £2,400 million for the year. That was 9.8 per cent higher than the year before. Yet inflation was falling steadily, being down to 9.2 per cent in the year to mid-May, the lowest rate since 1978.

Despite all the public clashes and painful climbdowns, it became graphically clear in September 1983 that Fine Gael and Labour still did not understand each other's priorities, or how they might be reconciled. The Cabinet was again trying to grapple with the provisional departmental estimates for 1984. Addressing a Junior Chamber meeting in Carlow, on Friday, 23 September, FitzGerald made clear his priorities: there was no room for increased taxation; the next year's budget would have to concentrate on spending cuts. On the following Sunday, on RTE radio, he went further. The budget would have to yield spending cuts of half a billion pounds. Some semi-state companies would have to be shut down if they were uneconomic.

Labour were furious. Spring felt his party was being pressurised publicly to go along with Fine Gael policy. A total cabinet split was the upshot. On the following Friday, 30 September, Spring decided they would boycott a cabinet session. Two of his ministers, Barry Desmond and Liam Kavanagh, were out of the country. He phoned up Frank Cluskey and asked him to meet him. They would not be going to Government Buildings. Labour felt that Jim Mitchell and Austin Deasy, in particular, were pushing for cuts. Spring now got in touch with FitzGerald. 'We are going to pull out of government', he told him. The two men met, and Spring laid it on the line. There was no way Labour was going along with half a billion pound spending cuts. Eventually, he and Cluskey returned to the cabinet table later that day. It was the most difficult showdown between the parties. But the upshot was yet another Labour victory. It was agreed there would be only one more ministerial statement on the estimates: a speech that night by Spring. Otherwise, there would be no other public comment until the estimates were finally decided.

The Labour leader delivered that speech in Millstreet. Earlier he had sent a copy to FitzGerald. It again hammered home the different priorities of the coalition partners. The government agreement to eliminate the deficit over five years was subject to 'prevailing economic conditions'. Spring said they had to strike a balance between borrowings and spending cuts. 'But in doing this, the government must consider where the cuts will fall. Will they be on staff, on services, on benefits, and what will be the implications of those cuts?' And they also had to look at possibly widening the tax base into capital taxation.

He was plainly making Fine Gael do what they had failed to do themselves: face up to the implications of reducing the budget deficit by cutting public spending. He also stressed that no government decisions had been taken. 'We are committed to correcting the public finances, but to do so in a way that does not impede our recovery and that does not damage the social fabric of our country. There are no easy answers to this dilemma, and no magic figures that can be pulled out of a hat. We will do it slowly and will do it with care. Any other way would be madness.'

It was a blunt put-down for Fine Gael. The implications were clear. Fine Gael was in government on the sufferance of the Labour party. The Labour party did not accept Fine Gael's economic policy and was therefore vetoing it. FitzGerald had a choice: to pursue fiscal rectitude or to keep power. He and his colleagues chose the latter option.

These inter-party rows brought home the different priorities of the two parties. Spring led a rank-and-file membership that was not nearly as committed to coalition as they had been, even in 1981. They did not want to merge their party and policy differences around the cabinet table. Therefore, Labour did not hesitate to go public on these policy showdowns. They wanted greater capital taxation and a bigger tax yield from farmers and the self-employed. On the other hand, Fine Gael were totally opposed to capital taxation. They saw the business and farming communities as their natural constituencies. The business sector, in particular, had some very discreet but effective ways of conveying their displeasure to Fine Gael politicians and backroom boys. In time, Labour came to realise that the senior party also had a bottom line in government: opposition to capital taxation. But if one party vetoed public spending cuts and the other vetoed tax increases, the result was utter stagnation and inertia.

Spring's Millstreet speech was a unique criticism of FitzGerald. The man in whom the public had reposed so much confidence as an economics wizard was being told by young Spring that his nostrums were madness. The public, too, were beginning to realise that the Fine Gael boss did not have all the answers. Just as Haughey had flattered to deceive with his January 1980 television broadcast, so now FitzGerald was proving a disappointment. Of course, the constraints imposed by Labour were a part of the problem. But there were no real indications that Fine Gael on their own would have made much more progress.

There were occasions, indeed, where Fine Gael backbenchers actually turned to Labour ministers to head off unpalatable decisions. It was Labour which effectively saved the Tuam Sugar Factory, much to the relief of many western Fine Gael deputies. Dick Spring would readily acknowledge there was no real political capital for his party in Galway East. On another occasion, Jim Mitchell criticised the lavish Great Southern Hotels, which the government was threatening to close. Michael Begley, Fine Gael's South Kerry deputy, was none too happy. He went to Spring and suggested he go to Ballyfermot and make a speech critical of government backing for factories there. One of the Great Southern Hotels was in Begley's constituency.

The Millstreet speech did not mark the end of conflict between the parties. However, the ultimate showdown was much more a clash of two men who epitomised the different approaches of Fine Gael and Labour. John Bruton and Frank Cluskey were tough, abrasive defenders of their respective views. Ironically, although they clashed fiercely, Bruton came to have great respect for Cluskey. He would stick with a decision when it was agreed. But there could be no agreement between them on the question of how natural gas from the

Kinsale Head field would best be distributed in Dublin.

As Minister for Energy, the matter came under Bruton's control. He had inherited a major refinancing package for the almost bankrupt Dublin Gas Company. This would enable it to distribute the new gas supply. By the autumn of 1983, the financial rescue package amounted to £126 million in bank loans, state grants and rebates on the cost of natural gas. But Cluskey, a staunch socialist, was opposed to baling out a private company: he wanted the government to go all the way and nationalise it. Bruton was equally ideologically convinced — against nationalisation. He argued that while the state's involvement was indeed very great, it was still limited. Nationalisation would mean having to compensate the shareholders. Moreover, the company would be ultimately liable for the £60 million in banks loans in the package. The proposed arrangement would also give the state up to 80 per cent of the eventual profits of Dublin Gas. The nub of the matter, however, was that Bruton favoured less — not more — state enterprise.

Through successive cabinet sessions there was no resolution of the conflict. Cluskey's Labour colleagues were supporting him, but purely as a matter of party solidarity. None of them had the same ideological hang-ups on the issue. The stalemate was suddenly broken on Thursday 9 December when Cluskey resigned from the government over the Dublin Gas Company deal 'and its implications'.

The government was stunned, and Spring and his colleagues became especially windy. Cluskey, a former party leader, on the backbenches would be the immediate focus of adulation by all the party's anti-coalition elements. The former minister immediately maintained that there was more at stake than Dublin Gas. The government's entire policy on natural resources was at issue. There were dark suggestions that Bruton was about to make concessions to the multinational oil companies regarding off-shore exploration.

Spring moved quickly after the resignation. He said that his party's continuation in government was not in doubt, but he also pressed FitzGerald for a reallocation of government portfolios to reassure his party. He wanted nothing less than control of the Department of Energy. Naturally Bruton

244

strongly and strenuously objected. FitzGerald wanted Spring and Bruton to discuss the matter directly, but the Labour leader would not. It was a matter for the Taoiseach to resolve. Bruton was adamant that, as Minister for Energy, he decided policy. He was totally opposed to a portfolio switch so directly linked to Cluskey's departure. Perhaps in six months time, but not just then.

In the end, however, FitzGerald insisted that Energy must go to the Labour Party. Bruton was so angry that he considered resigning. But resigning was not his style, and in the end, he ate humble pie and got on with the job. The upshot was a re-shuffle announced by FitzGerald to the Dáil on 14 December, exactly a year since he became Taoiseach. Spring became Minister for Energy. His Environment post went to Liam Kavanagh, and junior environment minister, Ruairi Quinn, took over at Labour.

Bruton retained Industry, and in an ironic twist, he also got Cluskey's former departmental responsibilities at Trade, Commerce and Tourism. In fact, Labour would have pre-ferred to acquire Industry, since it controlled the proposed National Development Corporation. But Cluskey's resignation forced the issue, and pressurised them to demand Energy.

Another indication of the shock-waves now felt by the government was a belated re-writing of the budget. Before Cluskey had left, about 90 per cent of it was agreed. It in-cluded a proposed cut of £30 million in the projected food subsidies bill of £96 million in 1984. Now, after Christmas, Labour nervousness led to pressure to rescind this move. Joe Bermingham and Mervyn Taylor pressed Spring on the matter, and the upshot was the retention of the full subsidies. The dates of social welfare increases were altered slightly to make up the loss in revenue. Pressure by Fine Gael to extend VAT to footwear and clothing was also abandoned.

Thus any prospect of a really serious start to tackling the budget deficit was postponed for yet another year. The deficit had finally overrun its target for 1983 and ended up at £1,085 million, £135 million more than the revised target set in July. The second Dukes budget, on 25 January 1984, was described by him as a 'neutral' package. There were marginal income tax improvements, and the food subsidies were retained in full. The deficit was set at £1,089 million for the year.

Eliminating the current budget deficit would be easier stated than achieved. The so-called 'neutral budget' had nothing to do with this central policy target. It was all about preventing further inter-party unrest. Through it, the coalition rediscovered its unsteady equilibrium. Spring would later say of the 1984 budget: 'We divided nothing equally.'

14

'We Knew We Couldn't Trust You'

Alice Glenn was nobody's fool. In October 1982, she sat at the Fine Gael árd-fheis listening to a debate on the proposed constitutional amendment on abortion, and she knew some of her colleagues were trying to weasel out of promises they had previously made. Most of all, she knew that Garret FitzGerald was opposed to the referendum. Alice thought that it was time to give Garret a little reminder.

When her turn came to speak, she recalled that 'Garret FitzGerald was the first leader of any party — back in April 1981 — to give a specific commitment to hold a referendum'. Therefore, the motion before the árd-fheis — expressing opposition to the amendment — was nothing less than a subtle attempt to undermine the leader! Just who was trying to undermine whom at this point is not at all clear, but Alice Glenn was putting down her marker.

If FitzGerald now found himself hoist with his own petard, he only had himself to blame. Back in April 1981, in the run-up to the June election of that year, he and Gemma Hussey had met a small delegation from the recently formed Pro-Life Amendment Campaign (PLAC) and without consulting anyone else in Fine Gael, or even playing for time, they had there and then given a commitment to hold a referendum. The June 1981 election manifesto duly announced that

> Fine Gael is unalterably opposed to the legalisation of abortion, and in government will initiate a referendum to guarantee the right to life of the unborn child.

The PLAC movement was a coalition of various existing bodies, including the Irish Catholic Doctors' Guild, the Irish Association of Lawyers for the Defence of the Unborn, the

Irish Pro-Life Movement, the Guild of Catholic Nurses and — most vociferous of all — the Society for the Protection of the Unborn Child (SPUC). They were concerned lest the existing clamour for contraceptives and some form of divorce be followed by a call for the legalisation of abortion. As they saw it, the danger was that the Oireachtas could repeal the existing legal prohibition on abortion — an Act of 1861 — without direct recourse to the people. Moreover, it was feared that either a Supreme Court or a European Court judgment could overturn the 1861 Act. The referendum was designed to block these possibilities.

FitzGerald's hasty concession to PLAC was motivated by a number of factors. At that stage the proposed PLAC amendment read:

> The state recognises the absolute right to life of every unborn child from conception, and accordingly guarantees to respect and protect such right by law.

As FitzGerald saw it, this would merely have the effect of taking power from the Supreme Court and giving it to the Oireachtas. He saw nothing wrong with that. In addition, he personally abhorred abortion. There was also, however, a political consideration: with an election imminent, he was concerned at how a rejection of PLAC's request might affect the voters. He did not want to be smeared as someone who was 'soft' on abortion. Fine Gael had good reason to be nervous about this: the echoes from the Maria Stack affair of the previous March could still be heard.

Despite the specific commitment to a referendum in Fine Gael's election manifesto, the 'Programme for Government' agreed with the Labour Party in the wake of the June 1981 victory made no reference to it. Labour would not stand for it and FitzGerald was not concerned to press it.

In August 1981, Dr Julia Vaughan, the chairperson of PLAC, wrote to FitzGerald — by now the Taoiseach — to enquire what had happened to the promised amendment. He replied that the Attorney-General, Peter Sutherland, was examining the matter.

Six weeks later, on Sunday, 27 September, FitzGerald declared in an RTE radio interview that he wanted 'to lead a crusade, a republican crusade to make this a genuine republic, on the principles of Tone and Davis'. Stressing his own Northern Protestant background on his mother's side, he declared that one of the primary reasons he was in politics was to tackle the partition of sectarianism we had built up against the North. Referring to Haughey's Family Planning Act, he said: 'we expect the Northern Unionists to join a state, which in 1979, was bringing in laws based on the theology of one church. Now that has to change, and what I want to do is lead public opinion towards that.'

He spoke of a comprehensive review of the constitution, including the possible removal of Articles 2 and 3 which enshrined the territorial claim to the north. PLAC leaders instantly became concerned that this approach would submerge their demand for an immediate anti-abortion amendment. Julia Vaughan wrote to the Taoiseach in November looking for a meeting.

Their fears were well founded. Immediately after the 'constitutional crusade' broadcast, FitzGerald set up a special committee under the Attorney-General, Peter Sutherland, which embarked on an article by article review of the constitution. Many leading academics were involved. It was all linked with FitzGerald's and Sutherland's attempts to build bridges with northern unionists. Sutherland had felt strongly that the April commitment on the pro-life amendment was wrong, and made this clear to FitzGerald. From the outset of the PLAC campaign there were complaints that it was a sectarian demand: it would seek to enshrine an article conforming specifically to Catholic teaching on abortion. With the constitutional crusade so firmly and dramatically launched, there was little doubt that FitzGerald now wanted to get away from the April commitment.

PLAC finally got their meeting with him on 10 December. They pressed him to enact their specific amendment to the constitution, and not to wait on any overall review he might have planned. He kicked for touch by promising to come back to them by the following February. Some PLAC people were in no doubt that the Taoiseach was trying to back away from his pre-election commitment.

The whole affair got submerged by the dramatic fall of the government in January 1982. However, PLAC and SPUC again canvassed many of the candidates in the ensuing February election, and PLAC also wrote to Haughey and FitzGerald seeking fresh commitments to the referendum. Haughey said he would enact it in 1982, if returned to power. FitzGerald showed a more indefinite approach this time, saying it would be done in the lifetime of the next Dáil. A fortnight into office, Haughey informed Fine Gael backbencher Liam T. Cosgrave that a referendum to guarantee the right to life of the unborn child would be brought forward that year, and he invited PLAC to submit possible drafts to his Attorney-General.

Fine Gael backbencher, Alan Shatter, a lawyer, urged Haughey to use the occasion of the referendum for other necessary amendments also. The Taoiseach replied that he had given a specific commitment, as had his predecessor, 'to bring forward legislation to enable the constitutional referendum to take place on this specific issue without regard to other matters'. That undertaking had been given in the context of the general election, 'and on the basis of which I now feel committed to implement it in the Dáil.'

By July, there was a growing body of opposition to the proposed amendment. Some members of the medical profession were concerned about a possible assault on established medical practices, involving ectopic pregnancy for instance. Other doctors were expressing concern over the future of certain contraceptives, including the IUD, which some people considered abortifacient. Protestant churchmen were concerned about enshrining in the constitution a specifically Catholic interpretation of the beginning of life.

The core of the conflict was the PLAC view that life begins at the moment of conception, and should be totally protected from that stage. The Protestant churches were not at all as dogmatic. In the case of say, profound foetal abnormality (as in anacephalic cases), or where there could be dangers to the mother's physical or mental health, they saw a conflict of rights. PLAC would admit of no such dilemma.

By now, it was also evident that Garret FitzGerald was anxious to disengage from his earlier commitments. He now favoured a complete overhaul of the 1937 constitution. Indeed any other stance, especially given the growing Protestant unease, would have made a total nonsense of his constitutional crusade. The state of play was summed up in July 1982 by journalist, Pat Brennan, writing in *Magill* magazine:

> The total capitulation of the politicians was the first real victory for the Pro-Life Amendment Campaign, and it was a more substantial victory than many larger, more representative, popular movements have ever hoped to gain.
>
> But PLAC suffered a real setback when all the main Protestant churches came out publicly against the referendum. Neither Charles Haughey nor Garret FitzGerald want to be seen to be insensitive to the sincerely held views of the Protestant churches. However, they have backed themselves into a corner, and there is no way the Pro-Life campaigners, having won the battle so far, are going to let them out.

Whatever scruples the Fianna Fáil government had about the minority churches they did not get in the way, however, of pressing on with the amendment. The task was assigned to Michael Woods, the Minister for Health. On 1 October, he announced that the necessary legislation would be introduced in the Dáil term beginning at the end of that month.

Before that, the Fine Gael árd-fheis was scheduled for 16-17 October, and the agenda contained a motion from Dublin South expressing opposition to the amendment. FitzGerald and the front bench decided that they would neither support nor oppose the amendment as such, but instead would back a more wide-ranging review of the constitution, of which this could be one element.

On the Saturday evening of the árd-fheis, FitzGerald gave his presidential address in an atmosphere which was virtually that of a general election rally. The party had launched its major economic document, 'Jobs for the Eighties', only the previous Thursday, and there was widespread confidence that they would topple Haughey's minority government when the Dáil resumed. In his speech, FitzGerald made much of the Constitutional Crusade: 'The time has come to dismantle the

251

mentality of partition and restore the genuine republic, a republic of pluralism and tolerance.' But he also noted that there were some people who apparently saw a contradiction between that objective and the proposal 'to strengthen the protection of life in our constitution'. This, he declared, was to create a false dilemma:

> *Any* constitutional review must in all common sense tackle the defective form of the existing provisions of our constitution which purport to protect *only* the life of the citizen: a proposition which surely no person, and no church, would wish to perpetuate. All life, whether of citizens, or of people of other nationality, whether born or unborn, should be protected by our constitution.

FitzGerald went on to deny that the proposed amendment was 'an attempt to impose on others the specific theology of one church concerning the details of what constitutes abortion', saying that this false impression had been created by the government's deplorable failure to consult the various churches from the start. Finally, he went on to condemn 'an insidious whispering campaign designed to suggest that some people in our party, or that I myself, support abortion', and he reiterated his own total opposition to it.

FitzGerald's performance on the abortion issue was a mixture of sophistry and evasion. If this speech were to be taken at its face value, he was in fact launching a campaign which would obscure his real intentions: he wanted a pluralist constitution, yet he appeared to regard the pro-life amendment as being non-sectarian. He failed completely to state whether he was still committed to the specific pro-life amendment which he had explicitly endorsed a year earlier. He was trying to keep all his options open.

The next day, the árd-fheis debated the Dublin South motion opposing the referendum. This time, in contrast to FitzGerald's performance the night before, the speeches were clear and unambiguous. Young Fine Gael, in particular, were extremely direct in their support of the Dublin South motion. One of their leading members, Barbara Cahalane, spoke of the party's TDs who had succumbed to the hysteria being generated by the PLAC:

> I abhor their lack of courage. It is the sort of spineless-
> ness that I would normally associate with another party.
> It is leading from behind. . . . Let us in Fine Gael have
> the courage to reject this amendment and instead take
> on the problem of preventing abortion in a positive way.

It was at this point that Alice Glenn materialised on the platform to deliver her little reminder to Garret.

Jim Mitchell replied to the debate. He reiterated Fine Gael's
opposition to abortion and their commitment 'to achieve the
required protection of all human life, born or unborn'. Rather
incongruously, he added that 'Because our commitment is so
clear and unequivocal we refuse to be harrassed or stampeded
into supporting any amendment which could be left open to
the construction by some that it was sectarian'. This brought
some interruptions from the floor. A few delegates began to
shout comments. 'We knew we couldn't trust you.' 'Keep
your word.' Sitting beside Mitchell, FitzGerald looked dis-
tinctly uneasy. Mitchell went on to talk about the party's
commitment to a united Ireland, to pluralism, to the Constitutional Crusade, and to an overall review of the constitution. He suggested that the presidential and European
elections scheduled to take place eighteen months later
would be a suitable occasion on which also to put constitutional amendments to the people: it would allow time
for balanced consideration 'of the complex side factors of
the amendment'.

Like FitzGerald's presidential address, Mitchell's speech
was less than frank and contained more than a little sophistry.
Nevertheless, he had succeeded in abandoning the earlier
commitment to the pro-life lobby and had established a
clear-cut and specific alternative. Fine Gael wanted a longer
time span for debate, and a multi-amendment approach to
the constitution. Alice Glenn and the PLAC people mightn't
like it: it was a fundamental U-turn on FitzGerald's commitments of June 1981 and February 1982. But at least the
debate had not split the party, and had left it with an alternative policy to Fianna Fáil's — albeit one which held many
hidden dangers.

All in all, it had been the liveliest session of the two-day árd-fheis.

As the political parties awaited the probable collapse of the Haughey government on the resumption of the Dáil on 27 October, the referendum controversy raged apace. Not only churchmen, but lawyers, doctors, teachers and other leading professions were dividing into pro- and anti-amendment groupings. However, despite the bitter atmosphere being engendered, Charlie Haughey informed the Dáil that there would be a Referendum Bill that term.

On the night of 2 November, the eve of a two-day confidence debate which looked certain to end in defeat for Fianna Fáil, the government issued the proposed wording of the anti-abortion amendment. It read:

> The state acknowledges the right to life of the unborn and, with due regard to the equal right to life of the mother, guarantees in its laws to respect, and, as far as practicable, by its laws to defend and vindicate that right.

Fine Gael announced that it was referring the wording for consideration to its former Attorney-General, Peter Sutherland, and would give its verdict in a few days. However, with an election beckoning, short-term electoral considerations were now going to challenge that loftier approach to the issue announced just a fortnight earlier at the árd-fheis.

From the very outset the proposed wording came in for serious criticism from anti-amendment sources. On the very night of its publication, for example, Senator Mary Robinson was speaking at a meeting of 'Teachers Against the Amendment' (that reflects the kind of division that arose on the issue). She saw the wording full of uncertainty, and thought that it would throw the whole business back into the lap of the courts. The wording failed to define when life began, or what 'due regard' for the mother's life might mean. It could also threaten the constitutionality of the 1861 Act, which was an unqualified prohibition without regard to the right to life of the mother. She also felt that the wording could be seen as sectarian.

In brief, there was no shortage of cogent opinions which cast fundamental doubts on the Fianna Fáil wording. There was plenty there for Fine Gael to think about and to reflect on. Yet less than twenty-four hours later, as the Catholic bishops and PLAC and SPUC were welcoming the wording, Fine Gael also unreservedly approved it. They even went further.

FitzGerald made himself available for an RTE news programme, where he announced that he was relieved at the wording. It was along the lines he had pressed for, and Fine Gael and himself would be able to give it their total support. 'We were concerned that it should be drafted in such a way as to protect life, rather than be negative and sectarian in nature.' There was no possible disagreement with the government, he stressed.

Fine Gael's dramatic about-turn was inspired by political opportunism. Confident that they were about to topple the government, most Fine Gael politicians did not want to risk a single vote being lost: suggestions that they were soft on abortion would lose quite a few. When the wording was first published, FitzGerald had contacted Sutherland, who refused to give an opinion and urged that no precipitate statement should be made. He also reiterated his long-standing opposition to the whole idea. The party leader was later to confirm this to the parliamentary party when the subject had become deeply divisive.

The next morning both the front bench and the full parliamentary party considered the issue. The proposed wording was approved with unseemly haste. It was imperative to get it out of the way. However, two of the party's young barristers, George Birmingham and Alan Shatter, urged that they should take more time over it. They would be seen to be serious if they gave it more consideration. But others were more impatient. Gemma Hussey expressed great relief at the wording. It was agreed to go for the fullest endorsement of it.

The following day, the government fell, and another election campaign was under way. Haughey identified his newly minted economic policy, 'The Way Forward', and the pro-life amendment as the major issues. 'I don't trust him', he said of FitzGerald's approval for the amendment and Fine Gael's commitment to a referendum by 31 March. Elsewhere FitzGerald was reiterating his acceptance, and described the wording as 'very sensible'.

255

In contrast was the line taken by the new leader of the Labour Party. When Dick Spring launched his election programme, he had been Labour leader for just nine days. He was faced with many media forecasts of annihilation for his party at the polls. But he was not panicked into endorsing the amendment.

He reiterated his party's opposition to abortion, and called on Haughey to desist from making it an election issue. He also denied the outgoing Taoiseach's allegation that Labour wanted the amendment dropped as a precondition to possible coalition with Fine Gael. Spring also said he had reservations about the proposed wording, since it appeared to be open to many interpretations. He indicated his preference for a general review of the constitution.

It was a very brave stance, contrasting sharply with the Fine Gael cave-in. He was running the risk that his reservations would be equated with being pro-abortion by the more hysterical advocates of the amendment. In fact, in his preparation for that vital first press conference as party leader, Spring had spent about 90 per cent of his time on the amendment. Fine Gael knew it could carry its party with a pro-amendment stance, but he risked serious Labour divisions whether he came down for or against it. He consulted widely with various experts. These included his doctor brother, Arthur, and two barrister friends, John Rogers and Dermot Gleeson. The general consensus was that there were serious defects with the amendment. But given the nationwide hysteria on the subject, his policy stance took real guts.

During the ensuing campaign, the amendment was not really an issue. Fine Gael's acceptance of the Fianna Fáil wording therefore had the merit of not allowing Haughey to debase a campaign into an irrelevant catfight about abortion. It is difficult, therefore, to make a complete judgment of the Fine Gael failure to stand their ground at this juncture. Many of their deputies were mighty glad to be able to point to their endorsement when the amendment was raised on the doorsteps. The subsequent political wisdom of their parliamentary party was that it had been necessary to prevent Haughey blackguarding Fine Gael, since they were just as opposed to abortion as Fianna Fáil.

For his part, FitzGerald decided to refer again to the issue in a statement on 19 November — five days before polling. He was replying to three occasions where Haughey 'had personally vilified my motives or actions', with deliberately false statements.

Haughey, he said, had sought to mislead the people concerning his views on the abortion referendum. 'As I have said repeatedly, the constitutional amendment will be brought before the country by my government by 31 March next.'

When the election duly returned a FitzGerald-led coalition, he had no option but to persist with the amendment. It appeared in the Programme for Government, with the promise of the referendum by 31 March, although the Labour Party reserved the right to a free vote. The commitment was very specific. The necessary legislation would adopt the 'pro-life amendment published by the outgoing government which has the backing of the two largest parties in the Dáil'.

The political embarrassment it contained for the government was dramatically underlined on 17 January, when the new Minister for Health, Barry Desmond said that he would not be introducing the Amendment Bill. In fact, he stated he would be voting against it. Desmond stressed his opposition to abortion, but made it clear that he wanted to repeal most sections of the existing family planning legislation, and favoured non-medical contraceptives being available without prescription.

Another member of the government was also busy. The Attorney-General, Peter Sutherland, had commenced a detailed examination of the Amendment Bill of his own volition. He sought the assistance of expert legal colleagues and representatives of some of the main churches, including the Catholic Church. He also got copies of US Congressional hearings on the abortion issue. Personally, he was totally opposed to abortion, but also believed the existing constitution adequately ruled out its possible legalisation.

Soon he came to the conclusion that the proposed wording was dangerously defective. It was riddled with ambiguities. By the end of January he had given his opinion to FitzGerald. The Taoiseach was now faced with a dreadful dilemma. He could, of course, have buried Sutherland's opinion and simply gone ahead with the existing wording. Not to do so would bring the wrath of the pro-amendment lobby and Fianna Fáil crashing down on him. In the end he decided to accept the objections raised by Sutherland. At this stage also the attorney-general had devised the essentials of an alternative wording: one that would exclude the courts from ever deciding on abortion, but rather leave the matter to the legislature.

By the beginning of February, with the Amendment Bill due to come before the Dáil soon, it was plain that all the main Protestant churches were strongly against the wording. Dean Victor Griffin of St Patrick's Cathedral in Dublin, said that while the pro-life people pushing the amendment were stating it was not sectarian, 'if it had been left to the Protestant churches, it would never have been pushed at all. So to that extent it is sectarian.' He added that it gave a 'particular confessional dimension to the constitution'.

This was deeply embarrassing to FitzGerald. All the ghosts of his earlier pluralist commitments and sentiments seemed to appear to him in the Dáil on 2 February when Tony Gregory questioned him about the proposed referendum. Did he intend to include other constitutional amendments with the pro-life one?

> *Taoiseach:* No.
> *Mr Gregory:* Does this indicate a significant change of policy and direction on the part of the Taoiseach, given the opposition of the Protestant churches to this sectarian amendment. This would seem to be contrary to the Taoiseach's much talked about Constitutional Crusade with the apparent aim of reconciliation?
> *Taoiseach:* I thought it better to take a number of amendments together. But events developed in a different way and as a result, this amendment is being taken at this stage.
> *Mr Gregory:* . . . Does he not accept that this amendment at this time will exacerbate . . . divisions and go contrary to his own often stated policy? . . . .
> *Taoiseach:* I hope that will not be the case . . .

The painful dilemma was back. Fine Gael was about to enter

a convulsive, self-destructive period; one that would blight its subsequent performance in government, and seriously damage FitzGerald's credibility and self-confidence. He had made a major blunder of leadership and — worst of all — the consequences were going to drag on for a long, long time. On Sunday 6 February, Dick Spring disclosed that he would be voting against the amendment in the Dáil. It was bad law and divisive and alienating of the minority. He said the existing law covered the situation very well.

Dissatisfaction within the ranks of Fine Gael began to emerge that same day. One of the most able backbenchers, Maurice Manning, said on RTE that his party and Fianna Fáil should allow a free vote on the issue. He also suggested that the proposed referendum could be deferred from March to the autumn, and held in conjunction with the expected presidential election. And he expressed concern about the opposition of the Protestant churches. But the party's chief whip, Seán Barrett, said that no member of the party had questioned the amendment commitment at parliamentary party meetings since the election.

At this stage government TDs especially were being subjected to the most vitriolic mail from pro-amendment people around the country. Any opponents or waverers on the measure were specially singled out. Manning was one of these. His radio interview triggered a fresh onslaught. One letter came from a parish priest in Co. Tipperary, who signed his name. It reflects the hysteria and abuse of language then prevalent. It read:

> Your cringing interview on RTE last Sunday re the forthcoming referendum to help guarantee the right of life of the defenceless, unborn child saddened and indeed appalled me. And of course your use of the opposition in-word 'sectarian' was sad in the extreme. If it is sectarian to be pro-life amendment, surely it is also sectarian (Protestant sectarianism) to be against it. Are you courting the Protestant vote or what?
>
> Remember also the issue is *not* the stopping of Irish women going to England for abortions — that's a red herring. The issue is that the slaughter-house of the

unborn may *never* be set up in *Ireland* legally. That's the issue at stake. If to ensure that this may not happen is *bad law*, then I'm a monkey's uncle.

For forty years I have voted Fine Gael. If the liberal, anti-Roman Catholic views on grave moral issues such as divorce, contraception, and abortion – i.e. Garret's Crusade – get any further footing in Fine Gael manifestos, my vote and the votes of many more will *not* support the party.

P.S. Of course you're against abortion like the Protestant churches *BUT....*

The Minister for Justice, Michael Noonan, introduced the second stage of the Amendment Bill on 9 February. He said the aim of the amendment was to prevent legalised abortion ever becoming part of our law. But the more startling point he made was that the government was open to possible alterations of the amendment wording. Sutherland's reservations had been taken on board by the government. But would the public accept their *bona fides* on the issue? Was the party weakening in its resolve? The pro-amendment lobby was vociferous in demanding that the wording be left alone. Fianna Fáil naturally came out against any change.

The following weekend, Young Fine Gael held their annual conference in Galway, and FitzGerald and most of his cabinet were there. The amendment was a prominent issue: the Young Fine Gael national executive had already come out strongly against it. As their national youth officer, Rona Fitzgerald, saw it, the executive regarded the amendment as being against everything they stood for in politics. It implied no trust in the people, and it was bowing to the wishes of a vociferous minority. The junior party also had good contacts with Northern Ireland. Motions on the North and law reform preceded consideration of the Amendment on the Saturday night, and heightened opposition to it.

There were to be only two speakers for, and two against, the amendment resolution. But such was the clamour on the matter that the 800 or so attendance decided that eight speakers would be heard. Eventually well over an hour was devoted to the subject. Young Fine Gaelers simply savaged

FitzGerald, and in the process, the eight or nine senior and junior ministers on the platform with him, including Alan Dukes, John Bruton, John Boland, Gemma Hussey and Nuala Fennell.

The speakers included Barbara Cahalane, who had already challenged FitzGerald on the issue at the árd-fheis. She said the issue reeked of the 1951 Mother and Child controversy with the Catholic Church and was an attempt to rebuild a confessional state. 'How will the Constitutional Crusade survive in that environment', she asked.

She was not the only one to note that dichotomy. Sally Ann Godson, another young Dublin delegate, looked directly at FitzGerald and pleaded with him to drop the amendment.

> You have won an election to a very large extent on the very grounds of your integrity and credibility. Can you not see that the amendment is a betrayal of the faith that has been put in you by members of the electorate and the members of Young Fine Gael?
>
> Can you not see that honesty pays off; that if you come out and say you were mistaken when you initially supported this amendment, you would in fact gain credibility.

Another delegate pleaded 'for God's sake cancel the referendum'. The conference overwhelmingly rejected the amendment, and just for good measure came out in favour of a divorce referendum.

To his credit, FitzGerald delayed his scheduled departure to another engagement. He did not seek to avoid the flak. He was visibly moved by the passion of the junior wing of the party which he had personally called into being and licensed to be outspoken, courageous and independent.

He disregarded much of the prepared script he had brought with him, and spoke informally. In effect, he asked their forgiveness. He said he understood their concerns and feelings, and defended their right to express them. They had reminded him why he was in politics and he thanked them for that. Despite the large gathering, it was a moving, even intimate, twist to a bitter evening. The hall was emotionally drained by it all, and there was little vigour for the dinner and disco

261

afterwards. This sense of despair, mingled with admiration for FitzGerald, also pervaded the next day's session of the conference.

However, some of FitzGerald's cabinet colleagues were not as happy with the notion of prostrating themselves before Young Fine Gael. They were probably also concerned to hear the party leader tell the Galway audience that more attention would have to be given to legal difficulties identified in the existing wording by the attorney-general.

When the parliamentary party met on the following Tuesday, 15 February, a number of ministers, including John Bruton and Paddy Cooney, were critical of the Young Fine Gael. National youth officer, Rona Fitzgerald, was made aware that many of them felt Young Fine Gael had too much autonomy. Peter Barry was another senior minister who was critical of the youth movement. However, Ms Fitzgerald took the view that the traumatic weekend in Galway and the showdown with the party leader, had brought the middle ground of the parliamentary party to its senses, and that the Young Fine Gael conference was responsible for the review of the entire issue which was now forced on the senior party. It would, she believed, culminate in their abandoning the original amendment wording, and opting for an alternative draft.

Even before that parliamentary party meeting, the newspapers were reporting that Peter Sutherland had identified two major weaknesses in the Fianna Fáil wording, and he reported personally on those to the meeting. He told the deputies that the wording was 'ambiguous and unsatisfactory', and could lead to greater uncertainty. 'In particular, it is not clear as to what life is being protected: as to whether 'the unborn' is protected from the moment of fertilisation, or alternatively is left unprotected until an independently viable human being exists at twenty-five to twenty-eight weeks.' And how would doctors have regard to the 'equal right' to life of the mother and her unborn when faced with the necessity of performing an operation to save the mother that inevitably meant the death of the foetus? Because of these possibilities – that the existing wording could actually facilitate abortions up to twenty-five weeks and, alternatively, could outlaw therapeutic abortions accepted by all the churches and the medical profession – Sutherland told the meeting that he could not approve the wording proposed.

Now the parliamentary party, no less than the Fine Gael cabinet members, were in a dreadful dilemma. Sutherland had outlined his objections with great clarity: he saw them as logical and possible interpretations of the proposed wording. FitzGerald now realised full well the great mistake that had been made in November. Sutherland told the meeting that he could come up with an alternative wording that would meet his objections; he had already given the government the basis for one. The majority of the party accepted this. They adopted a wait-and-see attitude.

After the meeting, a statement confirmed officially that the government were considering an alternative wording to the Amendment. It sought to contain the inevitable flak by re-affirming 'its decision to hold a referendum in the immediate future to honour its commitment to the strengthening of the constitutional protection of unborn children'. But it added: 'the parliamentary party will in the near future be considering any amendments that may be necessary to remove ambiguities, and to secure with certainty the achievement of the objectives of the bill. In the meantime, the second stage of the Eighth Amendment of the Constitution Bill will proceed'.

All hell broke loose on the pro-amendment side. The newspaper reports of the previous couple of days had put them on their guard. There had been suggestions from Fine Gael sources that the wording was defective, and would have to be abandoned. Now all they saw was yet another attempt by FitzGerald to wheedle out on his triple commitment to the amendment. Of course that was how Haughey also saw it. 'I did not make the amendment itself an issue in the recent general election campaign, but I did question the good faith of the Fine Gael leader in relation to it. Events have now shown I was right to do so.'

And Alice Glenn was not happy either. The existing wording, she declared, 'is just fine by me'. Michael Woods described FitzGerald as being 'devious and dishonest' on the matter. Michael Noonan, the hapless Minister now in charge of this unhappy piece of legislation, said they might have to overrun the March deadline but reiterated the government's commitment to it.

Something else was plain, however. Garret FitzGerald, who had been sold to the electorate in three successive general elections as the epitome of trustworthiness, now had a major credibility problem.

With the prospect of new wording, the national debate, already low on reason and tolerance, became bedlam. PLAC had a meeting with FitzGerald for three hours on 16 February, and afterwards their chairman, Julia Vaughan, said the existing wording was 'just and adequate'. However, the Director of Public Prosecutions issued a statement the same day warning that if the proposed text became law, he would have 'grave difficulty' in prosecuting abortion offences under the 1861 Act. Fianna Fáil accused the government of dragging the state's independent law officer into a political debate. From here on, it was all down hill into ever deeper division and bitterness.

The government wanted quickly to fill the gap it had created. Obviously, delay was damaging. But legal formulae are notoriously slow to get exactly right. So it proved here. Sutherland presented an alternative wording to the cabinet, following consultations with eminent figures in all the main churches, including the Catholic Church. He was guided by the principle of an amendment that would exclude the courts from having any possible right to terminate a pregnancy. After all, that had been the original motivation of PLAC. But he did not find it possible to enshrine in an alternative wording a positive right to life. He did not see how the state could in equal measure uphold the right to life of the unborn child and the mother.

Some members of the cabinet were unhappy. They feared that Sutherland's formula fell too far short of an explicit pro-life commitment. This led to Noonan being mandated to see if he could come up with an alternative to the alternative, in conjunction with the Attorney General. They wanted a wording that would meet the objections raised by Sutherland, and at the same time retain a pro-life commitment. However, this created even more damaging delay and Sutherland maintained from the outset that it was an impossible quest.

Every day that elapsed was read by the pro-amendment lobby as evidence of the government's reluctance to take the Amendment at all. The frenetic right-wing element in the vanguard of the amendment crusade were starting to go bananas. On 1 March, FitzGerald told the parliamentary party that the alternative wording would be ready in a fortnight. Bombarded by hysterical mail and personal representations, many backbenchers were getting very concerned. One of the party's noted conservatives on the subject, Tom O'Donnell, warned FitzGerald there must be no 'backtracking' on the pro-life commitment. Meanwhile the debate on the second stage of the bill continued. Fianna Fáil had a field day accusing the Fine Gael leader of breaking his solemn election commitment. Michael Woods said the government were floundering around 'leaderless and rudderless' on the issue. It was a perception many would accept.

FitzGerald actually visited one of the Catholic bishops as part of the negotiations on a possible agreed wording being pursued by the Minister for Justice. But the hierarchy refused to negotiate directly with the government and opted for an intermediary. In those talks Noonan and his officials decided it was possible to overcome Sutherland's objections and still retain a pro-life commitment. They sought to do this by proposing a constitutional guarantee of a right to life before birth, from the commencement of pregnancy (overcoming difficulties with the term 'unborn'), and qualifying this with a provision not to make unlawful medical treatment, or intervention, necessary to save an expectant mother's life. However, Noonan ran into one insurmountable difficulty. He failed to get Catholic Church backing. With the majority Church increasingly involved in the campaign locally, he was stymied. The whole saga was an immense distraction for a government charged primarily with sorting out the country's economic crisis. But it was the announcement of the establishment of the New Ireland Forum on 11 March that really put the business in perspective. This had been urged on the coalition by the SDLP leader John Hume, who wanted nationalist Ireland to spell out its blueprint for accommodating the Northern unionists. With all the churches of the unionist community opposed to the amendment, which was still official government policy, the contradiction was simply breathtaking.

FitzGerald also seemed unaware of another contradiction when he made his state-of-the-nation television address on 18 March. 'We won't be put off from what needs to be done, and said, by any fear of temporary unpopularity. We will act in the country's interests and will not be intimidated by any sectional or vested interests into abandoning this duty.' His complete entrapment in the amendment mire was the fruit of an abject surrender to a vested interest group, and it was done precisely for fear of unpopularity. Indeed, the following Sunday, in an RTE interview, the Taoiseach confessed they had gone along with Fianna Fáil wording in the November election for fear of Fine Gael being branded 'a pro-abortion party'. He went on:

> We agreed at the time that we would take it as a separate amendment. That was the position that was forced on us by Fianna Fáil and we agreed to do it. I think we are bound to stick by what we said we would do. It is not what I would have preferred. I wish it had not happened this way, but the particular clause [of the constitution] has to be changed.
>
> We have to define to whom the right to life applies and do it in a way which expresses the consensus of our people, and in the wording we use not to create any problems for any of the other churches.

There is no doubt that Fianna Fáil had sought to make the amendment an issue in the November election. But FitzGerald's statement omits some very pertinent details. He had enthusiastically welcomed the Fianna Fáil amendment a day *before* the Dáil fell, and that welcome was unequivocal, adding the commitment to a referendum by 31 March.

Finally, on 23 March, FitzGerald brought the alternative wording to the parliamentary party meeting. More correctly, he brought alternative wordings. By now many deputies were very short on patience and tolerance. They were under extraordinarily hostile pressure. Extremists were accusing them of being soft on abortion. 'Where is the wording' had been their increasing clamour in recent days. They wanted something clear and precise that would be accepted by the public and get the PLAC and SPUC people off their backs. They got nothing of the sort.

Firstly, FitzGerald put forward the Noonan wording as the preferred choice of the cabinet. But this was unacceptable to a minority who wanted to stick rigidly with the Fianna Fáil wording. In fact the cabinet had not yet really united on the subject. Bruton favoured amending the 1861 Offences Against the Person Act. Other ministers, like Jim Mitchell, had come up with other alternative wordings. The failure of the cabinet to deliver a simple, precise alternative provoked bitter and divisive debate. FitzGerald became the target of many of the criticisms. Some people were clearly settling old scores under the guise of being with the moral majority.

The upshot was that FitzGerald changed tack and proposed Sutherland's alternative wording. It stated: 'Nothing in this constitution shall be invoked to invalidate any provision of a law on the grounds that it prohibits abortion.'

A number of deputies including Alice Glenn, Oliver J. Flanagan, Tom O'Donnell, and Liam T. and Michael Joe Cosgrave strongly criticised this as not fulfilling the pro-life commitment. John Kelly complained that it was ridiculous to be asking the meeting to endorse a particular wording when it was not written down before them. He added to the confusion by making it clear that he regarded Sutherland's objections to the Fianna Fáil wording as 'piddling and perverse'.

On a show of hands, up to a dozen deputies indicated their opposition to the new wording. Afterwards FitzGerald sought to put an optimistic gloss on the proceedings, claiming overwhelming approval for Sutherland's wording. But it was denounced by the amendment lobby groups. SPUC found it 'totally and completely unacceptable, and a complete abnegation of the government's solemn commitment'. While Sutherland's version might tie the hands of the Supreme Court from ever approving abortion, they demanded a version which also tied the hands of the legislators in the Dáil from doing likewise.

The next day, the five leading Fine Gael backbench rebels —

Glenn, Flanagan, O'Donnell and the two Cosgraves (not related) — publicly indicated their opposition to the party's wording. A number of others were murmuring assent with them. Moreover, at this stage half the Labour Party deputies were against any amendment. Now Fine Gael was threatening to break three ways — a majority for their own wording, a minority for the Fianna Fáil text, and at least Monica Barnes and Maurice Manning against any amendment.

That day also saw the Dáil vote on the second stage. It was a bizarre spectacle. The government were now committed to changing the wording, and yet they joined with Fianna Fáil and eight of the Labour deputies to amass a vote of 140 — 11 in favour of the Fianna Fáil wording! Thus they rejected a Workers' Party motion calling for the issue to be referred to an all-party committee. The two WP deputies were backed by eight Labour deputies and Tony Gregory.

On 29 March, the Catholic hierarchy came out against the alternative wording. While appreciating the difficulties in framing the measure, the bishops' statement concluded: 'It is our earnest hope that at the end of the debate, our legislators will put before the people a form of amendment which will give them an opportunity to decide whether or not they wish to give to unborn human life the full constitutional protection already guaranteed to every citizen.' The three main Protestant churches stated their support for the Sutherland/government wording. There could be no more complete sectarian rift. A week later, on 10 April, the inherent conflict of the churches was dramatically exposed when the two most outspoken conservatives in the Catholic hierarchy, Dermot Ryan of Dublin and Kevin McNamara of Kerry, strongly defended the amendment. They made clear that there could be no exceptions to the ban on abortion. And in an unprecedented development, the country's Chief Justice, Mr Tom O'Higgins, made clear in the *Sunday Press* his unhappiness with the role in which he and his fellow judges were being cast. The amendment debate implied that they were liable to overturn the existing legislative ban on abortion.

Officially, the Catholic hierarchy was taking a quite restrained line with the exception of Drs Ryan and McNamara. But many pulpits on Sunday mornings were resounding to robust pro-amendment sermons, and denunciations of anyone who would be against it. The country was simply tearing itself apart. Nowhere was that process more evident than inside the Fine Gael party. By the time a further marathon parliamentary party meeting came round on 20 April, FitzGerald's 'overwhelming majority' for the government wording inside the party was crumbling. The five rebels were being joined by others. Claims by Seán Barrett that they still intended to apply the whip in the Dáil were taking on the aura of political desperation, or suicide. Defeat for the government in the Dáil was now opening up before them.

In an RTE radio interview, Oliver J. Flanagan was asked about FitzGerald's insistence that there would be no free vote. If anybody was to lose the whip, then it should be Dr FitzGerald, he replied, for not keeping his solemn commitment, and for his effort 'to terrorise every mother, and to terrorise every woman in the country'.

The party leadership was now in a serious quandry. They decided on a session where deputies could go and discuss their difficulties with FitzGerald. About a dozen took that course. Meanwhile, Haughey issued a statement deploring the Taoiseach's 'inconsistencies, contradictory statements and reversals of policy on the issue'. Fianna Fáil were plainly delighting in the government's, and especially FitzGerald's discomfiture.

Haughey threatened disciplinary measures against two deputies, David Andrews and Mary Harney, who expressed reservations about the whole amendment obsession. Andrews had called for an all-party approach. As Haughey saw it, sanctimonious Garret had brought this one on himself and he could stew in it.

In Fine Gael, it was notable that many of the deputies defying the leadership were not exactly devout Garret fans. But superseding that factor was genuine concern over reneging on a commitment given at successive elections, and in a most explicit form in the previous November's campaign. Many deputies, especially in rural areas, were being subjected to ever-increasing pressure from PLAC and SPUC supporters. Any equivocation at all could lead to veiled sermons on Sunday morning and charges of being pro-abortion, or soft on abortion.

Two years after the entire bitter episode was over, many deputies visibly paled when recalling this very unhappy time. Clearly, it was not merely dissidents who were unhappy with the leader's successive U-turns on the issue. Even John Kelly, who regarded the entire amendment as unnecessary, felt strongly that a solemn commitment given at the doorsteps in November should be honoured.

As the rift in the parliamentary party grew, some deputies began to blame Sutherland for the whole mess. He had promised a suitable alternative wording. Plainly that had not been forthcoming. The depth of opposition within the party to Sutherland's wording was summed up in a statement from Deputies Glenn, O'Donnell and the two Cosgraves.

> It does not fulfil the solemn commitment given to the Irish electorate by the Fine Gael party in three general elections.
>
> We cannot accept the fact of the total omission of any reference to the right to life of the unborn. We cannot accept the situation whereby the door would be left open to the Oireachtas to legalise abortion at some future date. This could be extremely dangerous in the event of a hung Dáil similar to the last two Dáils.

As more Fine Gael dissenters began to be named, the controversy became even murkier. Leaked documents began to fly testifying to the divisions between Noonan and Sutherland about the wording. They centred on Noonan's preference for a 'right to life' provision for the unborn child.

As possible defeat began to stare at FitzGerald he made a further dramatic comment. If his wording was defeated in the Dáil, he would withdraw the Bill altogether. 'I have to face the fact that the commitment I entered in good faith with regard to the Fianna Fáil amendment is one I cannot fulfil.' Support for the Fianna Fáil alternative was 'a moral responsibility which we could not, and would not take'. But that was to be a silly hope.

PLAC was buying none of FitzGerald's reservations. In a detailed statement, it said that 'it strains credulity to accept the suggestion that in the last quarter of the twentieth century, any court anywhere would wish to strike down established medical practice, held to be legal and ethically proper for over a century, and designed to save the mother's life, unless utterly compelled to do so. There is nothing whatsoever in the wording rejected by the Taoiseach which would so compel an Irish court.'

PLAC went on to claim that the problems that had arisen had nothing to do with the wording. They arose from the fact that Dr FitzGerald and his colleagues 'no longer wish to proceed with an amendment which would offer genuine constitutional protection to the unborn'. It urged the withdrawal of the 'worthless' Fine Gael amendment.

With the final, decisive vote on the Committee Stage of the bill scheduled for Wednesday, 27 April, yet another meeting of the parliamentary party was held the day before. The leadership was still suggesting forlornly that a three-line whip would be applied. But deputies who maintained their conscientious objection refused to climb down during another stormy four-and-a-half-hour session.

When the meeting finished shortly before midnight, the party leadership had caved in and accepted the inevitable. There were now eight deputies who would not back their own party's wording: Flanagan, Glenn, O'Donnell, the two Cosgraves, Joe Doyle, Michael Begley and Godfrey Timmins. The party faced certain defeat in the Dáil.

FitzGerald had been shocked when it emerged that so many were determined to defy the party whip, and incur automatic expulsion from the parliamentary party. 'I must ponder for a moment', he told the meeting. At this stage many TDs were scarcely on speaking terms with one another. This could crystallise in an outright party split. It was the most serious crisis faced by FitzGerald since he became leader. He now proposed that the rebels could abstain on the party's wording. They left the meeting to consider this. Michael Joe Cosgrave returned to give his colleagues their verdict. Seven of the eight would abstain, and Oliver J. would not. However, the following day, Flanagan also accepted this half-way house against expulsion.

It was now clear to all of them that their wording would be defeated in the Dáil the following day. This raised the issue of what they would do on the original Fianna Fáil

271

wording. It was impossible for the government simply to withdraw the entire measure, even if they had the courage to do so. They would have to win a vote in the House, and clearly that was as impossible as getting their own wording adopted. That left their attitude to the vote on the wording that FitzGerald had so recently said he could not morally support. The meeting had a vote, and the overwhelming majority were in favour of abstaining. Up to twenty indicated they would prefer to vote against. These included FitzGerald, but they had to bow to the majority wish to the parliamentary party. It amounted to a double rebuke for the leader: First, by the eight rebels who would be voting for the Fianna Fáil wording; and then by the bulk of the party who preferred to abstain, rather than vote against that.

The phlegmatic chief whip, Seán Barrett, acknowledged the outcome late that night when the in-fighting finally ceased. 'It now looks as if the majority of people in the Dáil will support the original wording of the amendment.'

When the final votes were reached on 27 April, the voting combinations were as unusual and diverse as the entire saga had been extraordinary and grotesque. The Fine Gael amendment was defeated by 87 votes to 65, with the eight Fine Gael rebels abstaining, and five of the Labour deputies (Spring, Desmond, Pattison, Moynihan and Kavanagh) voting for the Fine Gael wording. Then the original Fianna Fáil wording was put and carried by 87 votes to 13, with the eight rebels voting for it and 60 Fine Gael deputies abstaining. The total rift in Fine Gael was completed by its remaining two deputies, Alan Shatter and Monica Barnes, voting against. They were joined in the 'Níl' lobby by eight Labour deputies, the two Workers' Party deputies and Tony Gregory. This latter trio had voted against both wordings.

Finally, on the substantive vote on the bill before the house, the Fianna Fáil wording was carried by 85 votes to 11. Michael Noonan assured Fianna Fáil that the government would not be obstructionist in the Seanad, where it had a majority, but would facilitate the concluding stages of the bill.

FitzGerald, who had been seriously discredited, further angered his colleagues by promptly declaring that if the bill were enacted, he would advise the people to vote 'No' in the subsequent referendum. Many deputies, including some Ministers, blamed FitzGerald for walking them into the mess in the first place. Now they wanted him, for God's sake, to cut his losses and keep his mouth shut. They saw him persisting in his efforts to restore his *bona fides* with what one of them called 'his Dublin Four set of liberals'. And, of course, FitzGerald was mindful of his now battered Constitutional Crusade and, more important, the infant New Ireland Forum.

Voting day on the amendment was eventually fixed for 7 September, and the scene was set for an extraordinary summer campaign, with none of the major political parties participating. But there were myriad pro- and anti- amendment groupings. Sectional divisions finally reached the point which saw the emergence of a group called 'Handicapped for the Amendment'.

Rational debate went out the window, and the ready label of being pro-abortion, or soft on abortion, was pinned on anyone who begged to differ with the necessity for the amendment. The rapid sequence of three general elections inside eighteen months had enabled a small, very vocal group to pressurise the main political parties to do their will. The craveness of politicians at election time was never more graphically displayed.

And the politician whose reputation suffered most was Garret FitzGerald. Within the party those most disillusioned with him were Young Fine Gael, and in 1983 quite a few members drifted away from the organisation. The identity crisis now besetting the party in the wake of the amendment showdown was graphically underlined in a statement issued on 28 April 1983 by the YFG vice-president, Seán Tighe, from Sligo. It carried the punchy heading: 'Reform or die — Young Fine Gael calls on the government'. It said that the failure of the government to have the amendment wording changed

> marks another stage in the conflict between the conservative and progressive forces within Fine Gael. There are many other controversial issues which lie ahead of the government, and many social and economic reforms

which have to be carried out.

Fine Gael cannot allow itself to be immobilised by its anxiety to keep everyone happy, and to appease a reactionary minority. If these issues are merely consigned to all-party committees, never to be heard of again, the government can expect to face disaster at the next election.

The government must recognise the logic of its position: reform or die.

It set many senior party politicians into a rage. Rona Fitzgerald was again subjected to angry phone calls. Some deputies wanted YFG integrated into the senior party, or at least to have its press statements cleared by the party press office. But she resisted, and secured vital support from the party leader.

YFG did not leave it at that. In June 1983, it launched a major anti-abortion/anti-amendment campaign in every constituency in the country. It called up its 6,500 members for a national postering and leafleting campaign. This decision was taken by the YFG national executive, in pursuit of their conference decision in Galway. Needless to say, it again brought them into conflict with the senior party.

Rona Fitzgerald found herself before the national executive defending the right of YFG to their campaign. A split was threatening inside the national executive; some of the more conservative members wanted it to campaign *in favour* of the amendment! The compromise reached was that it would not campaign on the issue, but that individual members could speak out on it.

YFG ran a major campaign throughout the entire country. Only one constituency executive, that in East Limerick, opted out because they felt the issue was too divisive. But YFG headquarters, led by Rona Fitzgerald and national chairperson, Chris O'Malley, were determined that 'confraternity city', Limerick, would not escape. Flying squads went there at weekends to distribute leaflets.

On the debit side YFG was subjected to massive abuse. Party headquarters was deluged with vitriolic letters from pro-amendment people accusing them of being pro-abortion.

In their different localities many young members found themselves in conflict with the local Catholic priests, who were increasingly endorsing the amendment from their pulpits on Sunday, and with senior Fine Gael members.

They held meetings on a Euro-constituency basis to campaign against the amendment, and 50,000 leaflets were distributed. A major conference was held in Buswells Hotel, Dublin, in August, where Monica Barnes and Alan Shatter spoke out against the measure. Gemma Hussey and Alan Dukes were other notable figures to speak at YFG meetings on the issue.

In May, Fine Gael's press officer, Dan Egan, brought out the first issue of the party's revamped newspaper, now called *New Democrat*. The front page dealt with the amendment saga in a hard-hitting, slightly irreverent way. 'The debate itself has been like rolling over a stone – aspects and elements of our society have been exposed that would have been better left hidden', it said. 'Seán O'Leary in his Senate speech referred to [pro-amendment activists] as "a marauding band of reactionary red-necks". They will have a field day over the next few months trying to persuade the people to support their vision of Ireland.'

But it was the accompanying pictures of the eight Fine Gael rebels and the caption: 'The TDs with a conscience' that really got the party pot stirring. Other deputies, not appreciating Egan's irony, complained bitterly that they too had consciences. In the ensuing hubbub, Deputy Michael Keating, the only TD on the paper's editorial board, resigned after explaining that he had not seen the article before publication.

The whole dismal saga of the abortion referendum campaign, with its mixture of ignorance, bigotry, hysteria and farce, dragged on until September. When the votes were counted on 8 September, it was revealed that just over half the electorate (53.6 per cent) bothered to vote at all. Those who did gave a comprehensive endorsement – 841,233 to 416,136 – to the amendment wording.

Only 35.6 per cent of the electorate had endorsed the amendment, while 64.4 per cent of the people were unconvinced of its necessity, or decided to reject it. In the first nine months of 1983, 2,796 Irish women travelled to Britain to have abortions, a new record number.

The first period of FitzGerald and Fine Gael government in June 1981 had been thwarted by its minority position and the nation's financial crisis. Now, the second time round, the first nine months had been thwarted by the amendment. FitzGerald and the parliamentary party had paid dearly for their opportunistic U-turn of the previous November.

The controversy and internal division, also said much about the schizoid nature of the party on liberal/social issues. There was no doubt that FitzGerald had liberalised Fine Gael, and that the bulk of his new 1981-82 parliamentary recruits backed such a course. But he still had a sizeable conservative minority who would be very reluctant Constitutional Crusaders. FitzGerald had come so to dominate the party that his voice scorning 'laws based on the theology of one Church' probably misled many into believing that the entire Fine Gael parliamentary party were like-minded. The pro-life amendment controversy revealed the party with a conservative rump which was indistinguishable from Fianna Fáil.

Many Protestant churchmen had been appalled by FitzGerald's abject embrace of the Fianna Fáil amendment. It made nonsense of his Constitutional Crusade. Their view was put ascerbically by Rev. Desmond Gilliland, Secretary of the Methodist Church's Council for Social Welfare. 'Henry of Navarre said that Paris was worth a Mass. We're seeing a certain element of that now with Garret FitzGerald', he told Olivia O'Leary in the *Irish Times*.

For FitzGerald personally, the amendment was a disaster. It was he who had set such high pluralist standards for himself in the Constitutional Crusade broadcast. In that, he held out the prospect of a referendum to transform the constitution into a code of basic rights acceptable to Northern Protestants. How ironic that the referendum he ultimately delivered was one that enshrined specific Catholic theology in the constitution anew, a referendum which all the Protestant churches condemned as sectarian.

15

Shafting the National Handlers

It was all the fault of the Scruffy Murphy set, giving the impression that every political act by FitzGerald had to be vetted by them. It was time to bring them down a peg or two. A number of Fine Gael backbenchers (and at least one Junior Minister) had put the finger on Enda Marren, Pat Heneghan, Bill O'Herlihy, Frank Flannery, and other key strategists who had helped to bring a 'no win, no hope party to power'. They had given extensively of their time since 1979 to bring the party into the professional ranks, on a par with Fianna Fáil for the first time ever. But now, in the summer of 1985, they were the subject of huge resentment throughout the parliamentary party. In the view of many deputies, they had got too big for their boots, and it was time to teach them a lesson. Many deputies were convinced that these un-elected backroom strategists had a power and influence to which they could never aspire. They were parading themselves as confidants of FitzGerald. It was too much for the foot-slogging, door-knocking, clinic-weary backbenchers who never seemed to be chatted up by their leader.

There was now a firm belief that non-elected backroom people, like the Scruffy Murphy set, were the real power-brokers of the FitzGerald government. Indeed so great did the outrage inside the parliamentary party become that the Taoiseach found it politic to distance himself visibly from his key strategists. They were shafted, sent to Coventry, and they became very bitter about it.

The backroom boys had been dubbed the National Handlers early in the life of the government by *Irish Times* columnist, John Healy. Soon it really stuck, and came to connote all-powerful, Svengali-like manipulators of a bemused Taoiseach.

In fact, just as Conor Cruise O'Brien's creation, GUBU, became synonymous with the 1982 Haughey government, so did the National Handlers come to portray an essential image of the FitzGerald government.

Long before the second coalition took office in December 1982, media attention had focused on the key backroom boys in Fine Gael. The one singled out for attention was general secretary, Peter Prendergast. Fine Gael's many electoral innovations were rightly explained in terms of the influence of the professional PR and media people gathered together by Ted Nealon. But after the November 1982 success, the spotlight really began to linger on some of the Strategy Committee members: Prendergast, Derry Hussey, Seán O'Leary, Shane Molloy, Seán Murray, Marren, Heneghan, Flannery and O'Herlihy. Their tactical approach was brilliant, as evidenced, for example, in their attention to detail in preparing FitzGerald for his television debate with Haughey on the eve of the election. In December 1982, *Magill* ran a major cover story on the theme 'How the Fine Gael Whizz-kids sold us a Taoiseach'.

That was the real beginning of the media obsession surrounding the so-called National Handlers. Some of them, including Hussey, Molloy, Murray and O'Leary, quickly faded from the limelight, however. But the Scruffy Murphy set were never too far away from the political gossip columns of the national newspapers.

Scruffy Murphy's is the popular name of the discreetly located Patrick Murphy's pub, off Lower Mount St, in Dublin's southside office belt. Heneghan and O'Herlihy ran their PR partnership from Lower Mount St, and so Scruffy's was a convenient watering hole. Marren ran a large legal practice in nearby Northumberland Road. Flannery was chief executive of the Rehabilitation Institute in Sandymount. The four were good social friends, and met quite often over a pint in Scruffy's. Being a gregarious lot, they were the best of company, the kind of political insiders journalists liked to know. In fact, for O'Herlihy and Heneghan, daily contact with the media was their very livelihood.

But from the outset of the second FitzGerald coalition, Fianna Fáil sniped constantly at the alleged power and influence of advisers and 'faceless men'. When any of the Handlers received any patronage, as in the form of state directorships, Fianna Fáil screamed foul. There were a few. Murray was a government appointee on the board of Tara Mines; Flannery on the RTE Authority; and Marren on the board of Aer Rianta. When Public Relations of Ireland (O'Herlihy and Heneghan's company) secured a £14,000 contract with the Department of the Public Service in 1984, there were renewed screams about jobs for the boys. O'Herlihy was quick to point out that when Fianna Fáil were in power, a leading party supporter, Peter Owens, who also ran a PR and marketing company, received government contracts. Indeed, given the number of advisers Haughey recruited into his own Department of the Taoiseach in 1980, the charges against Fine Gael were a joke. When he became Taoiseach, Haughey's department had seventy-six staff. But by 1 December 1980, the number had soared to 174, the biggest Taoiseach's office in the history of the state.

Fianna Fáil had a particular obsession with Peter Prendergast, who became Government Press Secretary in December 1982. He was fiercely loyal to FitzGerald and, apart from Joan FitzGerald, probably the Taoiseach's closest confidant. Prendergast was a brilliant communicator. Available twenty-four hours a day, seven days a week, his opinion greatly influenced the shape and emphasis of political comment in all the media. To many in Fianna Fáil, he was the real Taoiseach. Haughey in particular saw Prendergast as some kind of Svengali, who powerfully manipulated every arm of government.

The Handlers were in no doubt about the opposition's motivation. O'Herlihy was adamant that there was a deliberate attempt to drive a wedge between FitzGerald and the Fine Gael party, on the one hand, and the Strategy Committee personnel on the other. They were the vital asset that had delivered power in 1981 and 1982. Neutralise them, and Fianna Fáil were half way back. It was a reasonable deduction by the opposition, and they were to succeed beyond their wildest dreams.

But the Scruffy Murphy set contributed greatly to their own downfall. First though, it is worth looking at the influence wielded by the Handlers before their fall from grace, and to contrast that with the performance of the government on key issues without them.

———————

From December 1982, the government retained a Communications Strategy Committee. In the early days it met every fortnight and, as its title suggests, it advised the government on the presentation and publication of government decisions. Chaired by John Boland, it had personnel from both coalition parties. Membership varied but the hard core comprised Prendergast; Labour's assistant Government Press Secretary, Fergus Finlay; Joe Jennings, head of the GIS; Ruairi Quinn, Minister for Labour; the general secretaries of both parties, and Flannery, Molloy and O'Herlihy. Boland also briefed Prendergast on an on-going basis on cabinet business.

One of the first major controversies to envelop FitzGerald's government was the decision to award TDs, ministers and judges a 19 per cent pay increase in November 1983. This was brought to the Communications Strategy Committee for advice. They recommended against paying such a large amount at once. But the politicians were strongly in favour of it. After all, it merely allowed them to catch up on wage rounds already conceded to public servants generally. But the committee was unconvinced: at least exclude ministers, they urged. But the cabinet disregarded the advice and went ahead.

Some Ministers suggested that when the public saw that even the Workers' Party and Tony Gregory were also taking the full increase, the flak would die down. It was not the case. Years later it was still recalled as one of the coalition's major public relations gaffes. The fact that the TDs were not taking their back-money, and that they had only been paid £13,800, was lost on a cynical public. Here was a government preaching pay moderation, and awarding themselves 19 per cent. That was how the public saw it. The strategists had been disregarded and the government had promptly walked themselves into a mess.

The strategists were not even *consulted* on the occasion of the government's biggest PR gaffe of all. That was the decision taken at a cabinet meeting on Thursday 2 August 1984 to halve the existing subsidies on butter, milk and bread. The move was reckoned to save about £20 million in the remainder of the year, and the money was needed to help pay the escalating cost of servicing US dollar loans, at a time when the dollar was soaring from strength to strength.

In many ways the episode bore an uncanny resemblance to Fianna Fáil's mini-budget package of July 1982. Both sets of cuts were announced on the eve of the August bank holiday weekend, and the coalition, just like their predecessors, left the task of explaining the measures to civil servants, although Fine Gael had specifically attacked this aspect of the Fianna Fáil cutbacks! Only Barry Desmond warned of the implications of what they were doing.

Ironically, Alan Dukes was not at the crucial meeting. He was already off on his holidays. The primary responsibility for pushing the cuts therefore rested with FitzGerald. It was a distressing time for him personally. His wife was extremely ill, and they were to travel to France the following morning for a holiday. Later he would accept his total misjudgment in failing to ensure that a senior minister went to the media to explain their case. Not only was there no minister to convey the news to the media, but no minister was available to participate in the main evening 9 o'clock news on RTE television, a point underlined on the bulletin.

There was a battle-weariness in the cabinet room at the time. They were immersed in the painstaking task of devising the national plan, and trying to agree public spending cuts. Nor were either of the two professional Handlers on call to deal with the matter. Prendergast was in London for a routine briefing session with the media there. He was aghast later that evening to learn of the announcement, and its manner of delivery. Fergus Finlay was moving house from his native Cork to Co. Meath, and he had taken a week's holidays to complete this task.

Once the news broke, Fianna Fáil were instantly on the attack. They concentrated their fire on the Labour Party. How could that party increase the price of the staple diet of working-class people? Spring soon felt the heat and realised that things were going dreadfully wrong. He had not realised that the measure would trigger such unrest. Only a week earlier, the ICTU general secretary, Donal Nevin, had stated on RTE that the subsidies were a blunt instrument, enjoyed by rich and poor alike. By the Friday morning, the Tánaiste — now in charge with FitzGerald off to France — realised the government were faced with a major crisis. He contacted John Boland, and they both agreed to act. On that day, and over the weekend, they did an exhaustive round of media interviews regarding their decision. Still, the damage had been done.

The final irony was that the budget deficit of 1984 eventually turned out at £1,039 million, £50 million *less* than budgeted for. There had been no reason, after all, to touch the food subsidies!

In the wake of this fiasco, the government needed a major success story. The launching of the national plan in October was a suitable subject for redemption. But this time the Handlers were consulted, their advice taken, and it turned out a resounding success.

The Communications Strategy Committee tossed around the question of how best to present the three-year plan. Firstly, what would they call it. Prendergast favoured the direct title 'The National Plan'. But Shane Molloy wanted something more descriptive, something that would convey the notion of being innovative, while still being bedded in the harsh economic times. 'Building on Realities' was his suggestion. Finlay suggested cutting this to 'Building on Reality', and that was the title that emerged.

Prendergast suggested the grandiose launch in the ornate ballroom of Iveagh House, headquarters of the Department of Foreign Affairs. FitzGerald and Spring would do this before an invited audience of leaders of the main sectoral groups: farmers, industrialists, trade unions and so forth. It would convey the impression of a government concerned for all their interests. And when the television cameras rolled, it was indeed an impressive ceremony. Not everyone was convinced it would work. Just as the proceedings were getting under way, another strategist, Seán Murray, just happened along. He was not involved in any way, and was quite aghast when he saw the strange bedfellows lined up before live television cameras to hear FitzGerald. What if

Mattie Merrigan, or Joe Rea were to interrupt and throw a tantrum? It could wreck the entire affair.

But the set-piece went a treat. The plan was sold positively, and had many innovative features. It did a lot to exorcise the memories of outrage at the food subsidies cut. It set up FitzGerald for a successful árd fheis the following weekend.

Fianna Fáil and anti-coalition commentators had no doubt what they had witnessed, nothing more than hype by the National Handlers. Plainly the government could not win. If they goofed with their policy announcements, they were wrong. If they presented them with style and aplomb, that too was out.

The 1985 budget was another outstanding presentational success by the Communications Strategy Committee. After the harsh 1983 measure, and the 1984 neutral package, it was time for something more innovative. The budget statement was broadcast live, and RTE had a panel of experts in the studio to dissect it. However, the standard formula of the budget was a long arid dissertation of the macro-economic state of the economy. Only towards the end, maybe an hour later, did the real public interest items arise. The taxation and social welfare changes, price increases, and so forth.

Committee people, like O'Herlihy, were convinced a great opportunity was being missed to sell the budget positively. What was needed was an indication at the very outset of the budget statement of whatever good news it contained. The idea was to influence RTE's panel of experts to endorse the budget. In the end, Prendergast rewrote the two opening pages of Dukes's financial statement. It set out the positive news of the budget. There were slight income tax concessions: PAYE and VAT bands were rationalised. There was a 6.5 per cent social welfare increase. RTE's panel reacted with surprise to the new format, and with approval for the measures. The budget got the most positive sell imaginable. It was months later before the public began to change their minds and detect that, really, it had just been more of the usual.

The government's renewed publicity successes over the national plan and the budget made Fianna Fáil more deter-mined than ever to neutralise the impact of the Handlers. A major controversy in March 1985 saw them redouble their efforts.

The question of political balance in RTE had always been a subject fraught with controversy. Every appointment affecting it was watched hawkishly by the political parties. They were specially on their guard that year, because both the RTE authority and its director-general were retiring.

The outgoing authority had been appointed by Fianna Fáil in 1980, and had a noted pro-Haughey complexion. However, the coalition had their own man, Flannery, *in situ*. The authority set about choosing a successor to George Water, the director-general who was to retire on 6 April. The appointment would have to be approved by the Minister for Communications. The three leading contenders were all senior executives inside the station: Muiris MacConghail, T. Vincent Finn, and John Sorohan. MacConghail was the popular favourite, and was the clear preference of the government. He had been head of the GIS during the Cosgrave coalition in the early seventies, and was perceived to be a Labour man.

It was also an open secret in government circles that Flannery would be appointed chairman of the new authority. Fianna Fáil were determined to upset the coalition's gameplan. They championed the cause of Sorohan as director-general, and Haughey personally canvassed some authority members to back him. Not that Sorohan was a Fianna Fáiler. He had in fact at one time worked for Labour's Health Minister, Barry Desmond. But Fianna Fáil wanted to stymie the MacConghail-Flannery grand design.

However, when it became clear in February that Sorohan was emerging as the nominee of the authority, Jim Mitchell intervened. On 1 March, he announced that he was appointing a team of consultants to review the operations and structure of RTE. In the meantime, he postponed the appointment of a new DG. All hell broke loose in the political arena. Fianna Fáil accused him of usurping the function of the authority and of deliberately politicising RTE. While there was real merit in a fundamental review of RTE's operations, the timing of Mitchell's move was totally political, and aimed at heading off the appointment of Fianna Fáil's favourite for the top job.

Such was the political row that ensued that FitzGerald was forced to give the most fundamental commitments on not politicising the state broadcasting station. It was vital, he told the Dáil on 7 March that RTE 'be free from political control, influence or bias'. Fianna Fáil might not have got their way entirely, but they had certainly baulked the government's intentions. It would now be impossible for Mitchell to appoint MacConghail, because the row had totally politicised the entire affair. The search had to be resumed for a demonstrably non-political authority and director-general. Gone too was Flannery's prospects of becoming authority chairman. He was perceived by Fianna Fáil as the coalition's hatchet-man.

To drive the point home about Mitchell's political interference, the RTE authority defied his instruction not to present him with a nominee for director-general. On 4 March, they had duly presented the name of John Sorohan as their choice. But Mitchell refused to appoint him and four days later, appointed Vincent Finn as interim director-general.

The government appointed a new authority for the station at the end of May, led by Cement-Roadstone chief executive, Jim Culliton. Flannery remained on board as an ordinary member. Later in 1985, Finn's appointment as director-general was made permanent. In political terms Fianna Fáil were the real winners.

The entire episode saw the opposition redouble their assault on the Handlers. It was very unpleasant stuff for the men concerned. Their really active role had been in the run-up to the three elections in a row. And their role since November 1982 had been quite marginal.

All the attention focused on the alleged power of these former election strategists was causing a growing tide of resentment inside the Fine Gael parliamentary party, most of whom had very little contact with FitzGerald. He would sweep by them in the Dáil corridors. And now there were these persistent reports of non-elective people reaching into the very heart of cabinet affairs, advising ministers and enjoying constant media attention. A mixture of envy and anger began to eat into some backbenchers.

But now some of the leading Handlers became the authors of their own downfall. It all had to do primarily with the Scruffy Murphy set. A week before the Fine Gael árd fheis in Cork, which took place on 17-19 May, *Magill* magazine carried a cover story entitled 'The National Handlers: the people who pull Garret's strings'. The cover picture reinforced this. It showed a wooden puppet of FitzGerald, with strings leading from his head, arms and legs. Part of the article, written by Olivia O'Leary, suggested that FitzGerald was a bit of a clot, always requiring careful coaching and handling. Without the Handlers, he was liable to shoot his mouth off and get himself and Fine Gael into all kinds of trouble.

She quoted various Handlers, all former members of the Strategy Committee. They included Marren, Flannery and O'Herlihy (Heneghan was not referred to at all), along with Hussey and Shane Molloy. They were presented as the people who had brought Fine Gael to power. Marren was quoted precisely to this effect: 'We brought a no-win, no-hope party to power.' It was not FitzGerald, or his 69 other TDs, but these brash know-all professionals. Marren was depicted as the Merc-owning habitué of the fashionable Berkeley Court Hotel. He was one of the privileged few who could lay claim to the corner table reserved for C. J. Haughey until 1.30 p.m. every lunchtime, and who regularly had a pint with Charlie.

Moreover, according to the author, 'Marren makes no secret apology for the fact that this government, like perhaps no other in Irish history, is obsessed with its own image', just as Fianna Fáil had been consistently alleging.

Flannery was represented as a key man to advise on how to wield power. 'Getting the message across is his constant obsession and FitzGerald is seen as a major obstacle in this regard. The one who unwittingly wrecks the rose garden. For instance, he works a full day before a major television interview and goes in tired. A tired Garret is a scattered Garret. By the end of the interview, nobody's quite sure what it is he's saying.'

The article referred also to the roles of general secretary, Finbarr Fitzpatrick and press officer, Peter White. But the power and real strategic influence was ascribed to the Handlers.

The appearance of the article caused uproar inside the Fine Gael parliamentary party and senior organisation. FitzGerald was very angry with his wooden portrayal. It was one of the predominant topics of conversation at the árd fheis. Fitzpatrick and White were also extremely angry. In Cork that weekend, there were persistent dark mutterings from TDs about the Handlers, some of whom — Marren, Heneghan, Flannery and Seán Murray — had turned up.

Back in Dublin, the role of the advisers was raised at a parliamentary party meeting. George Birmingham said he was outraged by the *Magill* article, and he strongly attacked the portrayal of the Taoiseach as someone needing his every political act vetted by non-elected people. Maurice Manning was another TD who strongly attacked the Handlers. The Scruffy Murphy set were feeling the heat.

FitzGerald tried to defend the role of the strategists at the meeting. He insisted they did not have a role in policy formation. Rather they simply helped out with the presentation of policy already decided by the government. This was indeed a more accurate description.

As we have seen, on the issue of the 19 per cent pay increase, the advice of some of the strategists was simply ignored.

But the *Magill* article brought the issue to a head. Such was the anger it engendered, and the hostility towards some of the strategists, that FitzGerald found it politic to distance himself visibly from them. The first casualties of the new departure were the group of strategists who, according to *Magill*, were 'referred to ominously as "the Committee".' Since coming to office in December 1982, this Committee had met on most Tuesday mornings in the Taoiseach's office between eight and nine o'clock. It was chaired by Derry Hussey, who set the agenda; the other attenders, along with FitzGerald, included Prendergast, Fitzpatrick, Heneghan, and White. Seán O'Leary and Peter Barry were also occasional contributors. The function of the committee was to assess public perception of ongoing government business. It was a very useful sounding board for the Taoiseach to glean impressions of how he and his government were performing.

The other key advisory committee, the Wednesday Communications Strategy Committee, was also lapsed for the entire summer. And when the Dáil resumed in the autumn of 1985, it met only fitfully, without any of the former regularity.

These dramatic developments went unreported by the media. The shafting of the Handlers was a Fine Gael secret. And while individual Handlers grew bitter and resentful about their fate, some media commentators continued to trot out the same clichéd stories of their continued powerful and influential role. Nothing could be further from the truth.

FitzGerald seemed to be fully aware of the trap he had fallen into. In September, he stated privately that the constant focusing on the Handlers was 'one of the cleverest things that Fianna Fáil have done. They have kept it up since we came into government, and now they have half our own party believing it too'. Nevertheless, he bowed to that mood.

Some of the strategists actually saw their business suffer because of the Handler publicity. In the summer of 1985, Public Relations of Ireland's annual £14,000 contract with the Department of Public Service was not renewed. In the autumn, they failed to secure a major PR account with a leading building society, though they were generally reckoned to have made the best presentation, because they were seen as 'too political'. Ironically this happened when they had already suffered the cold-shoulder from Fine Gael.

Frank Flannery also paid a high price for his prominent links with Fine Gael, and not merely the loss of the prestigious chairmanship of the RTE authority. As chief executive of the Rehabilitation Institute, he was very anxious to secure the franchise for running the first state lottery, which was part of the coalition Programme for Government. He saw it as vital to safeguard the existing lotteries, not only for his organisation but also for other community organisations like the Mater Pools and the Central Remedial Clinic.

A consortium of these three bodies, led by Flannery as spokesman, contracted the backing of the Ontario state lottery from Canada to draw up a thoroughly-researched and professional submission for the lottery franchise. Flannery lobbied the Fine Gael cabinet members intensively and also tried to sell his proposition to senior Labour Party representatives. But every media report of his application also referred to his advisory role in Fine Gael.

The other applicants for the lottery included the long-established Irish Hospitals Sweepstake, and the new semi-state postal organisation, An Post. The government dallied over allocating the franchise in the summer and autumn of 1985. While the Labour people found Flannery's case very persuasive, their ministers knew that if they approved him, rather than An Post, there would be a major outcry from the unions and their own parliamentary party. This factor lengthened the odds against Flannery. But it was his depiction as 'a leading National Handler', which was how media gossip columns constantly portrayed him, that did the real damage.

In the end, Alan Dukes and Barry Desmond made a joint recommendation to their government colleagues that An Post should get the lottery, and that was the decision announced on 17 October. Dukes said that An Post was chosen because 'a subsidiary of that body has more characteristics of a successful operation than any of the others'. Flannery was not convinced, and he strongly condemned the government decision. His Fine Gael connections had been *the* singular obstacle to his chances.

By this time, many of the limelight boys were deeply embittered at their being cast aside by the Fine Gael leadership. Some of them did accept that the blame lay primarily with the high profile of their Scruffy Murphy colleagues. The *Magill* article was cited and recited. In the absence of the Handlers, Fitzpatrick and White came to occupy a more prominent advisory role to FitzGerald.

The portrayal of FitzGerald as an inveterate bungler was a gross overstatement. After all, it was he who first brought the nascent Strategy Committee together in the dark days at the end of 1980, after the Donegal by-election defeat. He also remained a key member, along with other politicians like Peter Barry and Tom Fitzpatrick, until the election campaigns got under way. It was also his idea to retain the nucleus of the committee as his Tuesday morning advisory group.

True, he was liable to overreach himself, especially when faced with like-minded audiences. This vulnerability was especially noticeable with student and women's groups. Garret liked to be liked, and there was nothing that came easier to him than telling groups like these how much he agreed with their demands. But the Handlers' influence on him in government, even before they were shafted in the summer of 1985, was never what it was represented in the media. Only one of them was FitzGerald's real Handler. That was Peter Prendergast, his daily confidant and adviser. Finbarr Fitzpatrick was a key adviser on internal party developments.

There is little doubt that FitzGerald over-reacted to the controversy that enveloped the Handlers in May 1985. A government always needs advice on presentation, perception and the demands being made upon it. He was wrong therefore to yield so precipitately to the Fianna Fáil-inspired backlash against the advisers. The Handlers were a profound loss to Fine Gael. Their absence would become glaringly obvious before long.

The importance of the role the advisers could play was amply demonstrated in the autumn of 1985 in two very different ways. The Dáil was set to resume for the autumn term on 23 October. Fianna Fáil were 18 per cent ahead in the opinion polls. The government was assailed by a sea of troubles on all sides. The delicate Anglo-Irish talks were in the balance. Public sector pay was out of line, and major public sector strikes had commenced with a unilateral one-day strike on the 15th of the month. Backbenchers were disgruntled, wondering what had become of their invisible government.

What was the government to do? They had languished in a trough of despair since their trouncing in the local governments elections in June. They desperately needed a new initiative to convince the public, and especially their own supporters, that they had not thrown in the towel. Back in August, they had held a special cabinet session in Barretstown Castle to examine the jobs and taxation crises bedevilling the country. The intention was to come up with job creation and tax reform measures that would restore some lustre to the coalition. But on the eve of the Dáil meeting, these were still only a hotch-potch of schemes and ideas.

The Communications Strategy Committee was re-convened to see if anything could be done. There it was suggested that FitzGerald should open the new Dáil term by presenting the various schemes as a comprehensive package. The ingredients were hastily cobbled together. And when the Dáil resumed, FitzGerald made a statement on the first day back on 'employment and tax reform'.

A house improvement grants scheme, providing grants of up to £5,000 was the kernel of the package. There were also generous tax breaks to interest developers in the blighted inner city areas of Dublin, Cork and Limerick. The national gas grid was to be extended to Limerick and Waterford. A network of county sheriffs was to be appointed to crack down on tax evaders. A new authority would be established to develop the 27-acre Port and Docks Board site in Dublin.

The package sounded more impressive than it actually was. Most of the measures had not been worked out in detail. But one item, the home improvement grants, was a real winner. It was the first time the coalition was giving something back to the hard-pressed, house-owning, middle class. More importantly, it saw the government seize the initiative at the outset of the new Dáil term. The package was well received by the media. And in the weeks running up to the Christmas recess, the coalition retained the advantage, culminating in their finest hour with the Hillsborough Agreement and its aftermath. The strategy boys had got it right again.

By contrast, their absence was highlighted by another event, a special Leinster/Dublin Fine Gael organisation conference held at Kill, Co. Kildare on Saturday and Sunday, 7-8 December. The paid officials, Fitzpatrick and White, ran the show. A few of the Handlers dropped in on the Sunday evening, but they were on the sidelines just like any other delegate.

The event was a major disappointment. The very idea of such a conference three weeks before Christmas was wrong. Whereas up to 1,200 delegates were confidently expected, no more than 800 attended, despite the euphoria in the party over the recent Hillsborough Agreement. And the Handlers' finesse was also missed. The keynote feature of the weekend was a presidential address by FitzGerald on the Sunday evening. The actual venue was Goff's bloodstock sales ring. High above the arena, some twenty-five feet up, was the auctioneer's dias. This was the venue chosen for FitzGerald. Worse was the attempt at a dramatic entry. All the lights in the auditorium were turned off, and a single spotlight then picked out FitzGerald as he walked purposefully to the selected spot.

It had grotesque overtones of the circus ring. The following morning's newspapers carried pictures of Fine Gael TDs gazing skywards, trying to focus on their leader in the dark, high above them. Nor was FitzGerald's speech carefully crafted in the style of his árd-fheis addresses. It was a rambling economic dissertation, bearing all the hallmarks of being entirely FitzGerald's own work. There was even a feeble relaunch of the Constitutional Crusade. He dedicated Fine Gael to the 'objective of a pluralist society, founded on the Christian traditions of our people'.

The creation of a new Management Committee in the autumn of 1985, also served to illustrate the freezing out of the Handlers. This was really a successor to the Tuesday morning Committee. However, its membership was entirely from the paid ranks of the party. It comprised Prendergast, Fitzpatrick, White, Catherine Meenan, Seán Barrett, and FitzGerald himself. Its role was simply to check the Taoiseach's schedule, deciding which of the myriad functions he should attend, and how he should apportion his time.

Not everyone in the parliamentary party was happy at the exclusion of the Handlers. Peter Barry, in particular had a blunt, pragmatic attitude to them. When they were involved, as in the presentation of the national plan and the 1985 budget, these items had been splendidly successful. When they were excluded, as with the food subsidies, fiasco ensued. By the end of 1985, his view was that the strategists, masterly professional people who had given selflessly of their time to help make Fine Gael the largest party in the Oireachtas, had been treated disgracefully. He determined to restore them to favour.

By the start of 1986, the Strategy Committee were being invited back. Their assignment was to form a revived general election strategy committee, working to a deadline in the summer to autumn of 1987. All the old hands returned: Hussey, Heneghan, O'Herlihy, Flannery, Molloy, Marren and others. But FitzGerald made it clear to them all: this time there would be no shouting their mouths off about their role in Fine Gael. As for the media, it remained blissfully unaware of both the shafting and the subsequent rehabilitation.

16

The Rocky Road to Hillsborough

The Anglo-Irish agreement signed at Hillsborough, Co. Down on 15 November 1985 was the first unqualified triumph for FitzGerald's government after three years in office. That is not to say that it did not have some achievements. But by the standards FitzGerald had set when he succeeded Haughey, success or the lack of it was bound to be measured primarily in relation to bread and butter issues: the public finances, job creation and tax reform. By the end of 1985, the general verdict was that on all three fronts the government had been a failure. Unemployment had increased from 180,000 to 240,000. The current budget deficit had reached a new record of £1,284 million; moreover, this represented 8.2 per cent of gross national product, also a new record and higher than even the worst of the Haughey years. On taxation, the government had managed a number of small reforms in the collection system, but the radical structural reform which might have lowered the burden of the PAYE sector had not materialised.

Public support for the government, as measured by the opinion polls, declined steadily during those three years. As if to confirm these findings, all the elections held during the period confirmed that Fine Gael had big problems. In the Donegal South-West by-election of May 1983 Fianna Fáil actually increased its share of the vote to almost 56.5 per cent, despite (or perhaps because of) the recent turmoil in the party following the bugging and telephone tapping scandals. Fine Gael's vote dropped 8 per cent. Six months later, in November 1983, Fianna Fáil comfortably won the Dublin Central by-election, caused by the death of George Colley, despite the constituency party being badly divided along pro- and anti-Haughey lines. Fine Gael wasn't helped by the fact that the new £50 water charges in Dublin were beginning to bite. In addition the announcement of the TDs' 19 per cent pay rise in the middle of the campaign hardly impressed the voters in the poorest constituency in Ireland. In fact, Fergus O'Brien, the director of elections in Dublin Central, was consulted about the effects of the increase; he reckoned that Dublin Central wasn't winnable anyway and he advised the government to go ahead. Bad and all as the result was for Fine Gael, Labour suffered a shattering defeat, sliding to fifth place behind the Workers' Party and Sinn Féin.

In June 1984 the Fine Gael vote dropped nearly 8 per cent in the Laois-Offaly by-election, which Fianna Fáil won easily. But a rather more significant nationwide contest had taken place on the same day: the European Parliament elections. In 1979, Fine Gael had won just four of the fifteen seats but in the intervening five years the party had acquired a wealth of experience and know-how in election technique and, even with other trends running against them, they hoped to improve their position. Five months before the elections, FitzGerald set up four Constituency Review Committees, based on the Euro constituencies. The Committees' brief was to make a thorough examination of party structures both in the Euro constituencies and in the Dáil constituencies and make recommendations for improvement. They were also asked to have an eye to the following year's local government elections and to help identify good local candidates. In the short run their work bore fruit in the more professional selection of candidates for the Euro constituencies. For example, in Munster where the party had run four candidates in 1979, they now ran only two. The ideal arrangement was to have a Limerick and a Cork based candidate. Naturally Tom O'Donnell, the outgoing MEP, would be the Limerick candidate and in the end they shrewdly chose UCC Professor of Agriculture, Tom Raftery, both for his Cork base and for his good profile in agri-politics. It worked.

Similarly, in Dublin the choice of Mary Banotti as a northside candidate gave a much better balance to the ticket, as well as appealing to women voters and younger people. As in Munster, the policy was successful and Banotti took a second seat for Fine Gael. The party was unable to make any advance on its single seats in Leinster and Connacht-Ulster, but the success of Raftery and Banotti meant that Fine Gael had increased its Euro representation from four seats to six, a 50 per cent increase despite their share of the first-preference vote declining by 1 per cent to 32.2 per cent. It was a triumph for the new strategic maturity of Fine Gael, although the decline in support was undoubtedly worrying.

Just as worrying for the government, however, was the fact that Labour was wiped out in the Euro elections, losing all four seats which it had previously held. This confirmed the trend of the Dublin Central by-election, and inevitably there were loud murmurings from the anti-coalitionists in the party. In turn, Labour ministers sought to make the running in the cabinet, pressing for a national pensions plan and the long awaited family planning bill. The real problem with Labour, of course, was their woefully amateur organisation. For example, Brendan Halligan had been one of their Euro candidates in Dublin but dropped out before the contest and actually went on to predict that Labour wouldn't win any seats! For his pains, Dick Spring publicly called him 'a bollocks'. None the less, on the day of the count, Halligan was the Labour representative on RTE radio pontificating on the results as they came in.

As far as the Euro elections were concerned, Fine Gael felt that it had held the line. That, allied to its intensive constituency review, gave it some hope for the local elections of June 1985. The review had shown that party support was not holding up in the West — unsurprisingly, in view of the more liberal orientation of the party under FitzGerald — and this led to the specific appointment of a full-time organiser there. More serious was the evidence of decline in the Dublin region, where Fine Gael was discovered to be losing heavily in working class areas. Party membership was poor; and there was hardly any identity with the party in such areas, and many well-known deputies were found to be not really trying. By the end of 1985 Fine Gael had not made any real breakthrough in working-class Dublin. As FitzGerald noted wistfully, 'some of our TDs do better by not mentioning that they are Fine Gael.'

These straws in the wind suggested that the local elections of June 1985 would be tough for Fine Gael, but not even the most pessimistic government supporter could have forecast the eventual outcome. On a national basis, Fianna Fáil got 46 per cent of the vote, Fine Gael only 30 per cent and Labour 8 per cent. All over the country, there were Fianna Fáil gains. For the first time in decades, Fine Gael lost its dominant position in Dublin. If this kind of result was repeated in a general election, they would lose up to thirty seats: it could be 1977 all over again.

The two constants during the first three years of the coalition government were declining electoral support for both parties and a fundamental — and debilitating — divergence of opinion between them on policy matters. The poorer Labour performed in elections and in public opinion polls, the more pressure was applied to the party leadership by the anti-coalitionist left. But as 1984 wore on, the restlessness of the Fine Gael backbenches increased and started to become a significant factor for the government. While Fine Gael was having some internal successes — such as the spectacularly successful national lottery launched by Finbarr Fitzpatrick in June 1984, which in eighteen months had wiped out a party deficit of half a million pounds — the tensions were visible as well. Young Fine Gael continued to go its own way and was frequently an embarrassment to the senior politicians. It had already taken an independent line in the abortion referendum; its bi-monthly magazine, *Futureline*, pressed radical policies on minimum incomes, care for the homeless and the control of building land prices. In March 1984 their annual conference passed a resolution criticising the forthcoming visit of President Reagan to Ireland and the executive was mandated to protest at US foreign policy. Peter Barry was outraged and, for once, even FitzGerald was deeply embarrassed: the government was obviously concerned over the importance of American investment in Ireland. Not for the first time, Rona Fitzgerald came under pressure from the senior party, but Young Fine Gael stuck to its guns and a week before the visit they duly staged their protest outside the American Embassy in Dublin. They made it clear that they welcomed President Reagan as the leader of the American people, while putting on record their opposition to his foreign policy. They also held a public meeting on the eve of the visit which was attended by Monica Barnes and Senator Katherine Bulbulia.

Young Fine Gael highlighted a fundamental tension in the parliamentary party. Although 36 of the 70 TDs had been elected since June 1981, many of them were, like the longer serving deputies, deeply conservative. They had simply hitched their bandwagons to FitzGerald's star but few of them were actually social and economic crusaders. The smaller group of genuine radicals were, like Young Fine Gael, growing restive at what they regarded as Fine Gael's lack of reforming drive in government.

It is interesting to analyse the different voices with which the Fine Gael parliamentary party spoke under pressure. For example, in July 1984, in the wake of the Euro elections, the parliamentary party held a unique two-day meeting at Malahide to take stock of the government's performance to date. Many backbenchers gave vent to their frustration, but it was the liberal, radical wing of the party that tended to make the running. There were complaints that Fine Gael was becoming indistinguishable from Fianna Fáil. Alan Shatter, Nora Owen, Monica Barnes, Maurice Manning, Hugh Coveney, Richard Bruton and Mary Flaherty all stressed the need to pursue major social reforms, including such areas as contraception, illegitimacy, childcare, marital breakdown, joint property rights and reform of the court system. Hugh Coveney spoke for many when he said that the government always seemed to be 'one action plan away from action', a reference to the FitzGerald government's almost limitless capacity for discussion and analysis.

The 'Malahide Parliament' was a bruising affair, but at least most deputies left for home on the sweltering Friday evening confident that new bridges had been built to their ministers, and that they would be kept better informed. (One can imagine their consternation less than a month later at the debacle surrounding the announcement of the cuts in food subsidies.) The backbench conservatives were not, however, completely silent at Malahide. Oliver J. Flanagan, saying he spoke for 'the decent rural deputies', and Alice Glenn both reiterated their total opposition to any increased availability of contraceptives. By the time the parliamentary party next met in the wake of an election reverse — almost a year later, in June 1985 following the local elections — the conservatives were in full flight. At this meeting the only complaints about social reform were that it was on the government's agenda at all! This time, the cabinet members were told, it was time to get down to the nitty gritty: forget about social issues which don't win votes, and do something about jobs and taxation, which do.

By mid 1985, Fine Gael had become quite schizophrenic about social reform, one of the identifying marks FitzGerald had imposed on the party. The very large conservative flank of the party, which was not confined to rural deputies, was always equivocal. If social reform brought the party electoral kudos, they kept their mouths shut, and went with the tide. If it brought a backlash at the polls, they were instantly vocal in condemning an alleged obsession with 'peripheral issues'. The February 1985 Family Planning Amendment Bill played a pivotal role in the double-think.

That bill, to amend the existing law that confined contraceptives to married couples, was published on 7 February. It proposed their availability to all over the age of eighteen. The bill had been bogged down in cabinet for much of 1984 because the Minister for Health, Barry Desmond, wanted an age limit of sixteen. That was the marriage age. But there was strong opposition in Fine Gael especially, where there was immense nervousness at provoking any further clashes with the Catholic Church. This was a legacy of the bitterly divisive anti-abortion amendment debate. It was FitzGerald who finally persuaded Desmond to settle for an eighteen limit, the age of majority. With his facility for statistics, the Taoiseach uncovered the figures showing just a couple of hundred marriages of people under eighteen. Besides the Marital Breakdown Committee was also proposing that the age for marriage should be raised to eighteen.

After a meeting between FitzGerald and Spring in early February, it was finally decided to go ahead with the bill. FitzGerald informed the cabinet that they had to have done with the agonising. Some of his party ministers, like Paddy Cooney and Peter Barry, were very nervous of the opposition the measure would provoke. Fianna Fáil had themselves convinced that the government would be defeated, as various Fine Gael backbenchers wrestled in public with their consciences on the matter. But despite some very anxious days, the bill was safely carried, although three of the party's deputies — Alice Glenn, Tom O'Donnell and Oliver Flanagan — did vote against. However, FitzGerald and Fine Gael had at last cleared one of the major social legislative hurdles they had collectively set themselves. Now the party sat back to reap the popular reward for their efforts. But strangely, they earned no real kudos in successive opinion polls. The party's schizophrenia on social reform deepened.

The division between radicals and conservatives within Fine Gael mirrored the wider division between Fine Gael and Labour in government. Throughout the summer of 1984, the government was trying to formulate its national economic plan. It was the old issue again: how, and at what pace, was public spending to be cut. In September, FitzGerald admitted that the government would not now eliminate the budget deficit by 1987 because of the severe impact which this would have on the economy. Their revised target would be to get it down to 'a little more that 5 per cent by 1987'. At long last, after more than four years of sermonising, Fine Gael had confronted the implications of their most fundamental economic promise, and admitted that they were incapable of honouring it.

Yet, as FitzGerald also pointed out, even the greatly moderated target would require spending cuts of up to £700 million between 1984 and 1987. This forced Dick Spring's hand and the following night in Cork he made a major speech which was effectively a response to the Taoiseach, setting Labour's face against social welfare cuts and placing more emphasis on a widening of the capital taxation net. Spring specifically rejected one particular proposal.

There are those who would argue that in times like these, it is not unreasonable to expect wage and salary earners, who have never been required to pay before, to pay for access to the health services. That is something to which we could not agree under any circumstances.

'Those who would argue' were, in fact, Fine Gael colleagues around the cabinet table.

In an effort to cut borrowing, Fine Gael had proposed the idea of a nightly charge of £12.50 for beds in public hospital wards. Again, and not for the first time since December 1982, Labour imposed their veto and made it stick. Throughout 1985, party differences over the proposed National Development Corporation, and provision of legal local radio, dogged the coalition. Finally, after a year's inter-party wrangling, a local radio bill was published by Jim Mitchell at the end of June. It was planned to take the entire second stage on Friday, 5 July. The bill aimed to tackle the scandalous rash of illegal pirate local stations around the country. There was to be a two-tier system of local radio: one commercial, with RTE having a right to participate, and the other community based. The proposals had been approved at cabinet by the four Labour ministers.

But once the bill was published, there was a Labour back-bench revolt. Communications spokesman, Toddy O'Sullivan, and Frank Cluskey led the assault. It did not conform to the commitment in the 'Programme for Government'. The state must have a 51 per cent share in every licence granted for local radio, Cluskey asserted.

It was technically true that the bill did not conform with the December 1982 programme. That had simply stated: 'community radio to be developed in an orderly manner by RTE and local community interests'. The brevity of the policy statement, and the inter-party impasse that grew out of it, said much about the defective nature of the coalition negotiations, and the imprecision which flowed from them. The reality was that very little consideration was given to the issue. Afterwards, FitzGerald claimed that the clause was based largely on Fine Gael policy.

Yet the anti-Coalition element inside the Labour parliamentary party, now joined by Cluskey since his resignation, wanted state-controlled radio only. It was not what Fine Gael wanted; and it was not what the people wanted. Local commercial radio, with safeguards for genuine community involvement in the medium, was a sensible compromise. But not to the Labour ideologues.

The fact that the second stage debate actually commenced on the bill, but had to be aborted on 5 July, underlined other defects in the coalition. 'Labour cannot deliver' became the exasperated comment of many leading Fine Gael figures. It was Labour who had clamoured for the Contraceptives Bill, yet, they had failed to take two of their sixteen deputies through the 'Tá' lobby. Now on the radio issue, Labour's ministers had approved a measure at cabinet, but could not deliver their backbenchers in the lobby. Better no bill had been introduced at all, than to have this fiasco.

Afterwards Mitchell ruefully admitted that the bill would have to be amended if it was to secure Labour support. In his second stage speech he had spoken of the 'long-awaited' measure, and the 'extraordinary interest' in it. He warmly commended his 'two-tier structure of radio services, comprising local and community services', with the former run on 'a sound commercial basis'.

But the glowing blueprint was still-born. It was left lying there, testimony to the unworkability of the Spring-FitzGerald inter-party arrangement. Meanwhile, the gross illegality of pirate stations around the country continued to flourish. Allied to the constant public wrangling over the NDC, primarily between Spring, and Industry Minister, John Bruton, it left Fine Gael a thankless task, trying to uphold the credibility of the administration.

But another Labour proposal, first made in September 1984, revealed much about the Fine Gael party. Labour had always pressed strongly for a land tax. They were concerned with the extraordinarily low yield from farmer taxation and they also wished to compensate for the abolition of agricultural rates. Moreover, there was a sound economic argument that a land tax would lead to land being farmed more productively and would force land lying fallow into the hands of more enterprising farmers. However, the farmers were always a key Fine Gael constituency: their part defection in 1977 had cost the party dear, and since then Fine Gael was very wary of them. There may have been less than a quarter of a million of them in the whole country, but in multi-seat constituencies they were still capable of deciding the destiny of a fourth or fifth final seat, if they voted en bloc.

When media reports of a possible 1 per cent land tax began to appear, the IFA propaganda machine, led by its vociferous president, Joe Rea, swung into action. County executives were detailed to ascertain the attitude of local Fine Gael TDs and to publicise the findings in the local media. The next couple of weeks showed not only the power of the farmers' lobby, but the craven attitude of most rural Fine Gael TDs towards it. In Wexford the IFA issued a statement on behalf of the three Fine Gael deputies, Ivan Yates, Avril Doyle, and Michael Darcy (who was a junior minister) pledging the opposition of all three to the tax. Many other deputies made their opposition publicly known; one of them, Tom Enright of Laois-Offaly, said that half the TDs and senators in the parliamentary party were opposed to a land tax. All in all, it was a pretty complete collapse before a pressure group. FitzGerald himself tried to have it both ways, implying opposition to the capitulation, while still not criticising his TDs for it. 'They claimed to have been caught out', he said. 'I can't judge that. I'm not making criticism of the media. I am not judging deputies either, some of whom said they were conned'. Eventually, a modified form of land tax was included in 'Building on Reality'. The legislation to give effect to it was introduced in June 1985, only three weeks before the local government election, and contributed to a Fine Gael trouncing in many farming constituencies.

The incident also revealed the urban-rural tension inside Fine Gael. While rural deputies were lining up to assure local IFA executives of their opposition to a land tax, a group of Dublin TDs, together with Bernard Allen of Cork, were reminding Joe Rea of another reality of Ireland in the '80s: the plight of the urban poor, and the necessity for all sectors of the community to bear their fair share of taxation. Gay Mitchell, Richard Bruton and Mary Flaherty, whose constituencies had large working-class estates, went to the Farm Centre in Dublin to argue this minority Fine Gael view with Rea.

The land tax controversy, coming hard on the heels of the mishandling of the food subsidy cuts, alienated FitzGerald from almost every section of the population. The point was dramatically underlined on Sunday 23 September 1984, All-Ireland Football Final day. When it was announced over the Croke Park public address system that the Taoiseach was now taking his seat, he was audibly booed from all corners of the ground.

Fine Gael followers therefore pinned a lot of hope on the eventual launch on Tuesday 2 October of the national plan, titled 'Building on Reality'. The government claimed it represented three budgets rolled together, and set out the broad parameters of economic policy to the end of 1987. But it was no panacea for the country's basic ills. On unemployment, it grimly targeted a mere decline of 10,000 in the net jobless total by the end of 1987. Tax equity was scarcely addressed at all. Tax evasion was to be countered by publishing the names of culprits uncovered. But it was a proposed land tax of £10 per adjusted acre, up to holdings of 80 adjusted acres, which really made a joke of tax equity.

The grandiose launch of the plan did give FitzGerald and his colleagues a timely fillip for the following weekend's árd fheis. There, the party leader was jubilant, taking refuge again behind his reputation for honesty and integrity. 'I do not exonerate our government from some measure of clumsiness in handling policy decisions during the summer, although I believe that last Tuesday, we more than retrieved any such errors of judgement.'

As if positively seeking to put behind him the previous two years of wrangling with Labour, and consigning most burning subjects to commissions and review bodies, he committed his government to a new beginning. 'As far as I'm concerned, our future begins now', he declared to applause. 'The facile jibe of indecisiveness, levelled against us by some, is seen now to be hollow to the core. We have acted.'

The plan, and the árd fheis, marked a rehabilitation of

sorts for FitzGerald and his government. People might argue about the various targets in the economic plan. But there was a plan. And an MRBI poll later that month showed the Fianna Fáil lead over the Coalition was back to a manageable 8 per cent. But for the first time, Haughey had edged ahead of FitzGerald in satisfaction rating, 48 per cent to 47 per cent.

There was growing optimism in Fine Gael, however, as FitzGerald faced up to a major summit on the Northern Ireland problem on 29 November. There were real expectations of an historic Anglo-Irish accord to break the long cycle of death and violence. This stemmed in the main from the report of the New Ireland Forum the previous May.

The New Ireland Forum was the brainchild of John Hume, who had urged it upon all the southern nationalist parties from autumn 1982. They should spell out nationalist Ireland's blueprint for reconciliation with northern unionism. Fine Gael and the coalition government were reluctant to get involved, because the implicit emphasis of the Forum contrasted totally with the thrust of Fine Gael policy which was to secure political co-existence between nationalists and unionists within Northern Ireland. But Hume was nothing if not persistent and he prompted FitzGerald to formulate a proposal for a Forum of all nationalist parties opposed to violence. The Taoiseach put the proposal before the cabinet who promptly shot it down by a vote of twelve to three in February 1983. Only Peter Barry and Michael Noonan supported the Taoiseach; interestingly, both their departments were closely involved with the Northern problem in its diplomatic and security contexts.

This was a set-back for FitzGerald but he now proved that he could be as persistent as John Hume. The Fianna Fáil árd fheis was coming up that weekend and FitzGerald feared that Charlie Haughey would endorse Hume's call for a Forum. He used this argument to win over his cabinet colleagues one by one. Most ministers didn't want to get involved with the North at all. They had enough problems to solve in the South. Besides, they didn't want to do anything that might exacerbate the violence. But finally, by 24 February, FitzGerald had won. He made a statement calling for all-party talks in the Republic on an all-Ireland forum that would consider the possibility of peace and reconciliation in the context of a new Ireland.

Two days later, in his árd fheis speech, Haughey also endorsed Hume's call for a council for a new Ireland. He did not refer at all to FitzGerald's invitation to all-party talks. But inter-party discussions did get under way in March and they culminated in the formal announcement of a New Ireland Forum which would be established to examine how 'lasting peace and stability can be achieved in a new Ireland through the democratic process'. It was to report by the end of the year 'on possible new structures and processes through which its objective might be achieved'.

The Forum eventually got under way on 30 May 1983 at Dublin Castle. FitzGerald spoke of the need to examine any structure or solution that would meet the essential requirement of expressing and guaranteeing the two identities on the island: 'the Irish/Irish identity of nationalists' and the 'British/Irish identity of the unionist tradition'. Haughey, on the other hand, saw the aim of the Forum being 'to construct a basic [nationalist] position, which can then be put to an all-round constitutional conference, convened by the Irish and British governments as a prelude to British withdrawal'. These vastly different emphases were to overshadow all the work of the Forum, and the interpretation and application of its report. It didn't meet its 1983 deadline and finally ended — after many crises and near breakdowns — with the publication of its report in May 1984.

In contrast to the constant bitterness and rows that dogged FitzGerald's relationship with Haughey since 1979, both men got on well at the Forum. One incident captured the mood. Just before Christmas 1983, there was a row at a private session in Dublin Castle. Dick Spring attacked Haughey strongly as the source of a leaked story in one of the newspapers. Haughey suddenly became very distraught; indeed, he broke down completely. Ray MacSharry had to take him out and proceedings were interrupted for some time. When Haughey returned he explained that he was under a lot of pressure. The controversial book, *The Boss*, had just been published and his family had been very distressed by it. Suddenly FitzGerald remembered that he had recently told a reporter from the *Sunday Tribune* that his Christmas reading would include *The Boss*. He talked to Spring about this; Spring had also told the *Tribune* reporter that he would be reading *The Boss* at Christmas. FitzGerald decided to ring Vincent Browne, the editor of the *Tribune*, and asked him to delete *The Boss* from his and Spring's reading preferences, and this was duly done. They didn't want to hurt and embarrass Haughey any further.

Despite this increased personal goodwill, the differing party emphases in the Forum could not be fudged. The final report presented three possible options: a unitary state, federation, or joint authority. Fianna Fáil had wanted to recommend a unitary state as the only solution and after the report was published Haughey tried to suggest that in fact it *was* the only solution seriously on offer. Moreover, although the report recognised that Irish unity could only come by consent, Haughey managed to put a most jesuitical interpretation on this formula. Still, despite all the internal divisions within the Forum, its report did act as a major catalyst to the Anglo-Irish process, and led directly to the Chequers summit of 19 November.

Enormous, perhaps exaggerated, expectations had been raised in Ireland regarding the Chequers summit. But the outcome was disastrous for the government and for FitzGerald in particular. It was not merely Mrs Thatcher's dismissal of all three Forum options, with her brusque 'out, out, out' press conference. Compounding the debacle was that her haughty performance was followed by an utterly abject and bumbling press conference by FitzGerald.

Nationalist Ireland was outraged. FitzGerald had apparently been walked all over and didn't even make a whimper of protest. It was, in fact, a dreadful blunder because while the press conferences conveyed a totally negative impression, the agreed communiqué did point towards a radical departure on the North. It recognised the need to respect the culture and identity of the nationalist minority and to have them 'reflected in the institutions of Northern Ireland'. But at the time, this got lost in the tide of national outrage.

The following Wednesday, a shocked Fine Gael parliamentary party met. Many TDs were already harbouring misgivings about FitzGerald. He had not been the economic messiah they had expected. Now he had been humiliated on the national question. It was his blackest hour, worse even than the amendment debacle. Many deputies openly attacked him. In trying to put up a defence, he conceded that Mrs Thatcher had been 'gratuitously offensive'. Within hours, this remark was reported on RTE and carried in the newspapers. Key civil servants, desperately trying to restore normality with their British counterparts, were appalled.

There were some suggestions that FitzGerald, or one of his advisers such as Prendergast, had inspired the leak. This was incorrect. Others alleged that Maurice Manning was the leaker. This was also incorrect. It was, in fact, another backbencher who leaked the phrase to *Irish Press* reporter, Stephen Collins. It later led to FitzGerald warning the parliamentary party that it would be impossible for him to speak frankly if the proceedings did not remain confidential.

The entire Chequers debacle caused immense damage to FitzGerald. For the first time since he became leader, many backbenchers openly talked of the possibility of replacing him. They respected FitzGerald, but they had no real affection for him. He wasn't the kind of man to command loyalty, wasn't given to chatting with colleagues in the corridor, dropping down to the Dáil bar for a drink or two. As one junior minister explained, 'There's an awful lot of the Northern Protestant mammy in him.'

Nor was the anti-FitzGerald feeling confined to the backbenchers. In the aftermath of Chequers, Michael Noonan began to test the extent of the party's desire for a new leader. He talked to at least four prominent backbenchers. His line was that if Garret couldn't get it right on the North, what chance had he on other issues. Later, when reports of this move appeared in the media, Noonan denied them categorically. But the backbenchers in question were adamant about Noonan's overture.

It was immensely to FitzGerald's credit that he resisted all temptation to bow to domestic pressure in the wake of the 'out, out, out' summit. Soon he and his officials had the Anglo-Irish negotiations back on the rails and although they dragged on for another year, seesawing from one crisis and breaking point to another, he brought them to a triumphant conclusion at Hillsborough on 15 November 1985. Ireland was being treated as an equal by England. Dublin officials would help to administer the North from an office in Belfast. It was indeed an incredible breakthrough.

After the buffeting FitzGerald and his party had taken for most of 1984 and 1985, Hillsborough was like the first breath of spring. 'There are Fine Gael TDs going around now having orgasms about the North, and a couple of weeks ago they didn't want to know about the place.' Alan Shatter's cynical comment, made only a fortnight after the signing of the agreement, summed up the mood. Party deputies had good reason to be euphoric. On 25 November 1985, an opinion poll showed that Fianna Fail's lead over the coalition had been cut to 8 per cent, compared to 14 per cent in July. In other polls in the intervening period the Fianna Fáil lead had actually soared to 19 per cent. Even better, Fianna Fáil's strident dismissal of the agreement quickly revealed them to be completely out of touch with public opinion. Fine Gael, it seemed, had now become the true republican party. The success belonged pre-eminently to FitzGerald. He had finally delivered an historic breakthrough on one of his fundamental reasons for being in politics.

17

Back to the Future

Everywhere FitzGerald travelled in the days after Hillsborough, he was mobbed and applauded. There was a national wave of goodwill and appreciation for him and his government. Fine Gael wasn't slow to capitalise on this welcome upsurge in its standing. For the first time ever, a mail shot was sent to every registered party member — of whom there are over 30,000 — in the weekend after Hillsborough. It contained a resumé of the agreement, a letter from FitzGerald, and an invitation to one of a series of provincial meetings the following week. These were to explain the agreement and they were a huge success; every venue was packed out.

The government had a winning issue at last, and FitzGerald was their hero. He was the undisputed architect of the Anglo-Irish success. From the formation of the New Ireland Forum, when he overcame the opposition of his own cabinet colleagues, to his triumph over the Chequers debacle, he had confounded all his doubters and all the sceptics. Suddenly he was restored in the public's affection and he was once again the undisputed master of Fine Gael.

Even on the domestic front, things seemed to be picking up for Fine Gael. The home improvements grant scheme was a roaring success, and by the end of 1985 over 30,000 application forms had been requested. Deputies, senators and even some junior ministers were featuring them in clinic advertisements in their local provincial newspapers. Ted Nealon had a large advertisement in the *Sligo Champion* announcing that full details could be had at his clinics, and he had his biggest attendances ever. TDs were in excellent form as they headed home for Christmas. It looked as if the bad days were behind them, and 1986 might be the year when the party pulled itself together. In fact, the first quarter of 1986 turned out to be an unmitigated and uninterrupted disaster for FitzGerald and Fine Gael, in which the post-Hillsborough revival shuddered to a halt.

Fine Gael's troubles began on Saturday, 21 December 1985 when Desmond O'Malley, accompanied by another former Fianna Fáil deputy, Mary Harney, launched the Progressive Democrats. It was O'Malley's leap into the dark. In its initial composition, the party had a decidedly Fianna Fáil complexion, but the chairman was a young barrister, Michael MacDowell, who was a former chairman of FitzGerald's own Fine Gael constituency executive in Dublin South East. Moreover, if the leading personalities were ex-Fianna Fáil, the policy message enunciated was classic Fine Gael. O'Malley said that they stood for fundamental tax reform, support for private enterprise and a clear distinction between church and state. He called for public spending cuts and an attack on the current budget deficit. It was like an echo of FitzGerald in 1981.

Obviously the PD had an immediate appeal for disillusioned Fine Gael supporters. Their own party had failed to deliver on a very similar prescription for the country's ills in their three years in government. Initially, the PD got lots of media attention but political 'insiders' were inclined to be cynically dismissive. However when their first public rally, in the North Dublin suburb of Sutton, drew over a thousand people, both the major parties began to sit up and take notice. Further meetings around the country pulled equally large and enthusiastic crowds; suddenly, the PD had a bandwagon rolling.

However, it was the publication of an opinion poll in the *Irish Independent* on 17 January, less than a month after the formation of the PD, that underlined the serious threat the new party posed for Fine Gael. It showed PD with 19 per cent of popular support. Fianna Fáil had dropped 10 per cent to 41 per cent, and Fine Gael 8 per cent to 29 per cent. In other words, Fine Gael were nearly back at their bedrock support level inherited by FitzGerald in 1977. The poll also

310

revealed that the PD was drawing its support fairly evenly from both major parties.

It contained some chilling news too for Labour and for the existing Fine Gael-Labour coalition arrangement. Labour itself was trailing well down the field with only 6 per cent support. Even worse, however, was that although 24 per cent of Fine Gael supporters said that they would give second preferences to Labour, a further 22 per cent said that they would give them to the PD. Given that very many Labour seats were dependent on Fine Gael transfers, and that these had run at a rate of 86 per cent in the June 1981 general election, this switch of second preferences could spell near oblivion for Labour at a general election.

The following week, the new party picked up two more Fianna Fáil defectors, Pearse Wyse and Bobby Molloy, which gave Fine Gael something to smile about. The Fianna Fáil monolith appeared to be breaking up by the day. Privately, many Fine Gael ministers were pleased with the emergence of the PD whom they and many backbenchers saw as a potentially more congenial coalition partner than Labour. Indeed the February issue of *Magill* magazine carried an article which revealed that a majority of Fine Gael backbenchers preferred the idea of coalition with the new party than with Labour. Just over half the thirty-eight Fine Gael deputies surveyed could cite no major policy difference with the PD, while another one-third said that they would await detailed PD policies before committing themselves. Numerous deputies expressed their personal admiration for Des O'Malley. While almost half the TDs surveyed said that they were broadly happy with Labour's performance in government, a full 42 per cent of them also felt that Labour had held Fine Gael back. These included David Molony, Hugh Coveney, Ivan Yates, Alan Shatter, Richard Bruton, Joe McCartin, Madeleine Tayor-Quinn and Enda Kenny.

On Monday, 10 February the *Irish Times* published an opinion poll which had the most devastating implications for Fine Gael. Support for the party had plummeted to 23 per cent and it had already been passed out by O'Malley's seven-week old party, which was on 25 per cent. Fianna Fáil were also down, but they held a commendable 42 per cent. Labour were down to 4 per cent. The poll sent a shudder through every Fine Gael TD. The party chairman, Kieran Crotty, confessed that every TD's seat was now at risk. FitzGerald now tried to soothe his backbenchers, but even he was shocked by the disclosure that 47 per cent of PD supporters were formerly Fine Gael voters. Thirty-one per cent were Fianna Fáilers. FitzGerald decided there and then that something had to be done. He decided to reshuffle his cabinet.

FitzGerald had been toying with the idea of a reshuffle since before Hillsborough. He decided to wait until after the agreement in case it necessitated a full-time minister for the North. However the agreement wasn't signed until mid November, only a month away from the third anniversary of the formation of the coalition government on 14 December. The significance of that date was that the ten remaining senior and junior ministers who had not yet qualified for ministerial pensions would do so. To move in the immediate aftermath of the agreement but before that date, and to drop any of them, would only compound their disappointment. Yet if he were to wait until 14 December and then reshuffle, there would be a chorus of criticism that he had cynically delayed the change in order to let the lads in for the pension. However, the happy resurgence of Fine Gael popularity after Hillsborough suddenly banished the necessity for a reshuffle in FitzGerald's eyes.

It was generally assumed that any reshuffle would move Alan Dukes out of the Department of Finance. His public image was that of a remote technocrat, a mandarin loftily dishing out punishment to the punters. At the end of January, Dukes delivered his budget speech for 1986. It was easily the most creative budget that he had yet presented. For the first time, it afforded some relief to the PAYE sector. There was a full £120 million worth of tax relief, including the abolition of the 'temporary' 1 per cent Youth Employment Levy. The Labour input could be seen in increased taxation of the financial institutions. But the message simply never got across to the public. Since Duke's new style budget presentation of 1985, the national handlers had been shafted and he had reverted to a more traditional presentation. Even the little bit of good news that was given early in the speech was couched in dry, arid, civil service language. And so, an imaginative financial statement was grossly undersold, as Dukes droned on in the Dáil in his lifeless monotone for an hour and a half.

The next day, the Minister of Health, Barry Desmond, was making his contribution to the budget debate. He told the house that 'In 1986, we have reached the point where it is now necessary and appropriate to commence the programme of rationalising hospital facilities' and he announced that eight hospitals would be closed during the coming year, including two major psychiatric hospitals in Castlerea and Carlow. There was uproar in the Dáil.

Desmond was accused of having had no consultations and of having shown callous disregard for 'the weakest and the most vulnerable section of our society'. Government backbenchers, especially those from Roscommon and Carlow-Kilkenny, were appalled. They faced a torrent of criticism over the weekend and were left defenceless in any attempt to justify the government's plans. Desmond had indeed made it clear that there would be discussions on the proposed closures with the local health boards and that no patients would suffer, but his unilateral announcement was generally interpreted as unfeeling and precipitate.

Deputies had no sooner come back to the Dáil than another bombshell struck them on Tuesday 4 February. Fianna Fáil's education spokesperson, Mary O'Rourke, learned that the Minister for Education, Gemma Hussey, had that morning informed the head of Carysfort Teacher Training College in Dublin that it was to be closed; a similar letter had been sent to the College patron, the Catholic Archbishop of Dublin. Mrs O'Rourke raised the question in the Dáil and the minister had no option but to confirm the proposed closure. It was in the interests of 'a better reallocation of resources'. Again, as with the hospitals, there had been no consultation with the relevant authorities. College staff, the Archbishop of Dublin, student teachers: all condemned yet another unilateral decision. As with the hospital closures, it was the peremptory nature of the decision rather than the case for such action (which was a strong one) that was the real bone of contention.

Twice within six days the government had committed the most dreadful blunders in the most sensitive electoral areas — health and education. There was uproar at the Fine Gael parliamentary party meeting on the Wednesday and the cabinet came under massive assault. It was led in part by chairman, Kieran Crotty, a deputy for Carlow-Kilkenny, who obviously had a direct interest in the closure of the Carlow psychiatric hospital. Liam Cosgrave strongly denounced the Carysfort closure in his constituency. Peter Barry was heckled as he tried to defend the government's actions. The ordinary deputies were bitter and confused. On RTE radio that evening, Liam Skelly said Hussey was a disgrace. They especially attacked the lack of consultation on the closures. Many of them (and Labour backbenchers also) had meetings with Barry Desmond. The panic and despair felt by many deputies was pithily summed up by Maurice Manning, who declared that 'the ghost of Earnán de Blaghad still haunts this party.'

These traumatic developments were quickly followed by the devastating opinion poll on Monday 10 February which showed Fine Gael two points behind PD. What did it matter that on that very day Mrs Hussey announced that the government was going to give Carysfort a two-year reprieve so that existing students could finish their courses, and that she would begin discussions with the authorities there? It was too late. The political damage had been done.

It was in this atmosphere that FitzGerald decided on the cabinet reshuffle. That Tuesday evening, he told Dick Spring that he was going to reshuffle. It was a matter they had discussed a number of times the previous autumn. Spring now believed FitzGerald would get down to it in the coming weeks.

However, the Taoiseach had decided to act immediately. The conventional wisdom of a reshuffle in the autumn and winter of 1985 had been that it would at least embrace Dukes at Finance, and Noonan at Justice. Both needed to be rescued from negative departmental images. But now FitzGerald was reckoning in terms of much more sweeping changes. The events of the previous fortnight meant that

Desmond and Hussey would also have to be switched from Health and Education.

By Wednesday afternoon, FitzGerald had finalised the outline of his new government. He would move Bruton back to Finance, and attach Public Service to it. John Boland had delivered the public service reform package and completed the 25th wage round deal. It was a good time to move him to something more challenging. Bruton's planned return to Finance had all to do with the emergence of the Progressive Democrats, and the 47 per cent of Fine Gaelers amongst its followers. Bruton was quintessential Fine Gael, and in the same economic mould as O'Malley. He would be the direct foil to the PD leader.

FitzGerald would move Desmond to Justice, and Michael Noonan from there to Industry and Commerce, Bruton's former post. Gemma Hussey would get a new Department of European Affairs, with Peter Barry concentrating on the Anglo-Irish Conference. Alan Dukes would get Education, and John Boland would go to Desmond's dual briefs of Health and Social Welfare. It was an imaginative re-deployment of the team.

Soon the Taoiseach commenced negotiations with his Ministers. Dick Spring was fully apprised of the plans and endorsed the electoral necessity of moving Desmond. Around 5 p.m., Desmond was informed of the intention to move him. He immediately demurred.

FitzGerald had also commenced preliminary consultations with other Ministers. But now he had to attend a parliamentary party meeting, which was considering its attitude to a Labour Private Member's Bill on divorce which was due the following week. In the course of that meeting, the party leader surprised the attendance, including some ministers, by telling them that he would be carrying out a 're-structuring' of the government the following day. Everyone had thought the reshuffle was a dead issue. Hopes of preferment instantly swept through the ranks.

Later that night, FitzGerald resumed his consultations. Dukes readily accepted the offer of Education. Hussey was delighted with the offer of European Affairs and accepted. She rang a relative in Brussels to convey the good news and late that night had a celebratory drink with her husband, Derry, and Peter Prendergast in Government Buildings. But there was one major problem emerging. Desmond was adamantly refusing to move from Health and Social Welfare. He would not be made a scapegoat for agreed government decisions on hospital closures. He had also become obsessed with the notion that various vested interests — the doctors, the cigarette industry, the Catholic Church — wanted his scalp. The deputy Labour leader was determined not to be anyone's fall-guy.

All that night until 4 a.m. on Thursday 13 February, desperate efforts were made to resolve the obvious government crisis. FitzGerald and Desmond had angry, heated exchanges. The Taoiseach was determined to have his way: it had become one of the primary motives for the entire reshuffle. It was also his fundamental prerogative to decide who would serve, and where, in his government.

FitzGerald offered Desmond various alternative portfolios, Justice, Environment, or Social Welfare on its own. All were refused. Desmond made it plain that there was only one way he would go. He would have to be fired. But that would rock the very shaky coalition to its foundations once again. With virtually every Fine Gael deputy, including FitzGerald, contemplating the possibility of the PD as a potential coalition partner, it was no time to sack the deputy leader of the Labour Party.

The frenetic round of meetings by FitzGerald resumed later on Thursday morning. By lunch-time Dick Spring accepted that he had no option but to back Desmond, and he so informed FitzGerald. It was now a direct inter-party issue. It left FitzGerald in a terrible dilemma. To insist on his constitutional prerogative and fire Desmond would almost certainly spell the end of his government. Finally, he decided to yield to the Labour Party. Desmond would remain at Health, but he would lose Social Welfare.

But FitzGerald was also running into problems on another aspect of the reshuffle. It was not proving feasible to carve up Foreign Affairs to facilitate a separate Ministry for European Affairs. Peter Barry was opposed to losing half his portfolio. Thus, FitzGerald had to break the news to his long-time personal friend, Gemma Hussey. He was now offering her Social Welfare, Barry Desmond's part-time portfolio. She was completely shattered by this abrupt change of fortune, and was reduced to tears.

All around Leinster House, the news was out about the reshuffle crisis. The announcement had been postponed from the morning to 3.45 p.m., then postponed to 4.45 p.m., and finally was announced to the Dáil at 4.50 p.m. — ten minutes before the House rose — by FitzGerald. Desmond's obduracy had necessitated a massive shuffle of the reshuffle.

The eventual line-up announced to the Dáil was greeted with guffaws from Fianna Fáil, and consternation from the Fine Gael backbenchers and the press gallery. Bruton got Finance alright, but lost Public Service, which went to Labour's Ruairi Quinn. Noonan moved, as planned, to Industry and Commerce. But Desmond was still at Health. John Boland got Environment, and its former incumbent Liam Kavanagh got Fisheries, Forestry and Tourism. Paddy O'Toole got Defence. But it was when FitzGerald got to the final three ministerial changes on his list that the Fianna Fáil clamour of derision reached a crescendo. Social Welfare was being reassigned from Desmond to Hussey; Dukes was getting Justice, and Paddy Cooney was getting Education.

It was a case of back to the future for Fine Gael. Just before Christmas, advisers close to FitzGerald had been suggesting plainly that Cooney might be dropped from the government. He had just clashed openly with FitzGerald on divorce. Now he was being assigned to Education to improve relations with the Catholic Church for Fine Gael.

Along with him, Bruton and Boland represented a resurgence of the more right-wing of Fine Gael, clearly aimed at countering the popular march of the Progressive Democrats. But FitzGerald had failed to get the revised cabinet he wanted; his authority had been defied by Barry Desmond, and he had demonstrated his lack of guts to drop anyone. Many of the backbenchers privately equated this with cowardice.

Just three of the junior ministers were dropped. FitzGerald concluded his statement to the Dáil by telling them he had 'accepted the resignations' of Michael Darcy, Donal Creed and Joe Bermingham. Their replacements were Avril Doyle,

Enda Kenny and Toddy O'Sullivan. There was a bit of rejigging of other juniors. But as with all selections, there was grave disappointment among many backbenchers that they had been overlooked. And Darcy and Creed were both very angry at being fired.

It is difficult to imagine that things could really get any worse for FitzGerald. But he was now firmly in the grip of Murphy's Law, and anything that could go wrong, did. Firstly, the media was full of reports of the botched reshuffle, and his downfacing by Desmond. That Thursday night, he compounded his problems with an appearance on RTE's 'Today, Tonight' programme. There he frittered away much of his most fundamental and enduring asset, his reputation for honesty. He simply refused to tell the truth about the reshuffle crisis. He said he was 'very happy indeed' that Barry Desmond was staying at Health, and he paid tribute to him as 'a man of great guts, one of our hardest working ministers, who had done a magnificent job.' A week later, the Taoiseach told the Dáil that he made 'no secret of the fact that I pressed him quite hard' to change portfolios. He was certainly making one hell of a secret of it on 'Today Tonight'.

On the following Sunday, however, FitzGerald's account of events was called into question by the junior Fine Gael ministers who had been dropped. On RTE radio, Michael Darcy made clear that he had not resigned. 'I did not resign. I was sacked', he declared. And Donal Creed, the Cork North-West deputy said: 'I have a complaint if he [FitzGerald] said publicly that I had resigned, or that I handed in a resignation. If he made that statement that is not the position. He did not get any resignation from me. I did not resign, and if I was asked, I would not have done so'.

Fianna Fáil now focused on this in the lead-up to a no-confidence debate in the government they had tabled in the wake of the reshuffle, and which was debated on the Thursday and Friday, 20 and 21 February. But before they could get round to the no-confidence debate, the Taoiseach took the initiative on Tuesday afternoon, 18 February, when the Dáil resumed. He confessed that he had misled the House the previous Thursday when he said that Deputies Creed and Darcy had resigned.

In the absence of their resignations, he had terminated their appointments on Monday, and their replacements, Deputies Avril Doyle and Enda Kenny were only officially appointed from that day also. It demonstrated more bungling and ineptitude. 'I regret that on Thursday last I informed the House that the two deputies had resigned.' FitzGerald's cup of humiliation was overflowing.

On Wednesday, FitzGerald travelled to London for a scheduled meeting with Mrs Thatcher to review the Anglo-Irish Agreement. It had also been planned that he would unveil a waxwork model of himself at Madame Tussaud's. But it was time to stop these own goals. Peter Prendergast read the signs and saw the danger. Pictures of FitzGerald standing beside a waxwork model of himself at that time were likely to invite the query as to which one was the dummy. The waxworks appointment was scrubbed: the schedule was too tight to accommodate it, Prendergast announced.

———————

February 1986 had proved to be perhaps the most traumatic month in the history of Fine Gael under FitzGerald. But before the Dáil adjourned at the end of the month, there was one more obstacle to be negotiated. This was the tricky business of a Labour Party divorce bill. The origins of this lay in a private member's bill pressed to a vote by Michael O'Leary the previous November. This was the time in which the exploratory talks which eventually led to the formation of the PD were being held. Many Fine Gael people, including Peter Prendergast, believed that O'Leary wanted to get himself expelled from Fine Gael so that he could join O'Malley's new party. A free vote was allowed and there were no expulsions. But O'Leary's bill was a major embarrassment for Fine Gael. The party was formally committed to the introduction of divorce since 1978, but FitzGerald knew perfectly well that his party was deeply divided on the subject. He dreaded a repeat of the desperately divisive pro-life amendment. As we have already seen, the mood of the party since the local election thrashing of June 1985 had grown very conservative, nervous of liberalising social issues and putting the emphasis on taxes and jobs. John Kelly articulated the case against a divorce referendum. It would be beaten because, 'About half Fine Gael, all Fianna Fáil and the Roman Catholic Church would all be against it.'

But, in November, at the height of the controversy and embarrassment surrounding O'Leary's bill, FitzGerald changed his stance. He stated publicly, on the 'Today Tonight' programme, that he favoured removing the constitutional ban. On 6 December, Paddy Cooney told the Dáil that he was against divorce and claimed that a majority of Fine Gael TDs shared his view. FitzGerald replied pointedly two days later by saying that he was opposed to any undue delay in tackling the problem of marriage breakdown. 'Moreover, I believe that in this I speak for a majority within Fine Gael, whatever anyone else may say.' This was the clash of views that led many people to think that Cooney would be dropped from the cabinet in any reshuffle.

O'Leary's initiative had also put his old party, Labour, on the spot. Their response was to put down their own bill in place of his, and it was this bill that came before the Dáil for discussion in February. On Wednesday the 26th, the House voted on the proposal. FitzGerald had opted to vote against it on the ground that it would be wrong to change the law without ascertaining the churches' views. But the churches had long since made their views known to the Dáil Committee on Marital Breakdown and, besides, a year earlier FitzGerald had made a positive virtue of the fact that the government had amended the contraception law without deferring to the views of the Catholic Church. But he failed to bring his party with him. In the end, Fine Gael allowed a free vote, but the desire to show loyalty to the leader was reflected in the failure of any of the party's cabinet members or junior ministers to vote for the measure.

In the end, only eleven Fine Gael TDs voted for the bill. They were Alan Shatter, Michael Keating, Brendan McGahon, Mary Flaherty, Monica Barnes, Hugh Coveney, Liam Skelly, Maurice Manning, Richard Bruton, Nora Owen and Michael O'Leary. In short, less than one-sixth of Fine Gael TDs supported it.

The vote hardly represented a victory for Garret FitzGerald's nine-year campaign to liberalise Fine Gael. When it was over, Alice Glenn, the diehard of the party's right wing, turned to a Dáil colleague and crowed with pleasure. 'I have now proved that Fine Gael is a conservative party. Paddy Cooney was right.'

Just over two months later, on Monday 5 May, it looked as if Garret FitzGerald was poised to prove Cooney, Glenn and the other social conservatives of his party very wrong indeed. On that day, an *Irish Times*-MRBI poll revealed 57 per cent support for the coalition's proposal to amend the constitution to drop the ban on divorce.

It looked like a resounding justification for the latest twist in the saga of Fine Gael and divorce, and FitzGerald's persistent dithering on whether to take Fine Gael's eight-year-old pro-divorce policy at face value. In April, after concluding his consultations with the churches — with their inevitable failure to achieve a church-state consensus on divorce — FitzGerald, under pressure from Labour, had given the go-ahead to attorney-general John Rogers to draw up proposals for a divorce referendum. This stance was also supported by his own liberal wing, as fears grew at the top in Fine Gael that the party was losing some of its liberal supporters to the Progressive Democrats.

By March, opinion polls had shown half the electorate in favour of divorce, and little more than a third against. FitzGerald believed the time was right.

On Wednesday 23 April 1986, the government published its proposals to remove the constitutional ban, and to allow the courts to grant divorce. The proposal included the right to re-marry where a marriage had failed for at least five years; where there was no reasonable prospect of reconciliation; and where the dependent spouse and children were provided for.

At the outset, the measure was seen as a quite masterly balance between the political necessity of getting the measure passed, and allowing the electorate a voice in deciding the kind of divorce legislation that might be adopted after the constitutional ban was removed. Although the government adopted an officially neutral stance on the measure — odd, but enforced by Paddy Cooney's opposition — both Fine Gael and Labour were committed to campaigning for the referendum. Of course, the attitude of Fianna Fáil would be crucial.

But notwithstanding the restrictive nature of the proposal, Fianna Fáil was bound to be heavily influenced by the verdict of the Catholic hierarchy, which in the persons of the four archbishops, led by Cardinal Ó Fiaich, denounced the government measure as the basis for the most 'unrestrictive form of divorce in the world today'. In the event, Fianna Fáil copped out by being officially neutral, a stance which FitzGerald initially welcomed.

Repeatedly the Fine Gael leader had claimed that the timing of a divorce referendum was a matter of fine political judgment. Now, on Monday, 5 May, the first poll on the actual proposal appeared to confirm that on this key criterion, his performance had been masterly. Sampled on 28-29 April, the poll showed a majority everywhere, and among all the parties. Even Fianna Fáil voters broke down 49 — 46 per cent in favour. The overall findings were 57 per cent for; 36 per cent against, and a mere 7 per cent undecided.

The previous day, at the seventh annual conference of Young Fine Gael in Malahide, FitzGerald asserted confidently that the amendment would be carried. At this point it looked as if the contest would be a walk-over. There were very few anti-amendment voices, and the official neutrality of the Fianna Fáil party was regarded as crucial.

But on Monday 12 May, the first serious hiccup occurred in the Fine Gael campaign. At a private party meeting in Longford, Paddy Cooney, now holding the senior government portfolio of education, strongly attacked the referendum. He said that it was the most radical and significant proposal since the constitution was adopted. This led to some recrimination at the parliamentary party meeting two days later, the same day that the Dáil began debating the Tenth Amendment to the Constitution Bill to give effect to the government proposal. The formula adopted to cope with Cooney's dissent was to allow individual deputies to signal opposition in a personal capacity only, but not as members of Fine Gael. But such a specious distinction would fool nobody. It was clear that the Minister for Education was going to make it very difficult for many party colleagues, especially in rural constituencies, to campaign openly for divorce.

The changing climate of the campaign was also marked in the Dáil debate where Fianna Fáil speakers made a nonsense of their official neutral stance. With the exceptions of David Andrews and Charlie McCreevy, they lined up on the same side as the Catholic hierarchy in denouncing what their Justice spokesman, Michael Woods, likened to a Frankenstein that could stalk the land.

A fortnight after his first breach with his party, on 26 May, Paddy Cooney again made his views plain to an anti-divorce meeting in Longford. Early in June, the Junior Agriculture Minister, Paul Connaughton, publicly declared that he would be voting against the divorce proposal. His Junior Agriculture colleague, Paddy Hegarty, also made it clear that he would not be campaigning for the measure. With the exception of a few party deputies, notably John Bruton, Alan Dukes, Gemma Hussey, George Birmingham, Mary Flaherty, Monica Barnes, Alan Shatter and Nora Owen, the vast bulk of the Fine Gael parliamentary party decided to give the campaign a miss.

To make matters worse for the government, the anti-amendment campaigners were now running a very effective scare campaign to do with property rights, and social welfare entitlements in a divorce situation. Little was heard of the issue of civil rights for religious minorities, or the importance of demonstrating to Northern unionists that the Republic could be other than a theocracy. By 8 June, FitzGerald had become much more circumspect about the outcome and the implications for himself politically if the referendum was lost. He maintained, in an interview in the *Sunday Tribune* that day, however, that the result would be 'in the range of 55 per cent in favour, 45 per cent against'.

But it was becoming increasingly clear that the timing was not all it might be. In particular, it was very difficult to argue with those who criticised the government's failure to introduce first the various pro-family, pro-marriage measures promised in the wake of the referendum. These included raising the marriage age to eighteen, and introducing family courts and special conciliation services. There is little doubt that if these were first put in place, and the proposed legislation to protect the social welfare entitlements of people affected by divorce had also been published, then much of the anti-divorce hysteria could have been countered.

With so many government deputies sitting on the sideline, there was little surprise that the pro-divorce margin should begin to slip. By 15 June, a *Sunday Independent*-IMS poll showed the vote in favour to be down to 46 per cent; those against at 37 per cent, and an alarming rise in those undecided, up to 18 per cent. A week earlier, in the same paper, Paddy Cooney made his third and most dramatic assault on the referendum proposal. In a lengthy interview, he claimed that Fine Gael had only become a pro-divorce party a few weeks earlier; he denied that his stance contradicted any party ground rules, and said that some people contracting second marriages could be motivated by 'libidinous' considerations. He also said a future Dáil could cut the five year rule on divorce. His friend, Michael O'Leary, the deputy director of the Fine Gael referendum campaign accused him of 'demonism' and trading the politics of fear. Monica Barnes implicitly called on Cooney to resign. FitzGerald said nothing.

With some individual bishops growing increasingly more explicit in their calls for a 'no' vote — notably Archbishop McNamara of Dublin and Bishop Newman of Limerick — the tide was now beginning to run all one way in the final fortnight of the campaign, before voting on 26 June. A private Fine Gael opinion poll showed the issue at 50-50 and continuing to drift. FitzGerald accused opponents of the referendum of a 'quite unscrupulous campaign of distortion and misrepresentation'. But he also knew that he was losing the battle, and in the final days of the campaign tried to invoke a parallel with the issue of the minority in the North. On polling day, Fine Gael published newspaper advertisements with a picture of the Taoiseach, and a message: 'I call on the women of Ireland to vote YES.' And he assured them that he would not have been associated with any proposal that was against their interests.

But even before the votes were cast and counted, it was clear that he and his party and government were in for a startling defeat. A further *Irish Times*-MRBI poll the day before showed a dramatic swing in public opinion. Whereas the same company's poll on 5 May had shown a 57 – 36 per cent vote in favour, the figures now were 49 per cent against, 40 per cent for and 11 per cent undecided. An incredible swing of no less than 30 per cent had occurred.

To add to FitzGerald's woes, the same poll showed Fine Gael's popular standing back down at 25 per cent, and Fianna Fáil up to 51 per cent. The actual referendum outcome underlined the disastrous defeat it represented for the government, for Fine Gael and for FitzGerald especially. The people rejected their urgings by 63.5 per cent to 36.5 per cent.

It was the signal for renewed divisions and recriminations inside Fine Gael. All the bitterness overflowed at an acrimonious post-mortem parliamentary party meeting a week later, on Wednesday 2 July. Alice Glenn and Tom O'Donnell actually began a walk-out, only to be restrained by Paddy Cooney. There were bitter exchanges with the liberals in the party, Monica Barnes, Gemma Hussey, and Alan Shatter. The deep cleavage between liberal and conservative forces inside the party, which FitzGerald had for so many years struggled to mask, was out in the open. There was deep disillusionment on both sides. O'Donnell urged the abolition or reform of Young Fine Gael. Alice Glenn said they needed a leader who reflected both wings in the party. Peter Barry said it was the party's new TDs which had put Fine Gael into government. 'Any political party must change with the times, or else it dies', he declared.

FitzGerald committed the party to continue the battle for social legislative reform, and made it clear that as long as he was leader that course would be pursued. He attacked the quota-sitting mentality of many deputies, and said that as they faced into the general election of 1987, the biggest enemy they had was 'the attitude of our own parliamentary party'. It was a debate with loud echoes of battles fought by FitzGerald in the late seventies in the campaign to modernise Fine Gael, and to build it up to rival Fianna Fáil.

How does the balance sheet read? By his own standards, FitzGerald has had many failures in government. The three areas which he himself identified as central to the country's problems — taxation reform, jobs, and cuts in public spending — have all got worse in his time of office. This failure seemed all the greater given the degree of confidence which the nation was asked to repose to FitzGerald. In addition, he failed to move his party to the left, towards a more liberal, social democratic position.

Of course, the party had its problems, not least that of being yoked together in coalition with a Labour Party that was ideologically at odds with it on fundamentals. This effectively stymied any hope of public spending cuts although, as John Bruton pointed out, there were other, structural difficulties in the way of cutting public spending. It inevitably incurred massive opposition from vested interests — public sector workers or people enjoying a particular service. The public service was also highly unionised and any cuts were fought with tremendous vigour. And it took a lot of time and effort to amass all the data needed to decide whether particular services were worth retaining or scrapping.

Fine Gael glibly — perhaps wantonly — embraced the policy of eliminating the deficit in four or five years in the elections of 1981-2. But they never thought through the logic of their proposal. Alan Dukes summed up the position neatly: 'Fine Gael may not have worked out the full implications of eliminating the deficit. But more than any other party, we certainly are aware of the implications of not doing it.' And it did occasionally show flashes of meaning business particularly in the case of Jim Mitchell's determination to stop inefficiency and waste in publicly owned transport facilities: CIE, Irish Shipping and B and I.

Domestically, the government's greatest achievement was to help reduce the ruinously high rate of inflation which it inherited. By early 1986 inflation was less than 5 per cent and falling. Public service pay increases, which ran at 15 per cent in 1982, were only running at half that rate three years later.

Externally, the jewel in FitzGerald's crown was Hillsborough, probably the most significant achievement in

Anglo-Irish relations since 1922.

In the long term, however, FitzGerald and his party may be remembered for something else, something that a country ought to be able to take for granted but which Ireland seemed in danger of losing in the early eighties. He provided honest government. There were no scandals, no outrageous cases of nepotism or patronage. The administration of justice and the gardaí was above reproach. Of course, this is a negative achievement — the prevention or avoidance of abuses — but after the debilitating scandals and sinister machinations of the GUBU days, FitzGerald's government was like a breath of fresh air.

Index